PUBLIC POLICY AND PUBLIC CHOICE

SAGE YEARBOOKS IN POLITICS AND PUBLIC POLICY

Sponsored by the

Policy Studies Organization

Series Editor:

Stuart S. Nagel, *University of Illinois, Urbana*

International Advisory Board

Books in this series:

1. What Government Does (1975)
   MATTHEW HOLDEN, Jr. and DENNIS L. DRESANG, *Editors*

2. Public Policy Evaluation (1975)
   KENNETH M. DOLBEARE, *Editor*

3. Public Policy Making in a Federal System (1976)
   CHARLES O. JONES and ROBERT D. THOMAS, *Editors*

4. Comparing Public Policies: New Concepts and Methods (1978)
   DOUGLAS E. ASHFORD, *Editor*

5. The Policy Cycle (1978)
   JUDITH V. MAY and AARON B. WILDAVSKY, *Editors*

6. Public Policy and Public Choice (1979)
   DOUGLAS W. RAE and THEODORE J. EISMEIER, *Editors*

VOLUME VI. SAGE YEARBOOKS IN POLITICS AND PUBLIC POLICY

PUBLIC POLICY
AND PUBLIC CHOICE

DOUGLAS W. RAE
and
THEODORE J. EISMEIER
Editors

 **SAGE Publications**   **Beverly Hills / London**

For information address:

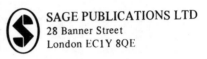

SAGE PUBLICATIONS, INC.
275 South Beverly Drive
Beverly Hills, California 90212

SAGE PUBLICATIONS LTD
28 Banner Street
London EC1Y 8QE

Printed in the United States of America

International Standard Book Number 0-8039-0725-7
0-8039-7026-5 pbk.

Library of Congress Cataloging in Publication Data
Main entry under title:

Public policy and public choice.

(Sage yearbooks in politics and public policy ;
v. 6)
    Includes bibliographical references.
    1. Elections--United States--Addresses, essays,
lectures. 2. United States--Politics and
government--Addresses, essays, lectures. 3. Policy
sciences--Addresses, essays, lectures. 4. Social
choice--Addresses, essays, lectures. I. Rae,
Douglas W. II. Eismeier, Theodore J.
JK1967.P8   320.9'73   78-27687
ISBN 0-8039-0725-7
ISBN 0-8039-0726-5 pbk.

CONTENTS

PART III Institutional Arrangements and Policy Decisions

SERIES EDITOR'S INTRODUCTION

This is the sixth volume in the series of Yearbooks in Politics and Public Policy published by Sage Publications in cooperation with the Policy Studies Organization. All volumes in the series have in common a concern for the nature, causes, or effects of alternative governmental policies. Some of the volumes have emphasized the nature of those policies, such as the one by Matthew Holden and Dennis Dresang, *What Government Does* (1975). Others have emphasized the causes or formation of public policies, such as those by Charles Jones and Robert Thomas, *Public Policy Making in a Federal System* (1976), and Judith May and Aaron Wildavsky, *The Policy Cycle* (1977). Still others will emphasize the effects or administration of public policies, such as Helen Ingram and Dean Mann's *Why Policies Succeed or Fail* and Robert Lineberry's *From Dollars to Distribution: Implementation between Policy Adoption and Consumption*. Another forthcoming volume cuts across these categories but concentrates exclusively on urban policy problems, namely Dale Rogers Marshall's *Urban Policymaking*.

The present volume edited by Douglas Rae and Theodore Eismeier, *Public Policy and Public Choice*, has as its theme a methodological orientation for analyzing public policies, rather than an emphasis on substantive principles such as the above-mentioned volumes. In that sense, it is the third volume emphasizing methods, in the series. The first such volume was Kenneth Dolbeare's *Public Policy Evaluation* (1975) and the second was Douglas Ashford's *Comparing Public Policies: New Concepts and Methods* (1978). The Dolbeare volume concentrated on social science research methods which attempt to relate input variables to policy outputs or to relate policy outputs to impact variables. The Ashford volume uses a comparative methodology in which the units of analysis tend to be two or more countries considered simultaneously. The distinctive methodological orientation of the present volume involves conceiving political decision makers as seeking to maximize their perceived benefits minus costs. The orientation then uses that general conception and other premises for deducing various conclusions as to how political decision makers are likely to behave under varying circumstances.

The public choice perspective has its origins in the reasoning of microeconomics in which the decision-making behavior of producers, consumers, and other economic actors are conceived as attempting to maximize their utilities, income minus expenses, revenues minus costs, or similar economic variables. A number of economists, political scientists, and other social scientists have extended that basic conception to the nonmarket behavior of such political decisionmakers as voters, legislators, administrators, judges, and people who are regulated by or recipients of governmental programs.

One way to classify public choice models is in terms of the purpose of the analysis, which could be either for predicting or explaining behavior or for the purpose of prescribing or recommending behavior. Most public choice studies involve a combination of those positive and normative purposes, although one or the other may tend to dominate. From a methodological perspective perhaps the most useful way of classifying public choice models is in terms of their structure, rather than who the actors are (which gets into substance rather than methodology) or whether the purposes are predictive or prescriptive (which tends to be a blurred classification since the same study can often be used for both purposes). In structural terms, public choice models can be classified as optimum choice, level, or mix models or interaction-equilibrium models.

Optimum choice models involve a decisionmaker who is faced with discrete alternatives of which each choice has a separate degree of benefits or costs, with those benefits and costs possibly discounted by the probability of some relevant event occurring. A good example of an optimum choice situation is that faced by a voter choosing among candidates, with each candidate representing a different payoff in terms of the voter's interests and each candidate having a different probability of being elected. The rational voter would generally vote for the candidate whose payoff discounted by his probability of winning is the highest. An important problem in that kind of analysis is how do voters determine the relative payoffs of candidates. More specifically, to what extent do they rely on a candidate's issue positions, party affiliation, or demographic characteristics. Another related example also used in this book involves the discrete choice of members of the general public, especially poor persons, deciding whether or not they should support an income distribution system that allows some people to become much richer than others. It seems that many American poor people are supportive of that kind of unequal system because they perceive they have a fair probability of becoming well off or at least that their children do. The perceived "get rich" payoff discounted by its probability of occurring in the presently unequal system is thus higher than the perceived expected value of a more equalitarian one. A third example in this book involves a would-be presidential candidate trying to decide whether or not to fight for his party's nomination. The decision to do so, rather than withdraw, is a function of his perception of the value of the nomination in terms of the probability of winning the presidency discounted by the probability of obtaining the nomination, relative to the cost of fighting for the nomination. These three examples are discussed in the chapters by Achen, Hochschild, and Brewer/Nelson, respectively.

Optimum level models involve a decisionmaker who is faced with a policy that can generally take an infinite number of alternatives, but doing either too much or too little would be unduly costly in terms of the decisionmaker's interests. A good example of that kind of model is involved in determining how much a governmental budget should be in terms of total taxing and spending, assuming the taxes are roughly equal to the expenditures. If the budget level is too low, the policy makers may lose votes because of a lessening of government services. On the other hand, if the budget level is too high, the policy makers may lose votes because of the burden of the high taxation. One could conceivably arrive at an optimum budget level by obtaining data for many gubernatorial elections as to (1) the percentage of the two-party vote obtained by the incumbent party and (2) the percentage that state government spending represents of the income of people within the state. One could then fit a quadratic curve to that data and observe where the curve reaches a peak, which would represent the optimum budget level for maximizing votes. One could also vary the analysis to consider other factors that influence the two-party vote besides government spending. Problems like these are addressed by Niskanen and Eismeier in their respective chapters.

Optimum mix models involve a decision maker who is faced with the question of how to allocate scarce dollars, time, or other resources among various activities or places. A good example involves members of Congress trying to decide how to allocate their time between constituency/campaigning activities; and congressional work. One could conceivably arrive at a optimum mix between those two activities by obtaining data for many members of Congress in a recent congressional term as to (1) the percentage of the two-party vote which each incumbent received at the end of the term; (2) the percentage of his total working time spent on con stituency/campaigning acitvities; and (3) the percentage of his total working time spent on congressional work activities. Information on the first variable could be obtained from voting statistics; information on the second and third variables, from interviews or mailed questionnaires. One could then fit a diminishing returns curve to that data in order to observe the nonlinear elasticity coefficients of those two activities. With that information, one could then allocate one's time to those activities in proportion to their elasticity coefficients and thereby maximize one's votes. As in the optimum level analysis, one could vary the data inputs in order to consider other factors that influence votes received besides constituency/campaigning and congressional work. Problems such as these are addressed by Cavanagh in his chapter.

Interaction-equilibrium models involve multiple decision makers relating to each other in a conflict, cooperation, bargaining, or other interactive context as individuals or groups seeking to arrive at an equilibrium through a convergence of interests or a domination by one set of individuals over the rest. A good example of the bargaining-convergence kind of equilibrium model is the out-of-court settlement situation in civil or criminal cases. There the individual decision makers tend to have in mind limits (as to how far they are willing to go to avoid a costly trial), which reflect their perceptions of the damages or sentence which would be received if the defendant loses, discounted by the probability of the defendant losing. With those limits in mind, their initial offers tend to be distant from their limits, but tend to move toward those limits. A convergence equilibrium is reached when both sides feel they have come out ahead relative to how far they were willing to go. A good example of the coalition-building kind of equilibrium model is the legislative situation, in which (1) unstable initital coalitions form on a legislative issue, (2) those coalitions seek to add uncommitted legislators as well as take legislators from existing coalitions, and (3) a dominant coalition develops that captures at least 51% of the vote, thereby arriving at an equilibrium on that issue. Coalition-building models have often inadequately considered the institutional rules of legislative bodies in trying to predict or explain legislative behavior. The chapter by Shepsle emphasizes the importance of rules relating to the decentralization of decisionmaking to committees, committee jurisdiction, and the controlling of amendments.

One especially interesting aspect of what is referred to above as a public choice perspective involves comparing the optimum or rational choice, level, mix, or equilibrium with the actual choice, level, mix, or equilibrium. For example, one might find the "optimum" percent of defendants to hold in jail prior to trial is about 4% in order to minimize the sum of the holding costs and the releasing costs. Yet in the sample of cities from which that optimum was generated, the average might be 27%. That kind of discrepancy can be explained in two general ways. The researcher may have failed to capture the goals or values of the decision makers, such as the desire to avoid the embarrassment of making a releasing error (i.e., releasing a no show) when there is no embarrassment in making a holding error (i.e., holding a defendant who would show). On the other hand, the decision makers may be misperceiving the relations between their actions and their goals, as when they think there is a greater likelihood of defendants, failing to appear than there actually is. To remedy that kind of discrepancy involves changing the values or perceptions of the decision makers or else changing what values and perceptions the researcher is attributing to them.

Accounting for the variance between the "optimum" and the "actual" illustrates how a public choice perspective can have both theoretical importance in understanding why decision makers decide the way they do and practical importance in seeking to improve political decision making in light of given goals. A public choice perspective can help suggest predictive hypotheses, prescriptive proposals, ways of organizing ideas into categories, criteria for testing proposals, explanations for data-based findings, and also suggest data to gather in policy studies research. I hope that this volume will stimulate more applications of a public choice perspective to important policy problems by both policy studies and public choice people.

Stuart S. Nagel
Urbana, Illinois

VOLUME EDITORS' INTRODUCTION

This book has a simple premise: there are gains from trade to be made by linking the study of public policy with the study of democratic institutions and processes. The potential gains, we think, are substantial. To begin with, our ability to explain and appraise public policies and policy-making institutions will almost certainly be enchanced by paying more systematic attention to processes of individual and collective political decision. "Policy analysis," Richard Nelson has argued, "is now well understood to be a much less neutral, much more active, aspect of the 'steering' process than policy analysts originally liked to tell themselves. With the development of this self-understanding it has become increasingly apparent to members of the profession that it is important to know how policy is actually made, to understand the forces that bear on the process and the parts that cannot be moved, to know where the moveable levers are and how they can be maneuvered" (1977:30). Political science has an important role to play both in developing such knowledge and, more importantly, in applying it in the design of decision-making institutions.

At the same time the theory of democratic institutions stands to profit considerably by paying more attention to the real world of public policy making. With political scientists showing a growing interest in formal models of political institutions and with economists extending their "science of choice" from the private to the public realm, the last decade has brought impressive advances in the methodological sophistication of the theory of public choice. Yet for the most part such theorizing has remained untempered by evidence about the workings of democratic processes. Thus critics have argued, with some justification, that the theory of public choice still represents at best a set of internally consistent but empirically brittle propositions about political decision (see, e.g., Toye, 1976). If this indeed is a problem, one remedy may be a greater concern with the substance of public policy.

The articles in this volume analyze the choices of citizens and politicians, the consumers and producers of public policy. Each of the articles bears in some way upon the relationship between democratic political processes and public policy decisions. Beyond this shared interest in policy choice in democratic institutions, the work reported here varies considerably both in substance and methodology. In our view such diversity is a definite virtue, for the variety of issues addressed here should serve to illustrate the wide range of public policies in which a public choice perspective can be of both explanatory and evaluative usefulness.

Questions about how citizens form judgments on political matters have, of course, long been grist for the mill of political science. More recently, however, questions about citizens' policy judgments have gained a new prominence in the controversy over "issue voting". The volume leads off with Christopher Achen's assessment of this controversy. Achen starts by arguing convincingly that the statistical logic supporting most arguments about issue voting has been faulty and that as a result recent evidence about the rise of issue voting by the American electorate is weak. He then goes on to suggest alternative statistical methods which are better suited to the task of teasing out the effects of policy issues on voting decisions.

Jennifer Hochschild's work also deals with the demand side of the policy-making process. Hochschild begins with an intriguing question—Why is it that in the United States even those who stand to benefit the most from the redistribution of wealth and income apparently do not support such policies? To answer this question, Hochschild argues, it is necessary to go beyond simple assertions about objective self-interest and instead look at the structure of belief systems in mass publics. Using both survey data and evidence from her own in-depths interviews, Hochschild develops a framework for explaining patterns of choice about economic justice and about the government's role in promoting it.

The next two articles are concerned with elections as referenda on the policy performance of government. As part of his more general effort to develop a model of the behavior of the American presidency, William Niskanen presents here an analysis of the effects of economic and fiscal policies on the popular vote for President between 1896 and 1972. Niskanen finds that, on average, American voters have rewarded incumbent parties for presiding over a growing economy and for managing to hold the line on spending and taxing. On the other hand, voters have punished incumbent parties for presiding over a faltering economy and for increasing the size of the federal budget. One important implication Niskanen draws from his analysis is that the federal government has been "overspending," producing budgets which are greater than the vote-maximizing level of taxing and spending.

The reaction of voters to the rising cost of American government is also the subject of Theodore Eismeier's work. After decades of explosive growth in public spending, taxpayer hostility to rising taxes has reached the point of rebellion in many parts of the United States. Eismeier examines one form of this rebellion by estimating the electoral consequences of tax increases in gubernatorial elections between 1948 and 1974. Like Niskanen, Eismeier finds that voters have punished incumbent parties for increasing taxes, but he also finds that strategy can make an important difference in rendering tax increases more palatable to voters. He then relates this evidence to two broader questions: How do voters judge the fiscal performance of government? What constraints do these judgments put on public policy choice?

In the final three articles in this volume we turn from questions about individual choice to questions about institutional arrangements and their relation to policy decision. Ross Brewer and Garrison Nelson examine patterns of decision making and conflict in American nominating conventions between 1896 and 1976. Employing several measures of political conflict, Brewer and Nelson find that the degree of conflict at conventions is related both to the perceived availability of the nomination and to the perceived value of that nomination. While no strictly causal inferences can be drawn from this analysis, it provides a suggestive insight to the economy of national party politics.

Thomas Cavanagh presents a purposive model of legislative behavior delimiting two arenas of congressional performance: the electoral and the institutional. Every congressman, Cavanagh argues, must make strategic choices about allocating his resources between those activities which help him get reelected and those which contribute to effective decision making within Congress. Cavanagh then matches his theoretical expectations against evidence about how congressmen do allocate resources between these often conflicting demands. He concludes by analyzing how these patterns of resource use have contributed to the increasing advantage of incumbency in congressional elections.

In the concluding article of this volume, Kenneth Shepsle presents a formal model of institutional choice. Most formal models in political science, Shepsle contends, have been "highly atomistic and institutionally sparse" and as a result have added little to our understanding of the ways in which institutions make policy. Shepsle attempts here to develop an institutionally richer model of public choice. His framework focuses on three institutional features: committee system, jurisdictional arrangements, and amendment control rules.

REFERENCES

NELSON, R. R. (1977) The Moon and the Ghetto: An Essay on Public Policy Analysis. New York: W.W. Norton.

TOYE, J.F.J. (1976) "Economic theories of politics and public finance." British Journal of Political Science 6 (October): 433-448.

Douglas W. Rae
Yale University
Theodore J. Eismeier
Hamilton College

1

ISSUE VOTING: WHAT COUNTS AS EVIDENCE?

CHRISTOPHER ACHEN

University of California, Berkeley

INTRODUCTION

Liberal democratic theory presupposes that the ordinary citizen is capable of forming judgments on political matters and voting accordingly. The empirical accuracy of this assumption has always been in dispute, never more so than in recent decades. Modern opinion polling methods have given researchers a wealth of new information with which to carry on the debate, and statistical methods applied to survey data have been used to support the arguments of all sides.

In recent years, most studies of American voting habits have concluded that issues play a large part in voters' deci-

AUTHOR'S NOTE: *I would like to express my thanks to Jack Citrin, Lloyd Etheredge, John Jackson, Gerald Kramer, John McCarthy, David Mayhew, Douglas Rae, Steven Rosenstone, Edward Tufte, Ray Wolfinger, and Gerald Wright for helpful comments on earlier versions of this paper.*

sions. Key (1968) showed that citizens switching their party choice between two Presidential elections tended to express views that fit their new affiliation better than the old one. Other scholars, such as RePass (1971) and Broh (1973), reported success in predicting vote intention with models based on issue preferences, and Shapiro (1969) said that voters appear to be "rational." In an influential book, Nie, Verba, and Petrocik (1976) have argued that the American electorate has abandoned its intellectual torpor and now more often conditions its votes on the policy positions of parties and candidates.

These new evaluations of voter competence contrast sharply with the dominant view of 10 years ago, expressed so persuasively in *The American Voter* (Campbell, Converse, Miller, and Stokes, 1960). At that time, public opinion researchers taught that party identification dominated the vote and that issues, when they were understood at all, had little impact. This pessimistic judgment of mass man-made democracy's prospects (and those of "the people") seems doubtful, leading many public opinion researchers to seek escape from the statistical logic. Lately, routes out seem to have been discovered, but the trustworthiness of those paths remains in much dispute.

In the issue voting literature, substantive conclusions often turn on the resolution of disputes over data analysis. If the suitability of a methodological procedure can be established, the findings follow easily. Unfortunately, from a statistical point of view the logic of quantitative work in this field is frequently weaker than it need be, and many of the techniques in use are themselves the subjects of contention. Indeed, some central disputes in the field—such as the debate over the alleged rise in issue voting—rest primarily on methodological disagreements. How is the strength of issue voting in the 1950s to be compared with its contemporary strength? Are the measures in use comparable across samples from different time periods? Resolution of such questions is obviously logically prior to the substantive discussion, yet the topics have been treated only scantily in the literature. With questions such as these unanswered, conflicting substantive findings are inevitable. In general, writing on issue voting is notable for its technical ingenuity and clever intuitions, but much less so for the patience and care that would put its findings on solid foundations.

Certain statistical issues recur often enough in discussions of issue voting to be worth special attention. This article examines three of them, each distinguished by its importance to the assessment of voter rationality and by the widespread uncertainty over its proper resolution. My intention is to summarize the methodological research that bears on these three topics and to refer the reader to recent substantive work in the issue voting field that meets reasonable statistical canons. No attempt will be made to summarize the issue voting literature; the task has been well-performed by Kessel (1972), and more recent references can be found in Margolis (1977). The summary is restricted to those difficulties of *inference* that afflict the issue voting field.

THREE RULES ABOUT EVIDENCE FOR ISSUE VOTING

The first rule is obvious, but its implications are not well understood.

(1) *Statistical evidence that issues influence voting will be accepted only if party ID has been properly controlled.* Current researchers know that issues cannot simply be correlated with the vote, with no attempt made to partial out the effect of party identification. *The American Voter* (Campbell, Converse, Miller, and Stokes, 1960) long ago argued that party ID is itself the cause of opinions. If party ID determines both issue positions and vote intention, then a correlation between votes and issues will be induced. Votes will vary

with issues preferences, even if issues have no real impact. Without controls for party ID, therefore, the close relationship of issues and votes proves nothing.

The most common technique for controlling party ID is normal vote analysis (Converse, 1966a). In this procedure, issue voting is assessed as a deviation from the "normal vote," the vote that would occur if nothing but party identification were at work. Researchers use certain regression analyses to predict the vote by party ID alone, then examine the deviations or residuals to see whether they correlate with issue positions. If the liberals on an issue vote more Democratic than expected from their party IDs and the conservatives vote more Republican, the deviations from normal expectations are a measure of the issue's impact. A few prominent articles employing this technique include Converse (1966b), Boyd (1972), Miller, Miller, Raine, and Brown (1976), Re-Pass (1976), and Miller and Levitin (1977).

From a statistical point of view, this procedure contains an unfortunate bias. Roughly speaking, the bias may be summarized as follows. If a group of party identifiers, say the Independents leaning Republican, is small and/or responds strongly to the national trend in the vote, their normal vote estimate will be biased toward whichever party has been winning recent elections. Likewise, if another group, say the strong Democrats, is large and/or responds weakly to the national trend, their vote estimate will be biased toward the recently losing party (Achen, forthcoming). The bias is not always large, but under plausible conditions, it can amount to five or more percentage points, more than enough to disguise most issue effects.

When issue voting is studied by normal vote analysis, therefore, substantial error can be introduced. The normal vote calculations "overcontrol" for party ID, in the sense that some of the short-term forces in recent elections are erroneously attributed to the normal vote. If issue impacts are assessed as deviations from these erroneous normal vote estimates, the result, of course, is biased, undependable estimates. Normal vote analysis simply cannot be trusted to assess the effect of issues correctly.

(2) *Statistical evidence for issue voting will not be admitted if it involves comparing correlation coefficients, gammas, standardized betas, or other correlational measures across samples or across time.* This statistical fallacy appears frequently. Indeed, the evidence for the new sophisticated voter virtually depends on it. The problem, of course, is that correlational measures can increase over time while the strength of the relationship remains stable or weakens. That is, two relationships with the same regression slopes can have different correlations if the dispersions of their independent variables differ (Hanushek and Jackson, 1977, pp. 21, 59, 78, 95; Blalock, 1961, pp. 114-126; Duncan, 1975, ch. 4). Gammas, standardized betas, and other measures of association have the same flaw. Since virtually all opinion measures have different variances now than they did in the 1950s, comparisons are impossible. Worse yet, the Michigan SRC changed its coding scheme for opinion variables in 1964, using response scales with fewer categories from that date. The new format raises the variance of respondent opinions relative to the scale length and guarantees that "Issue voting" or "Issue consistency" as captured by correlational measures will show a permanent upward jump in 1964, even if voters remain as somnolent as before. This upward skip, offered by Nie et al. (1976, p. 129) as evidence for a growing issue consciousness, demonstrates instead only the existence of a new question format (see also Bishop et al., 1978; Sullivan et al., 1978).

If what one means by "the rise of issue voting" is that, all else equal, voters now respond more strongly than before to issue differences among candidates or parties, then one is claiming that (unstandardized) regression slopes have

changed. Correlation measures fail to bear on the question.
The point is not an academic quibble: the lone two studies
that have addressed this matter found that the case for more
issue-conscious voting collapsed when the statistical error was
corrected (Declercq, Hurley, and Luttbeg, 1976; Popkin,
Gorman, Phillips, and Smith, 1976).

(3) *Studies of issue voting will stand in evidence only if
they have sorted out the directions of causation among
issues, party ID, and the vote.* Most research makes use of
measures of closeness of the voter to the party or candidate,
either by asking the respondent whom he trusts or with
whom he agrees on certain issues. Sometimes the respondent
is asked to place himself and the candidates on an issue scale.
In each case, a measure of the perceived closeness of the
voter to the candidates is derived from his responses and used
to predict his party or vote. The difficulty here is that the
voting intention and party ID probably influence the perceived distance to the candidates: if a voter likes candidate
Jones or belongs to his party, he will rate Jones nearer
himself on the issues than the candidate actually is. This is the
phenomenon of cognitive dissonance reduction (Festinger,
1957). Shapiro's (1969) analysis showed that party ID often
influences perceived candidate position, and the effect might
have been stronger if he had used vote intention rather than
party ID as the correlate. In short, perceived closeness to the
candidates on issues may influence voting, but vote intention
and party ID may in turn affect perceptions of candidate
positions. Simultaneous, reciprocal impacts may be occurring.

Under these conditions, cross-tabulations or regressions
showing that issues are related to voting (even with party ID
controlled) are inconclusive: statistically speaking, single-
question techniques are biased estimators of simultaneous
equation models. One cannot know whether voters support a
candidate because he seems to have their views or whether he

seems to have their views because they support him (Brody and Page, 1972).[1]

A few sophisticated studies have attempted to disentangle the complex interrelation between issues and voting by examining aggregate election data. Independent measures of the issue positions of candidates, instead of voters' perceptions, are used to estimate how much effect true candidate opinions have on voting. The implicit definition of "issue voting" is altered here: in these studies, a voter need not be aware of the candidates' views. If a machinist is swayed by a union's endorsement and that endorsement was given in return for certain policy stands taken by the candidate, then the voter has been influenced by true candidate positions. Hence, issue voting has occurred, regardless of what the voter knows beyond the union endorsement. Cognitive dissonance effects are irrelevant, simultaneity of causation is eliminated from the analysis, and ordinary cross-tabulation and regression methods are applicable.

Schoenberger (1969), for example, noted that GOP Congressmen who were prominent in their support of Goldwater in 1964 fared less well at the polls in the fall than did their more independent-minded colleagues. Similarly, Erikson (1971) demonstrated that Republican representatives with more liberal voting records do better at the polls. Here, objective measures of congressional positions (Presidential endorsements, roll call liberalism) seemed to influence voters, and neither study is subject to the criticism that cognitive dissonance effects have prejudiced their findings.

The use of aggregate data to eliminate simultaneous causation is not without difficulties of its own, however. Neither GOP Congressmen who sign a pro-Goldwater statement nor GOP Congressmen with unusually liberal voting records are likely to represent a random sample of districts. These people may do better or worse at the pools for reasons having more to do with the character of their constituencies than with their policy positions. Put another way, studies of this sort are essentially ecological analyses: the inference is from behavior of an aggregate to the behavior of individuals, from margins in election returns to issue voting by citizens. "Ecological inference" is a difficult business, and parameter estimates are typically biased. (See Stokes, 1969, pp. 62-83, and the references in his footnotes.) Indeed, it would be possible to obtain biased results in cases like these even if statistical controls for the nature of the congressional districts were introduced, something which has not been done in either article. Thus escaping simultaneity by embracing aggregate data will change the inferential lacunae, but not eliminate them. For that, more powerful techniques are needed.

BETTER STATISTICAL PROCEDURES

Two of the rules above are essentially negative: normal vote and correlational measures should be abandoned in the study of issue voting. But the third is a standard to meet: the interconnectedness among party, issues, and vote need explicit statistical recognition. For the researcher who wishes to do more than look this difficulty in the face and pass on, what methods are available?

Two procedures exist to cope with reciprocal causation in statistical models of issue voting. The most straightforward conceptually are the simultaneous equation estimation methods from econometrics. (An elementary treatment is Duncan, 1975.) These techniques specifically permit relationships in which, for instance, issues influence party ID and vice versa, so that the causal links in each direction can be evaluated.

Jackson (1975a) used simultaneous equations in his study of the 1964 Presidential election. His results show that party identification has some impact on issue positions and on evaluations of the parties for their ability to handle political problems; these are the consequences of cognitive dissonance reduction. The "rational" links, however, are generally stronger: issues influence party evaluations, which in turn modify the party ID. In addition, party evaluations strongly affect the voting decision, dwarfing the impact of party ID. Assessing all these causal paths jointly is the considerable achievement of Jackson's work.

Simultaneous equation techniques show great promise for the study of issue voting. Any simultaneous equation model, however, requires the researcher to specify in some detail his beliefs about the processes at work. Inevitably, different scholars will make somewhat different assumptions. In Jackson's case, the most controversial decisions would appear to be two: first, vote or vote intention is not allowed to influence party evaluation. A voter is not allowed to let himself like GOP foreign policy because he is going to vote for Goldwater. In a Presidential election, it seems entirely possible that this cognitive dissonance reduction effect might be rather large. If so, Jackson's method would artificially inflate the effect of party evaluations on the vote and depress that of party ID.

Second, Jackson's model assumes that all issue dimensions are weighted equally. That is, each issue is assumed to be equal to every other in its impact on party ID, evaluations, and the vote. We cannot assess the distinct impact of each issue taken separately, nor allow for different individuals to weight the issues differently. An election determined by foreign policy matters is not distinguishable from one settled by social welfare debates, nor from one in which half the electorate votes its foreign affairs views and the other half, its social welfare beliefs.

Difficulties of this sort unfortunately occur rather frequently when simultaneous equations are applied to survey data. So far, any model with strong, stable results is likely to have achieved them in return for making some implausible assumptions. Much good data analysis remains to be done to learn the leanest set of assumptions that will produce usable results.

To avoid the strictures imposed on simultaneous equation models, a researcher can also employ time series techniques. A panel study contains the necessary data. In this approach, a respondent's current party ID and issue positions are regarded as a function of his party ID and issue views the period before. In this way, simultaneous causation is avoided, and the simpler time series or ordinary regression methods become applicable. Jackson (1975b) has also explored the use of this method, finding, once again, that even in the 1950s, issues determined party ID more than the reverse. However, this article does not discuss issue voting. Indeed, modeling the vote decision in this framework is probably impossible: votes are presumably determined by current issues and party ID, not those of the last time period, which in some panel studies may be as long as two years ago. Thus time series methods likely will be of more value in studying the origin of party ID rather than of the vote. Within those limits, however, the use of over-time data shows considerable promise.

Neither time series nor simultaneous equation methods promise instant solutions to the inferential difficulties of the issue voting field. Jackson's ingenious applications of both methods go far toward meeting the statistical demands of the problem, and his results constitute some of our best current knowledge of the effects of issues on party ID and the vote. Nevertheless, much remains to be done in loosening the restrictions of both techniques. So far it has proved impossible to look at issues one by one in a credible statistical framework. For example, at present no one can estimate with any certainty how strongly social welfare views influence elections or how weighty are short-term issues such as Korea or Watergate relative to long-term liberal/conservative dispositions. Knowing that these are probably simultaneous equation problems leaves one some distance off from their solution. Here, as usual, a competent statistical method is just a good map. Without it, however, one will arrive at the destination only by chance. Buying a cheap, outdated map is a false economy.

CONCLUSION

Voting research too often allots careful attention to preliminary conceptualization and data collection, while giving relatively little thought to the statistics used to summarize the findings. All too frequently substantive ingenuity is led astray by an untrustworthy statistical procedure. The normal vote and correlational measures are simply undependable guides to inference. The use of better statistical methods, such as time series or simultaneous equation techniques, would restore a sense of direction. No other single change in work habits holds out as much hope of finding a way through the welter of conflicting claims endemic to the issue voting field.

NOTE

1. Nie *et al.* (1976, p. 173) argue that the objection based on reciprocal causation is not fatal, since a stronger inflence in either direction constitutes "issues growing in importance." But this argument seems to be a play on words, for we would not ordinarily say that a variable such as issues is of growing consequence if it submits increasingly to the domination of another variable such as party ID.

REFERENCES

ACHEN, C.H. (forthcoming) "The bias in normal vote estimates." Political Methodology.

BISHOP, G.F., R.W. OLDENDICK, and A.J. TUCHFARBER (1978) "Effects of question wording and format on political attitude consistency." Public Opinion Quarterly 42: 81-92

BLALOCK, H.M., Jr. (1961) Causal Inferences in Nonexperimental Reseach. Chapel Hill: University of North Carolina.

BOYD, R.W. (1972) "Popular control of public policy: A normal vote analysis of the 1968 elections." American Political Science Review 66: 429-449.

BRODY, R.A. and B.I. Page (1972) "Comment: The assessment of policy voting." American Political Science Review 66: 450-458.

BROH, C.A. 1973 Toward a Theory of Issue Voting. Sage Professional Papers in American Politics 1, series no. 04-011. Beverly Hills: Sage Publications.

CAMPBELL, A., P. CONVERSE, W. MILLER, and D. STOKES (1960) The American Voter. New York: Wiley.

CONVERSE, P. (1966a) "The concept of a normal vote." In A. Campbell, P. Converse, W. Miller, and D. Stokes, Elections and the Political Order. New York: Wiley.

––– (1966) "Religion and politics: The 1960 election." In A. Campbell, P. Converse, W. Miller, and D. Stokes, Elections and the Political Order. New York: Wiley.

DECLERCQ, E., T. L. HURLEY, and N. LUTTBEG (1976) "Voting in erican Electoral Behavior. Sage Contemporary Social Science Issues 24. Beverly Hills: Sage Publications.

DUNCAN, O.D. (1975) Introduction to Structural Equation Models. New York: Academic Press.

ERIKSON, R.S. (1971) "The electoral impact of congressional roll call voting." American Political Science Review 65: 1018-1032.

FESTINGER, L. (1957) A Theory of Cognitive Dissonance. Evanston, Ill.: Row, Peterson.

HANUSHEK, E. and J. JACKSON (1977) Statistical Methods for Social Scientists. New York: Academic.

JACKSON, J.E. (1975a) "Issues, party choices, and presidential votes." American Journal of Political Science 19: 161-184.

––– (1975b) "Issues and party alignment." In L. Maisel and P.M. Sacks (eds.) Electoral Studies Yearbook. Beverly Hills: Sage Publications.

KESSEL, J. (1972) "Comment: The issues in issue voting." American Political Science Review 66: 459-465.

KEY, V.O., Jr. (1968) The Responsible Electorate. New York: Vintage.

MARGOLIS, M. (1977) "From confusion to confusion: Issues and the American voter (1956-1972)." American Political Science Review 71: 31-43.

MILLER, A.H., W.E. MILLER, A.S. RAINE, and T.A. BROWN (1976) "A majority party in disarray: Policy polarization in the 1972 election." American Political Science Review 70: 753-778.

MILLER, W.E. and T.E. LEVITIN (1977) Leadership and Change. Cambridge, Mass.: Winthrop.

NIE, N.H., S. VERBA, and J.R. PETROCIK (1976) The Changing American Voter. Cambridge, Mass.: Harvard University Press.

POPKIN, S., J. GORMAN, C. PHILLIPS, and J.A. SMITH (1976) "Comment: What have you done for me lately." American Political Science Review 70: 779-805.

RePASS, D.E. (1976) "Comment: Political methodologies in disarray." American Political Science Review 70: 814-831.

——— (1971) "Issue salience and party choice." American Political Science Review 65: 389-400.

SCHOENBERGER, R.A. (1969) "Campaign strategy and party loyalty: The electoral relevance of candidate decision-making in the 1964 congressional elections." American Political Science Review 63: 515-520.

SHAPIRO, M.J. (1969) "Rational political man: A synthesis of economic and social-psychological perspectives." American Political Science Review 63: 1106-1119.

STOKES, D. (1969) "Cross-level inference as a game against nature." In J.L. Bernd (ed.) Mathematical Applications in Political Science, IV. Charlottesville: The University Press of Virginia.

SULLIVAN, J.L., J.E. PIERESON, and G.E. MARCUS (1978) "Ideological constraint in the mass public: A methodological critique and some new findings." American Journal of Political Science 22: 233-249.

2

REDISTRIBUTING WEALTH:
POSITIONS, PAYMENTS,
AND ATTITUDES

JENNIFER L. HOCHSCHILD

Duke University

WHY DOES THE DOG NOT BARK?

"Is there any point to which you would wish to draw my attention?"
"To the curious incident of the dog in the night-time."
"The dog did nothing in the night-time."
"That was the curious incident," remarked Sherlock Holmes (Conan Doyle, 1965: 347).

Holmes solved his case when he realized that Colonel Ross's watchdog once had not barked when the evidence suggested

AUTHOR'S NOTE: *Many thanks to readers of earlier drafts, especially Deborah Baumgold, C. Anthony Broh, Lloyd Etheridge, Charles Lindblom, Douglas Rae, Ned Woodhouse, Charles Whitmore, and the members of the Project on American Democratic Institutions, Yale University.*

that it should. Watson's awe at Holmes's reasoning suggests that we are not in the habit of closely examining something that did not occur. There are obvious reasons for this. But, as Holmes points out, when evidence leads us to expect something which does not happen, then an explanation may be required.

Such an important nonevent is the absence of a widespread leftist movement among poor Americans. As Sombart and Marx asked, "why is there no socialism in the United States?". More precisely, why do the nonwealthy apparently not support the downward structural redistribution of wealth? Since most of the population have less than an average amount of wealth—the median level of holdings is well below the mean—why is there no political movement among this majority for the equalization of holdings?

THEORETICAL EXPECTATIONS

Classical and liberal political philosophy, psychological theories, empirical observation, and current politics all suggest that redistribution should be a major political issue. Aristotle worried that the many poor would revolt against the few rich in a democracy:

> In democracies, changes are chiefly due to the wanton license of demagogues. This takes two forms. Sometimes they attack the rich individually, by bringing false accusations and thus force them to combine .... Sometimes they attack them as a class, by egging on the people against them [1972, bk.5, ch.5].

More recently, John Adams and Lord T.B. Macaulay concurred. Adams wrote:

> Suppose a nation, rich and poor, high and low, ten millions in number, all assembled together; not more than one or two millions will have lands, houses, or any personal property ....

Would Mr. Nedham be responsible that, if all were to be decided by a vote of the majority, the eight or nine millions who have no property would not think of usurping over the rights of the one or two million who have? . . . Perhaps, at first, prejudice, habit, shame or fear, principle or religion, would restrain the poor from attacking the rich, and the idle from usurping on the industrious; but the time would not be long before courage and enterprise would come, and pretexts be invented by degrees, to countenance the majority in dividing all the property among them, or at least, in sharing it equally with its present possessors. Debts would be abolished first; taxes laid heavy on the rich, and not at all on the others; and at last a downright equal division of everything would be demanded, and voted [1972: 8-9].

A century later, Lord Macauley warned:

Institutions purely democratic must, sooner or later, destroy liberty or civilization or both . . . . If we had a purely democratic government here [in Great Britain] . . . either the poor would plunder the rich and civilization would perish or order and prosperity would be saved by a strong military government, and liberty would perish . . . . Distress everywhere makes the laborer mutinous and discontented, and inclines him to listen with eagerness to agitators who tell him that it is a monstrous iniquity that one man should have a million while another cannot get a full meal . . . . It is quite plain that your government will never be able to restrain a distressed and discontented majority. For with you the majority is the government, and has the rich, who are always a minority, absolutely at its mercy. The day will come when in the State of New York a multitude of people, none of whom has had more than half a breakfast, or expects to have more than half a dinner, will choose a Legislature. Is it possible to doubt what sort of a Legislature will be chosen? [1977: 460].

Not only opponents of redistribution assume that political democracy will lead eventually to economic equalization. Some people hail the American polity for precisely that reason. For example, Stephen Simpson wrote:

We are bound by the highest and most sacred ties of moral, religious, and political obligation to bring the condition of the people, in respect to the wages of labor and enjoyment of competence, to a level with their abstract political rights, which rights imply necessarily the possession of the property they may produce, on principles of equity congenial to the equal rights guaranteed by the organic law .... Let the producers of labor but once fully comprehend their injuries and fully appreciate their strength at the polls, and the present oppressive system will vanish like the mists of the morning before the rising sun. The power to remedy the evil is unquestionable; it resides in the *producers* of wealth, who constitute so overwhelming a majority of the people, when not carried away by the infatutation of faction [1954].

One hundred years later, Senator Huey Long's "Share the Wealth Society" claimed a nationwide membership of at least 3 million members, a figure confirmed fearfully by a secret poll conducted by the Democratic National Committee in 1936 (Farley, 1938). Long had been elected governor and senator and intended to be elected President, largely on the basis of growing support for his redistributive program (Long, 1933, 1970). It would have provided for a minimum family estate of $5,000 a maximum estate of $5 million with capital levy taxes on wealth above $1 million, a minimum yearly family income of one-third the mean family income, and a maximum family income of 300 times the mean. It also called for social welfare programs for the poor and unemployed to be paid for by higher taxes on the rich. Long's lieutenant, Gerald L. K. Smith, claimed "we're getting 20,000 new members a day. When we have enough millions, we'll make ourselves heard. We'll change things in this country" (Deutsch, 1935: 27). Furthermore, "we did not create a state of mind, we merely discovered and recognized a state of mind that had been created by conditions" (Smith, 1935: 15).

It is not surprising that so many thinkers (Bagehot, 1867; George, 1939; Long, 1933; Sinclair, 1933) have argued in the face of continual disconfirmation, that in a majoritarian political system, the poor majority would eventually dispossess the rich minority. Both normative and empirical strands of democratic theory lead to this expectation. Empirically, liberal theorists see people as motivated by the pursuit of private, self-interested goals; people are assumed to be rational and self-conscious in that they always prefer more, rather than the same or fewer, material goods, *ceteris paribus*. Thus everyone should favor redistribution from others to themselves; and a properly functioning democracy should translate these desires into political demands. The poor particularly might favor redistribution both because their absolute need is greater and because the rich have more efficient ways to get richer.

Normatively, liberal theorists, particularly Americans, value the ideal of equality. The public answer to the question, "How should equality be defined, with respect to what and for whom?" suggests increasing receptivity for redistributive public policies. The answer to "for whom?" has expanded over three centuries from propertied white males to the entire adult population; the answer to "with respect to what?" has expanded from narrowly circumscribed political rights to a wide range of civil and social rights. We now hear powerful arguments that the domain of equality must be expanded to include rights to economic and environmental well-being. Most important, the answer to "How should equality be defined?" is increasingly substantive equality of outcomes, either as an end in itself or as a prerequisite for liberty and true equal opportunity. Thus a strong redistributive argument falls well within the traditional American values of freedom, individualism, and opportunity (Jencks et al., 1972; Harrington, 1972; Schaar, 1967).

Psychological theory also predicts redistributive demands from the poor. Depth psychology agrees with liberal political theory that people are fundamentally selfish, atomistic, goal oriented, and materialistic—at least consciously. Social psychology stresses our profound and continual need for comparison with others and our past, our propensity to feel relatively deprived and envious, our focus on achieved over ascribed characteristics, our need to be validated by participating in socially rewarding—and rewarded—activities, our need for social and economic security, our altruism toward sufferers similar to ourselves, our propensity to attribute worldly success to personal traits and behaviors, and our need to perceive the world as just. All of this suggests that redistributive demands might come as the political working of psychological impulses. (Festinger, 1954; Merton, 1957; Pettigrew, 1967; Rainwater, 1974; Macauley and Berkowitz, 1970; Runciman, 1964; Rubin and Peplau, 1975; Jones et al., 1971).

Furthermore, other nations *have* moved in the direction predicted by Aristotle. Since World War II, Sweden, Denmark, and Great Britain have sought more economic equality through progressive taxation and social welfare policies. Nonwestern, nonliberal nations such as the People's Republic of China, Yugoslavia, and Tanzania have partially flattened wage and authority structures, at least in non-political institutions. We need not be surprised that Americans are not clamoring to follow the lead of Tanzania, but we do have close historical, cultural, and political ties with northern Europe. Why, then, are both masses and elites so much less egalitarian, particularly given our increasing dependence on the federal government for the redress of political, social, and economic grievances?

Finally, our current political and economic climates make redistributive demands plausible. The economic growth rate may be declining in the United States. In addition, in January 1975 over half of those with annual family incomes below $10,000 saw their financial position as only "fair" or "poor";

more than half of the population expected their family's financial situation to worsen or to stay the same. In 1978, respondents with incomes below $5,000 saw $10,348 as the "smallest amount a family of four needs to get along". At the same time, 54% of the population, including 65% of those with incomes below $3,000, expected prices to rise more than their incomes during the succeeding 12 months. At least one-third of the population consistently cites financial problems as their greatest worry (Gallup Opinion Index, 1975a, 1975b, 1976, 1977; Erskine, 1973). Decreasing economic growth can only exacerbate the economic problems of the poor and middle classes. What is more, relative deprivation theory suggests that the rise in prosperity and expectations in the 1960's will produce even greater discontent among the poor and increased demands on the government (Stouffer et al., 1949; Runciman, 1964; Festinger, 1954; Merton, 1957; Pettigrew, 1967).

EVIDENCE ON THE DISTRIBUTION OF WEALTH

One response to why does the dog not bark is that it doesn't really need to. That is, equality in the United States may fall short of theoretical expectations or desires, but nevertheless people are "Pretty equal". Compared to feudal, or some modern, societies, there are not great disparities of income and wealth; in fact, we are all middle class (Hartz, 1955). Others claim that compared with our efforts toward political and social equality, we naively or hypocritically deny the magnitude of economic inequality.

Income distribution data may be interpreted variously. The median money income for households in the United States in 1976 was estimated to be $12,686; the mean income was $14,922. Of all households, 18% had incomes less than $5,000, and 3.5% of the aggregate income. Fifteen percent earned over $25,000 and held 35% of the aggregate

Table 1: Percent of Households, Mean Income, and Aggregate Household Income in 1976 (in 1976 dollars)

				Total Household Income			
	under $5000	$5000–10,000	$10,000–15,000	$15,000–20,000	$20,000–25,000	$25,000–50,000	over $50,000
Percent of total households	17.9%	21.3	19.1	16.4	10.7	13.0	1.6
Mean household income	$2900	7360	12,340	17,290	22,240	31,910	69,720
Percent of aggregate household income	3.5%	10.5	15.8	19.0	16.0	27.8	7.4

Note: "The mean income of households with greater than $100,000 was assumed to be $100,000 exactly." This assumption depresses the measure of the degree of inequality shown in the "mean household income" row, since it does not take into account those households with incomes greater than $100,000. See U.S. Bureau of the Census (1978).

income (U.S. Bureau of the Census 1978). Table 1 shows the distribution of income in more detail. Note the wide range of incomes and the degree of skewness to the right.

Table 2 shows that income inequality before taxes and transfer payments has declined; the significance of the change is open to debate. The poorest 20% of the population continues to receive about 4% of the total income, and the richest 20% receives at least 40%. The largest change is a transfer from the richest (fifth) quintile to the third and fourth quintiles—from the wealthy to the upper middle classes—leaving the shares of the lowest two quintiles almost unchanged. Even though the absolute level of incomes has increased dramatically in the past 30 years, estimates suggest that the difference between the median and mean income for families has remained between $1,200 and $2,000 (U.S. Bureau of the Census, 1976).

Estimates about the effects of transfer payments and taxation are as controversial as evidence on pretransfer incomes. There is considerable evidence (Smeeding, 1977; Lampman, 1974; Plotnick, 1977) that government transfers reduce income inequality and raise close to half of the poor above the poverty level during any single year, but it cannot be shown that the amount of relative poverty has declined significantly over time. Morgan Reynolds and Eugene Smolensky (1973) have compared the size distribution of income in 1961 and 1970 after allocating all government taxes and expenditures across households. They conclude that "despite sizeable government efforts toward a more egalitarian distribution during the 1960's, . . . final distributions changed very little in ten years". They later suggest (1975) that this "disappointing" result is due largely to the fact that "most government benefits are distributed independent of income, and depend on characteristics like being a farmer, or aged, or a veteran, or driving an automobile, or going to a public college". Other studies suggest that the

Table 2: Percent Share of Aggregate Income Received by Various Quintiles, 1929-1976

Year	Lowest 10%	Lowest fifth	Second fifth	Third fifth	Fourth fifth	Highest fifth	Highest 5%	Highest 1%
1929		12.5%		13.8%	19.3%	54.4%	30.0%	14.6%
1935–36		4.1	9.2	14.1	20.9	51.7	26.5	12.5
1947	.72%	3.6	10.6	16.7	23.5	45.6	18.8	6.8
1957	.68	3.5	10.8	18.0	24.7	43.1	16.8	5.6
1967	.94	3.7	10.5	17.2	24.7	43.6	16.3	6.0
1976		4.3	10.4	17.0	24.7	43.6	16.5	

Note: The data from 1929, 1935-6, 1947, and 1957 are from Miller (1966) The data from 1967, the lowest 10%, and the highest 1% from 1947 on are from Budd (1970). The data from 1976 are from U.S. Bureau of the Census (1978). The lowest 5% of the population received .47% of the aggregate income in 1947 and .68% in 1969. See U.S. Congress (1972). Also see note to Table 1.

effect of taxes and transfer payments may in fact be redistributive upward, or may redistribute primarily within one
class. For example, social security transfers from young to
old middle-class citizens; low tuition at state universities transfers from old to young middle-class citizens (Pechman and
Okner, 1974; Abel-Smith, 1958; Boulding and Pfaff, 1972;
Gillespie, 1965; Hanson and Weisbrod, 1969; Dahl and Rae,
1975; Stigler, 1970).

Data on wealth are even more inferential and incomplete,
and much more unreliable than data on income. They suggest, however, much greater differences between the very rich
and the very poor. In 1962, the wealthiest 0.5% of the
population held 26% of all private assets; the wealthiest 8%
held 60%; the wealthiest 20% held 75%, and the poorest 25%
had no or negative net worth, since their debts equaled or
exceeded their assets (Thurow and Lucas, 1972). (Note the
discrepancy between Thurow and Lucas's and Smith and
Franklin's estimates of the holdings of the wealthiest 0.5% in
Table 4.) Table 3 provides greater detail.

Studies of the top holders of wealth argue that the distribution of wealth (1) became significantly more equal in the
1930's and early 1940's and (2) has remained essentially
unchanged since 1945 (Smith and Franklin, 1974). Using IRS
estate tax return data, the estimates in Table 4 have been
made of the holdings of the wealthiest. Even after progressive
taxation and efforts at downward transfers of income and
services, the wealthiest 1% of the population retains 25% of
the nation's wealth. And even these figures do not show the
full measure of the inequality of wealth, since they cannot
consider intangibles such as opporunity for further investment, security of assets, confidence in the future, and dispro-
portional benefits from some public goods and services (Miller and Roby, 1970). (Stanley Lebergott provides more
recent evidence on the distribution of wealth. Because of
different assumptions and measures, the 1962 and 1970 data

Table 3: Distribution of Wealth among American Families, 1962

					Net Worth of Family					
	negative	under $1000	$1000 –5000	$5000 10,000	$10,000 –25,000	$25,000 –50,000	$50,000– 100,000	$100,000 –200,000	$200,000 –500,000	over $500,000
Percent of total families	8.1%	17.3%	17.3%	14.2%	24.4%	11.2%	5.1%	1.0%	0.9%	0.5%
Percent of total net worth	–0.2%	0	2.1	4.5	17.2	17.1	15.0	5.4	12.9	25.8

Median wealth: $ 7,550
Mean wealth: $22,588

Data is from Thurow and Lucas (1972) and Projector (1964).

sets do not permit comparisons over time, but Table 4a reinforces the conclusion of Table 4 that wealth is much more unequally distributed than income.)

These data can be interpreted variously. Some claim that "available statistical data indicate that over-all income inequality in the United States has been diminishing since the 1920's," and that "the United States has traveled a considerable distance toward absolute equality of incomes" (Spengler, 1973; National Bureau of Economic Research, cited in Kolko, 1964). Others claim that "poverty and inequality are . . . integral to a society where the richest tenth receives 30% of the annual money income, as in 1961, or 14% of the nation owns 68% of the net wealth, as in 1962 . . . . The basic distribution of income and wealth in the United States is essentially the same now as it was in 1939, or 1910" (Spengler, 1973; National Bureau of Economic Research, cited in Kolko, 1964). Similarly, "America can be described as an unequal society that would like to think of itself as egalitarian" (Gans, 1973: XI).

Even avoiding the elaborate methodological and ideological foundations on which these claims are based, we can still note that there are enormous disparities in household income and (especially) wealth, that median wealth is well below the mean, that "Progressive" income taxes and transfer payments may not be redistributing downward, that 24.7 million people were below the government-defined poverty line in 1977, and the number and proportion of the poor are increasing, and that the wealthiest 0.5% of the population owns 20% of the nation's wealth (New Haven Journal-Courier, 1977).

ATTITUDES TOWARD DOWNWARD REDISTRIBUTION

Economic inequality persists in a society that prides itself on its social and political equality and majoritarian decision-making processes. And yet, the dog does not bark, at least

Table 4: Share of Wealth Held by Richest 0.5% and 1.0% of the Population of the United States, 1922-1969

	Year											
	1922	1929	1933	1939	1945	1949	1953	1956	1958	1962	1965	1969
top 0.5%	29.8%	32.4%	25.2%	28.0%	20.9%	19.3%	22.7%	25.0%	21.7%	21.6%	23.7%	19.9%
top 1.0%	31.6	36.3	28.3	30.6	22.8	20.8	23.6	26.0	26.9	27.4	29.2	24.9

Data from 1922 to 1956 from Lampman (1959). Data from 1958 to 1969 from Smith and Franklin: due to measurement problems, "the time series of wealth distributions understates the degree of concentration in any given year, but is consistent and permits comparisons over time" (Smith and Franklin, 1974: 163).

Table 4a: Distribution of Wealth among Families and Unrelated Individuals in 1970

	Adjusted Gross Income for Families and Individuals								
	under $1000	$1000 –5000	$5000 10,000	$10,000 –15,000	$15,000 –25,000	$25,000 –50,000	$50,000 200,000	over $200,000	top 1%
Percent of total families & individuals	8.3%	29.66	30.03	19.00	10.03	2.27	0.55	0.02	1.00
Percent of total wealth	1.32%	13.91	19.84	18.07	18.02	13.52	11.65	3.57	19.86

From Stanley Lebergott, *The American Economy: Income, Wealth, and Want* (Princeton: Princeton University Press, 1976): 242

not much. The poor do not demand the equalization of incomes or, more important wealth. Trade unions have sought better wages, working conditions, and benefits—not reductions in wage differentials or ties between corporate profits and wages (Hoxie, 1966; Perlman, 1970). Socialists have demanded public ownership of industries, the creation of opportunities to advance for oppressed groups, and changes in American foreign policy—not a fundamental reordering of property and wage relations (Laslett and Lipset, 1974; Shannon, 1955; Sombart, 1906; Samson, 1935). The United States has no viable leftist party; at best one wing of the Democratic Party acts as a mild social-democratic movement.

On the contrary, anarchists, not egalitarians, have dominated American radicalism. American radicals are more likely to oppose government interference in individual autonomy than to seek government aid in the creation of substantive equality (Jacker, 1968; Silverman, 1970; Rubenstein, 1970). Even egalitarian communal movements have insisted on voluntary membership and freedom from outside intervention (Nordhoff, 1965; Noyes, 1961; Fogarty, 1972).

Four questions on national surveys have asked about redistributive views. Two suggest reducing income differentials by transferring money from the rich to the poor. In 1937, 43% of the poor and 18% of the prosperous agreed that the "federal government should take money from those who have much and give money to those who have little". In 1974, 55% of those with incomes under $4,000, 44% between $4,000 and $10,000, 32% between $10,000 and $15,000, and 23% over $15,000 agreed that the government ought to use tax and welfare policies to "reduce the income differences between the rich and the poor" (Fortune, 1937; Hansen, 1976).

Support for steeply progressive taxation to alleviate poverty is strongest among the poor and has increased in all income categories. However, no more than 55% of the poor strongly support a program for their benefit. Other survey data support this finding; more poor than rich support anti-poverty programs but never do a majority of the poor do so.

Two other questions focus explicitly on achieving substantive equality through redistribution. As the emphasis on equalization increases, agreement at all income levels decreases. Again, more poor than rich favor redistributive programs, but fewer than half do so. Overall support for substantive equality has declined from 1939 to 1969 (see Table 5). (Other *Fortune* survey questions follow the trend

Table 5:   Attitudes toward Redistribution of Income and Income Level

| | Income Level* | | | |
	Poor	Lower Middle Class	Upper Middle Class	Prosperous
A. (1939) Do you think our government should or should not redistribute wealth by heavy taxes on the rich?				
Should	45.6%	33.5%	27.9%	17.3%
	Income Level			
	under $4000	$4000 –6000	$6000– 10,000	over $10,000
B. (1969) "Every family in this country should receive the same income, about $10,000 a year or so." (Agree-disagree) (N = 1017)				
Agree	14%	17%	16%	7%

*Sample includes only whites
Cell entries are percent of income category
Data is from *Fortune* (1939) and Feagin (1973). Other *Fortune* survey questions follow the trend of these two sets of questions; as the focus on substantive equalization becomes stronger and more concrete, support for it declines in all classes (see Hochschild, 1977).

of these two sets of questions; as the focus on substantive equalization becomes stronger and more concrete, support for it declines in all classes, Hochschild, 1977.)

The outlines of the picture are clear but the details are lacking. Is changing support a function of question wording or of substantive changes in ideology or circumstance? Why do those who would benefit from redistribution, but not from welfare, support the latter but not the former? How do supporters and opponents within one class differ? What specific policies do supporters, and opponents, of redistribution prefer? Why do some of the wealthy support downward redistribution? Most important, why do so many people with incomes below the mean oppose policies that would benefit them substantially?

All of this, of course, is not new. But social scientists have explained the absence of American socialism with historical, institutional, and sociological reasons; they have largely ignored the more precise question of redistributive demands and relevant individual beliefs, perceptions and desires. Individual views are embedded in contexts; here I can examine only the views, not the contexts. Yet the extent of the harm caused by great economic inequality justifies even a partial explanation of its causes. The first-order effects of poverty are obvious—malnutrition and ill health, misery and bitterness, wasted talents and untapped energies, the costs of maintaining minimal order in ghettos and rural backwaters. More subtle but just as destructive are second-order effects of the "religion of inequality"; it "has the natural and necessary effect, under present circumstances, of materializing our upper class, vulgarizing our middle class, and brutalizing our lower class. And this is to fail in civilization" (Arnold, cited in Myers, 1945: 7). Inequalities in wealth persist through the welfare syndrome, class biases in education and job recruitment, unequal access to political resources and benefits, and unequal economic possibilities. These economic inequalities in turn perpetuate further political and social inequities and prevent true political liberty. If we can understand why people accept such a system, perhaps we can take more intelligent steps toward mitigating it.

REASONS FOR THE DISCREPANCY
BETWEEN THEORETICAL EXPECTATIONS
AND EMPIRICAL EVIDENCE

This effort at understanding is part of a research project consisting of intensive interviews with 27 white working adults with family incomes below $12,000 or above $30,000. Respondents were randomly chosen from selected neighborhoods in a Northeastern city and were interviewed for six hours apiece on their perceptions, explanation, evaluations, and desires about issues of distributive justice. The openended conversations range from the distribution of money and authority within the family, school, and work place, to views on "fair incomes," class structures, and government policies, to the meaning of words such as justice, equality, and democracy. The respondents' viewpoints and other evidence can be categorized according to four elements: (1) the general structure of positions in society; (2) the general structure of payments to positions;[1] (3) one's own place in the structure of positions; and (4) one's place in the structure of payments to positions. Logically, one can accept or reject the status quo for any of these elements independently of the others.

Four combinations of these four elements will be examined here. They are:

(1) "Acceptors": some people accept both the general structures of positions and of payments and they accept their own place in both structures. They seek no major changes.

(2) "the Ambitious": some people accept both general structures but reject their own location in both. They compete with other

individuals to change their personal situation, but they seek no fundamental structural changes.

(3) "Inconsistents": some reject both general structures, but accept their own location in both. They live with a basic inconsistency between their general and their particular viewpoints.

(4) "Radicals": some reject both general structures and they reject their own place in both. They seek fundamental political-economic changes in which redistribution is only one of several elements.

The purest redistributive viewpoint is:

(5) "Redistributionists": some accept the general structure of positions and their own place within it, but they reject both the general structure of payments and their own payment. The redistributionist standpoint will not be considered further in this article, although it will be in the completed research.

A final impediment to redistributive demands lie outside the set of economic concerns, and therefore the structures of positions and payments:

(6) "Nonmaterialists": some argue that the whole matter of economic structures is less important than other, nonmaterial concerns. They seek reforms such as increased political participation, more law and order, a better quality of life—issues affected by, but not directly related to, economic reforms.

Schematically, these viewpoints are shown in Figure 1.

Figure 1: Viewpoints on the Nature of Payments and Positions in Society and in One's Own Life

	General Structure of Positions	General Structure of Payments	One's Place in Structure of Positions	One's Place in Structure of Payments
Acceptors	+	+	+	+
Ambitious	+	+	−	−
Redistributions	+	−	+	−
Inconsistents	−	−	+	+
Radicals	−	−	−	−
Nonmaterialists	0	0	0	0

Key: + indicates acceptance
      − indicates rejection
      0 indicates indifference

The viewpoints treated here—acceptance, ambition, inconsistency, economic radicalism, and nonmaterialism—combine to form more than a list but less than a full theory. I shall consider their joint theoretical ramifications after examining each separately.

ACCEPTANCE

Each viewpoint has several components, some or all of which may be found in a single person's attitudes.

Identification with the employer. An element of the first viewpoint is identification with the employer; the poor and insecure see their relationships with those higher on the economic ladder as harmonious rather than conflictual.

Americans see high profits as a just return for an industrialist's efforts, and they believe that businesses use their profits in the public interest. In 1946, for example, most wage earners did not think a company making an exceptionally high profit should therefore increase workers' wages. Similarly, only 7% of the sample thought over half the labor leaders had a "sense of social responsibility," compared with 60% who thought over half the businessmen had such a sense. In January 1977, 37% of those with incomes below $7,000 thought big government would "be the biggest threat to the country in the future," compared with 21% choosing big labor and only 18% choosing big business as the biggest threat. In 1978, 51% of the population held government "most responsible for inflation"; business was blamed by 13% and labor by 20% (Gallup Poll, 1978). Even after the Bert Lance affair raised suspicions nationwide about the ethics of bankers, 39% of Americans including 35% with incomes below $5000 gave bankers "very high" or "high" ratings for their honesty and ethical standards. Comparable ratings for Congressmen were 16% over all and 23% among the poor. Only 13% total and 14% of the poor gave labor union leaders high or very high ratings (Gallup Opinion Index, Jan. 1978).

Acceptors among my interviewees sometimes question the ethics or practices of particular corporations—Lockheed, Penn Central, local steel manufacturers—but the right to private property is inviolable. They may wish for better wages, or more philanthropy, but they are shocked at the idea of redistribution through taxes on profits or inheritance. To some, violating private ownership is simply inconceivable, or at best un-American and undemocratic. Others, with no expectations of upward mobility, nevertheless put themselves in their employers' place. One unskilled worker, when asked about the fairness of corporate executives inheriting their place, answered, "Well, if their parents were wealthy and they inherited it, good, fine. Sure it's fair. If I had money, and I gave it to my children, they inherited it, that's good. Good luck to 'em."

Psychological explanations for these views range from the Freudian identification with authority and the "Cult of gratitude" among mobiles to theories of deference and the American worship of success. Structural explanations focus on the industrial and bureaucratic settings, where authority is faceless, organization is hierarchic, and minute divisions foster conflict among peers (Tumin, 1957; Rosenberg, 1953; Mann, 1973; Lawler, 1977). Finally, identification with the employer may be perfectly rational from the viewpoint of the vulnerable individual; it does not make immediate sense to bite the hand that feeds you.

Support for meritocracy. A second feature of acceptance is a belief in meritocracy and its consequences. People see the general distribution of persons and payments to positions as fairly derived, so they accept their own position and payment as fair. Involved in this perception are a belief in equal opportunity, a fear of substantive equality, and self-imposed limits on aspirations.

First, many see equality of opportunity as the only desirable form of equality. In addition, they believe that the United States in fact gives everyone an equal chance to find his or her proper level. One respondent, named Sally White, is an unsuccessful entrepreneur herself, but she insists that there are no longer barriers to equal opportunity for all because "you have your SBA to help people out. There's all kinds of help and there's education programs and this and that and training and, you know, job programs and, well, there's everything! There's *no* reason why people can't get out and work nowadays". Thus, if the poor have as good a chance for success as the rich, then economic failure is their own fault and a salutary lesson to others. Too much help through direct governmental redistribution would spoil the poor, reduce work incentives for all, and penalize the deserving middle classes (Lane, 1962; Potter, 1954; Chinoy, 1955; Sennett and Cobb, 1973; Huber and Form, 1973).

More specifically, most Americans attribute both poverty and success to personal traits. In 1969, 51% of those with incomes below $4,000 gave individualist explanations for poverty (laziness, wastefulness); 25% gave fatalist explanations (luck and illness); and 29% gave structural ones (poor educational system, exploitation by the rich). The comparable figures for those with incomes between $4,000 and $6,000 were 57%, 18%, and 20% (Feagin, 1973).[3] Three-quarters of those most disadvantaged by the political-economic system believe their situation to be unremediable by political action.

Recent polls do not permit a structural explanation of success. However, at least 80% of all income groups recently agreed that "people who are successful get ahead" through ability, not luck. In 1945, 69% of self-identified middle-class respondents thought ability determined success, compared with 52% of the self-identified working class respondents. Comparable figures for other explanations are 3% to 8% for luck, 6% to 16% for pull, and 18% to 20% for better opportunities (Gallup Opinion Index, 1970; Centers, 1949). Sally White again: "people *can* make money if they put their little minds to it and get off their little rear ends. I think what happens is people get lazy". Similarly, Maria Pulaski, who is sinking deeper and deeper into debt despite her full-time work as a cleaning woman at age 60, still believes that "if you want to do it, you'll do it. You'll try hard. You have to work for it, otherwise you don't get it. Education is good, but if you don't have the education you can still work and try to earn the money".

Second, a fear of equality and legitimation of huge income differentials reduce dissonance for the poor. Workers may be envious, but they are not hostile toward the rich; my respondents argued that professionals deserved compensation for their extra responsibility and schooling and their "higher" skills. Maria says her employers deserve their large salary because "they worked for it, why not? You work for it, it's fair. If I got a good education and I'm doing a different job, a harder job, I deserve more. I don't believe in this equal, all equal". Most of the poor do not understand progressive income taxes, although they want the rich to pay their "fair share". Research on belief in a just world—that people ultimately receive deserved rewards and penalities—suggests that upper-middle-class respondents in fact perceive more inequity and injustice than working class respondents (Coles, 1971; Rubin and Peplau, 1975; Lerner and Elkinton, 1976; Lane, 1962).

Many respondents fear that equalizing incomes would destroy the fabric of society. People would refuse to work, either because they could survive without working or because they would not receive enough money to make it worth while. Eugene Santaguida knows that he did not have the same opportunity to advance as someone born into "the Woolworth family," but he still insists that inequality is necessary:

> That's the way it's gotta be. Because it'd be a hell of a world to live in if we didn't have *some* rich and *some* poor. You gotta have

all classes. Who'd mow your lawn then? Who'd do your house-
work? Who'd go picking up the garbage? You gotta have people
with money that you have to look up to and do work for them.
We don't, most of the people don't like rich people; that's what's
gotta be.

Finally, the poor aspire to less in their careers and incomes. They may desire the same things as the rich, but they
limit their expectations of achievement and environmental
support as they approach adulthood, when goals and results
must be compared. This self-restriction is fostered by an
educational system that tracks students and an occupational
system that requires educational and social credentials
(Stephanson, 1957; Rosenbaum, 1976; Bowles and Gintis,
1976; Thurow, 1976). These internal and external restrictions obviously reduce redistributive demands; psychologically, it is only sane to accept an apparently unchangeable
system.

Redistribution = welfare = charity. The connotations of
redistribution itself suggest another reason for acceptance;
redistribution is a fancy term for welfare, which is a fancy
term for charity, and most Americans want no part of it.
Responding to needs by equalizing incomes is demeaning to
the recipient and philanthropic to the donor, rather than
being a restitution to correct past injustices.

Welfare recipients may be seen as dishonest, promiscuous,
and lazy; welfare payments therefore should be cut back and
more tightly administered. A more subtle view holds that
welfare recipients are disadvantaged, deprived, and helpless
rather than evil; welfare payments therefore are charitable
and should be "rehabilitative". Those who hold either view
would be horrified at the idea of receiving welfare themselves. For example, if Salvador Tivolli, who formerly labored
in a munitions factory, had to accept welfare, he would "feel
ashamed or something, ya know what I mean? Because

there's always a way of makin' a living, I don't give a damn what anybody says". If a guaranteed annual income is seen as an extension of welfare, and redistribution as an extension of both, few self-respecting people would demand, or even accept, redistribution in their favor. Only a sophisticated elite and the radicalized poor see welfare as a right or restitution, or as a self-defense measure of an imperfect capitalist system.[4] Similarly, very few people see downward redistribution as a corrective to the government subsidies and services that currently redistribute upward.

Americans do support state aid to individuals facing certain debilitating handicaps (the blind, the old) or exceptional circumstances for which no one, even the provident middle-class citizen, could be expected fully to prepare for (severe illness, natural disaster). Thus some redistribution in kind is seen as the right of citizens in an affluent state, not as charitable dispensations from patron to client. Of course, these transfers often benefit primarily the middle class, such as social security, wage and price controls, and national health insurance. Thus people resist downward redistribution, support horizontal redistribution, and are ignorant of upward redistribution.

Misperceptions of the distribution of wealth. Finally, Acceptors overestimate the number of their economic peers and underestimate the amount and range of wealth and poverty. In my sample, doctors and lawyers in the top decile of the distribution of wealth see themselves as middle class, as do cleaning women and some laborers; the incomes of self-identified middle-class respondents ranged from $5,000 to $75,000 (Pen, 1971; Schreiber and Nygren, 1970; Rainwater, 1974). Perceptions of the full distribution of wealth among my interviewees appear as shown in Figure 2. People at point A know they are at the bottom. They are aware that others are vastly wealthier than they, but they do not distinguish much between incomes of $15,000 and $50,000 a year.

Figure 2: Perceptions of Household Income

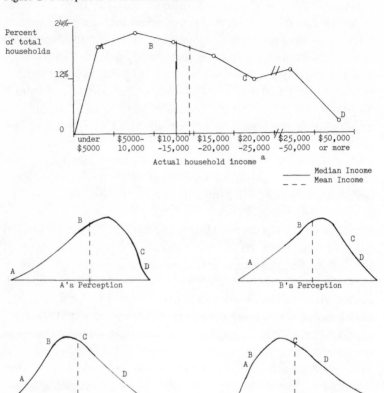

aU.S. Bureau of the Census (1978)

They can barely imagine a $500,000 yearly income. They, like the others, have difficulty conceiving a radically different distribution of wealth and income, but if they understand it they know that they would benefit from downward redistribution. They do not demand it, however, for reasons suggested above and perhaps because of experience with the present welfare system (Katz, Gutek, Kahn, and Barton,

1975; Davis, Gardner, and Gardner, 1966; Gitlin and Hollander, 1971).

People at point B misperceive the most; their subjective status is much higher than their objective status measured by income or occupation. They know there are many poorer and many richer, and they may resent both extremes (Litwak, Hooyman, and Warren, 1973). However, they feel more threat from the closeness of the poor than the distance of the rich, so they identify with the middle class to which they aspire and reject "welfarism". Partly because they are unaware of the skewed distribution of wealth, they expect to be donors rather than recipients of redistribution. They therefore oppose it.

People at point C perceive the distribution most accurately. They are less insecure about their position than people at B, so they need not cling as strongly to the fear and envy of the poor. But their greater self-confidence and their typical upward mobility lead them to covet an even better position. Thus they neither see themselves as beneficiaries of redistribution nor are they willing to pay for it.

People at point D know they are well-off, but they neither see themselves as the economic elite nor do they realize the extent of poverty. They oppose redistribution on both self-interested and moral grounds; they usually rose from an "average" middle-class background and believe that they did so by their ability and effort. Thus their humanitarianism is blurred by skewed perceptions, and their material interests and ethical principles coincide in fostering opposition to redistribution.

PERSONAL AMBITION

A framework of mobility. Some people accept low positions and payments because they obscure and deny conflicts between themselves and the rest of society. Others also oppose redistribution, but for different reasons. They too

accept the given structures of positions and payments; how-
ever, they reject their own situation within these structures.
They are personally ambitious, but politically conservative.
The Ambitious deflect class conflict differently from the
Acceptors—they substitute real but superficial struggles for
more fundamental ones.

Within a static structure of positions and payments, individuals may make various movements. They can remain
where they began, whether rich or poor, secure or insecure;
they can move upward; or they can move downward. Liberal
theory assumes that everyone wants a high income in a
reliable and prestigious occupation. However, not everyone
can have a steady income above the mean and a secure job.
The basic conflict, therefore, lies between those with reliably
high incomes and everyone else.

The people considered here think only of moving among
positions and payments, not of changing the structure to
eliminate the differences among them. In an economy that
grows more slowly than the population or its desires, most
movements must be conflictual. Downward movement may
not directly match upward movement, but seldom can all win
and none lose. This could occur only under one of three
conditions: (1) everyone becomes satisfied with the status
quo, or mutually acceptable and noncoercive trades are
made; (2) income and status are redistributed so that everyone has the same amount of both, would mutually acceptable
trades be permissible? (Nozick, 1974); and (3) people believe
that new opportunities for generating wealth and status are
completely open, so that upward movement forges a new
path without impinging on others' choices or possibilities
(Locker, 1967; de Tocqueville, 1969).

Since none of these conditions obtains, movement among
positions and payments creates conflicts that obscure redistributive demands.

Movement within one stratum. Conflict among members
of the same stratum, especially the poorest, is the most

pernicious both personally and structurally. This is not merely a problem of false consciousness, but rather one of the industrial reserve army. When jobs are scarce, two unskilled workers have a critical conflict of interest; within this structure the insecurity of any unemployed person arises directly from the existence of others in the same situation. There are simply too many people for too few positions, and the focus is on the assignment of people within the given structure of payments and positions, not on changing it. The poor are unaware both that this conflict is avoidable and that it is the most harmful and needless for them.

Division among the poor and powerless can be based on race, sex, region, employment status; it occurs among individuals and between organized groups or nations. Salvador Tivolli grumbles about his problems in receiving disability pay. "I just got a notice from the social security, I'll have to go to the lawyers *again* now. I tell ya, boy, ya gotta be *black* ya gotta be *black* to get anything today". Esther McLean's husband, a welder, is shocked (and she is secretly pleased) that his company just hired a woman to replace a laid-off worker. Explanations for intraclass antagonism are psychological (invoking theories of learned helplessness, defensive reference groups, envy, alienation, personalism, and lack of abstraction), historical (tracing the formation of nation-states, trade unions, racial and sexual taboos), and economic (analyzing marginality, capitalist efficiency, political power and impotence.) But all conflict among the poor diverts attention from the social structure and redistributive possibilities; it is perfectly reasonable and understandable, but finally self-destructive.

Successful movement. Upward mobility—which defines liberty as freedom from restraint by others, equality as equal opportunity to become unequal, and fraternity as an atavistic drag on competition and progress—is the step beyond conflict within one stratum. At age 27, Sally White is now unemployed after holding six clerical jobs in 10 years, mostly in small companies that have failed. Nevertheless, she says, "I have no doubt that I will, you know, make out well. Because I'm very ambitious, so if there's something I want, I'll do it." She "really hopes" there will always be rich people in this country, "because if there wasn't, it'd take away all my hopes of ever being there. Really, it would take away my feeling to push myself, you know. What would be the sense of pushing if I couldn't get rich by doing it?".

Upward mobility takes two paths. Contest mobility— movement from a low-paying, low-status, insecure job to a lucrative, insecure job with uncertain status, to a lucrative, prestigious, secure job—is the Horatio Alger story (Turner, 1966). Using luck and skill, individuals rise by breaking rules and creating new channels for achieving success. A group can make this move (witness the Irish creation in the nineteenth century of a new type of politician), but chances diminish as numbers increase. Although widespread contest mobility requires a fluid and rapidly expanding economy, at least 70% of all classes of Americans recently sampled approve of this kind of mobility and rated its chances for success very highly (Turner, 1966).[5]

The other path is sponsored mobility—from low-paying, insecure, low-status jobs, to low-paying, secure, respectable jobs, to lucrative, prestigious, secure jobs. It is equally unac- commodating to redistributive demands, and more likely in the present economy. In this case, the elite or its agents select certain persons, sponsor them through a cumulative tracking process, and finally induct them into a higher status. As trade union history and affirmative action programs suggest, the second path is more feasible for groups than the first path. Over 90% of both the American and the British sample approved this type of mobility; but more Americans rated one's chance for success very highly—91%, compared with 75% of the Britons (Turner, 1966).

Most Americans see upward mobility as a fact as well as a norm. The longer the time period considered, the more

mobility they perceive in their own lives; 67% of the lower
class and 77% of the upper class see themselves as better off
than their parents were at the same age (Erskine, 1969).
Americans *are* now more affluent; however, people mistake
absolute for relative improvement, so they are unaware that
their position in the total range of inequality has not
changed. They also attribute their share of a society-wide
economic growth to individual achievement rather than to
political and economic forces beyond their control.

As many manual workers as professionals are optimistic
about long-term success, even though fewer workers are
pleased with their movement in the near past. A reanalysis of
the 1939 Roper survey found that among employed respondents, blue collar workers were the least pleased with their
own past progress and future prospects, but the most optimistic about their children's opportunities. Only wage
workers and the unemployed had an optimism toward the
future that was not congrument with their own evaluations
of the past (Verba and Schlozman, 1977).

More recent surveys maintain the trend toward low-income
optimism. When perceptions of the near past and expectations of the near future are compared, respondents with
incomes below the mean ($13,800 in 1975) are more opti-
mistic than those above the mean (see Table 6). When expectations for the nation's near and distant future are compared,
low-income respondents are again much more optimistic than
high-income respondents (Gallup Opinion Index, 1975).

All three sets of data suggest that low-income respondents
are less realistic than high-income respondents, in that their
expectations are less warranted by their experience. An individualistic optimism strong enough to withstand experience,
and strongest among those who would benefit most from
redistribution, has obvious antiredistributive effects.

Albert Hirschman's "tunnel effect" may explain this low-
income optimism. Until recently, the expanding and increasingly service-oriented American economy permitted upward

Table 6: Perceptions of Improvement in Financial Standing and Income Level, 1975

				Income Level			
	under $3000	$3000–5000	$5000–7000	$7000–10,000	$10,000–15,000	$15,000–20,000	over $20,000
A. (1975) Would you say that you and your family are better off or worse off financially today than you were twelve months ago?							
Better off	12%	7%	17%	18%	26%	27%	35%
B. (1975) Looking ahead, do you think that twelve months from now, you and your family will be better off financially or worse off?							
Worse off	22%	18%	28%	31%	37%	34%	39%
C. Optimism bias	+10	+11	+11	+13	+11	+7	+4

Cell entries are percent of income category
Optimism bias is B-A, or the difference between expectation of future financial improvement and perception of past financial improvement. Positive values indicate optimism; negative values indicate pessimism. Data is from Gallup Opinion Index (1975).

mobility without an equal and opposite downward effect. Under these conditions, people who see others progressing will expect their own position to improve accordingly, despite their current immobility (Hirschman and Rothschild, 1973).

Once one expects progress, emotional dynamics and perceptual blinders mitigate against redistributive demands, even if one's expectations are not fulfilled. Grateful and insecure mobiles go through anticipatory socialization, typically adopting the conservative, individualistic attitudes that they see as representative of their new class (Lopreato, 1967; Lipset, 1963; Lipset and Zetterberg, 1959). Sally White describes people like herself as "more or less upper-middle-class workers. Semi professionals or whatever. We've always been workers, we've always been money-makers. We've always been onto the newest idea: 'Let's see how to make money here' ".

However, Table 6 suggests a caveat. In no case do a majority of those with incomes below the mean see their past, their immediate future, or their long-term future in a rosy light; and fewer poor are gratified or optimistic than rich. Thus, arguments about the inverse relationship between unsupported belief in upward mobility and opposition to redistribution apply to only a minority of the relevant population. Others, the Acceptors, may simply be satisfied with their situation or unable to imagine a better one. Still others, competitors within one stratum, concentrate on remaining where they are. Finally, some perceive change in their life, but in a negative direction. We now turn to this group.

Unsuccessful movement. It is initially surprising that the downwardly mobile, who are failing in the system by their own standards, are not prime candidates for redistributive appeals. However, few people believe that they are on a permanent downslope even when they recognize a recent decline. Harold Wilensky found that more skidders than nonskidders identified themselves as middle or upper class, and expected their children to be the same (Wilensky and Edwards, 1959). Table 7 shows that 42% with incomes below the mean believe that their financial position has worsened recently, compared to 28% of the wealthiest; yet only 11% of the lower class and 2% of the upper class believe that they are worse off than their parents (Gallup Opinion Index, 1975; Erskine, 1969). Similarly, more poor than rich expect the near future to be worse than the present, but in all classes many fewer are pesimistic about the future than are discouraged with the past. Most important, those with incomes below the mean are less likely than those above it to extrapolate pessimistically into the near future even if they are discouraged with the recent past (see pessimism bias).

This optimistic bias can be explained both structurally and psychologically. First, the few who plummet from success to failure usually have some obvious personal defect that explains their fall to others and themselves. Most commonly, downward mobility is from low white collar to high blue collar occupations, and it is often blurred enough by compensating factors to make it palatable (Parkin, 1971). Second, even those aware of their downward movement see their fall as temporary and they cling to old convictions. They maintain distance between themselves and their new peers by exaggerating the manners and attitudes of the higher, more conservative classes.

Skidders will be radicalized only by adopting an ideology that simultaneously recognizes skidding and restores self-respect. It must both define skidding as a structural phenomenon, not a personal failure, and substitute another indicator of status for income or occupation. An intelligent redistributive ideology fulfills these criteria, but encounters a vicious cycle. It is too threatening for skidders to adopt it until it is more generally accepted, and it will not be widely acceptable until it is adopted by more people, especially skidders.

Table 7: Perceptions of Worsening of Financial Standing and Income Level, 1975

				Income Level			
	under $3000	$3000–5000	$5000–7000	$7000–10,000	$10,000–15,000	$15,000–20,000	over $20,000
A. (1975) Would you say that you and your family are better off or worse off financially today than you were twelve months ago?							
Worse off	51%	47%	42%	44%	42%	40%	28%
B. (1975) Looking ahead, do you think that twelve months from now, you and your family will be better off financially or worse off?							
Worse off	37%	35%	33%	33%	28%	34%	23%
C. Pessimism bias	–14	–12	–9	–11	–14	–6	–5

Cell entries are percent of income category
Pessimism bias is B-A, or the difference between expectation of future financial improvement and perception of past financial improvement. Positive values indicate Pessimism; negative values indicate optimism. Data is from Gallup Opinion Index (1975).

[69]

Thus some opposition to redistribution derives from acceptance of the general structures of positions and payments. Acceptors either cannot imagine a different social system and personal situation or they simply reject it. The Ambitious seek a better personal situation, but only in the context of the given structures. Other people, however, do not accept these structures, but they too do not support redistributive policies. We turn now to them.

INCONSISTENTS

Inconsistents reject the general structures of positions and payments but accept their own place within those illegitimate structures. Their standpoint may be manipulative, acquiescent, or alienated. The people in this category are the most attractive, and frustrating, to redistributionists. They have the ideological prerequisites for making radical demands, but there is a slippage between their perception of the polity and their conclusions on what they can or should do about that perception.

Dissatisfaction with the general political situation is common. In 1977, 22% or less of those with incomes below $10,000 had "a great deal" or "quite a lot" of confidence in labor unions, big business, Congress, the Supreme Court, or free enterprise, compared with over 34% with confidence in medicine and organized religion. Fewer than 20% of the poor want their son to enter the corrupt and crooked business of politics. Of the population 67% believe that some Senators and Representatives won election by "unethical and illegal methods in their campaign," and 20% believe this about a majority of the members of Congress. "Dissatisfaction with government" and "corruption in government" are among the top five national problems; in 1974, 48% of the population blamed government for inflation, compared with 16% blaming big business and 19% blaming big labor (Gallup Opinion Index, 1973a, 1973b, 1974, 1976, 1977; Erskine,

Table 8: Personal and Societal Satsifaction and Income Level, 1975

				Income Level			
	under $3000	$3000 –5000	$5000 –7000	$7000– 10,000	$10,000 –15,000	$15,000 –20,000	over $20,000
(1973) On the whole, would you say you are satisfied or dissatisfied with . . .							
A. your standard of living: Satisfied	60%	54%	66%	70%	73%	77%	89%
B. the future facing you and your family: Satisfied	46%	38%	51%	50%	52%	58%	70%
C. the way this nation is being governed: Satisfied	21%	24%	29%	23%	25%	29%	34%
D. the honesty and standards of behavior of people in this country today: Satisfied	20%	26%	22%	22%	20%	24%	23%

Cell entries are percent of income category. Data are from Gallup Opinion Index (1973).

1974). More pointedly, satisfaction with both one's own life and the national situation declines with income; but for all levels, personal satisfaction exceeds societal satisfaction (see Table 8). Clearly, many who fear for the political and economic state of the nation nonetheless are content with their own economic lot. However, the nature of this discrepancy is suggested only in more focused studies.

Manipulators. Manipulators are the most purely self-interested among opponents to redistribution, since they have neither the narrow perceptions and constrained desires of the Acceptors and Ambitious nor the alternative values of the Radicals and Nonmaterialists. They are willing to live with an illegitimate system because they derive benefits from it. They are self-conscious free riders:

> a worker who thought he would benefit from a "proletarian" government would not find it rational to risk his life and resources to start a revolution against the bourgeois government . . . . As in any large, latent group, each individual in the [working] class will find it to his advantage if all of the costs or sacrifices necessary to achieve the common goal are borne by others . . . . There are *no* individual economic *incentives* for class action [Olsen, 1968: 106, 108] .

Richard Christie demonstrates that self-interested manipulators, or high Machiavellians resist social influence, try to initiate and control structures, are cynical about others, and will "exploit whatever resources the situation affords". They are more successful at manipulating their environment to their own advantage than are low Machiavellians. They are particularly successful in using competition and entrepreneurship to achieve great economic success; but in situations where cooperation will produce greater results, high Machiavellians are more cooperative than low Machiavellians. No significant relationships between gross demographic variables, ideology, or political party identification and

Machiavellianism have been found, although social class differences have not been carefully studied. Machiavellian orientations may be increasing over time (Christie and Geis, 1970).

In my interviews, manipulators appear more among the
wealthy than the poor. However, several low-income respondents distinguished between a norm of egalitarianism desirable in an ideal world and their perception of the real world
today. They argue that it is inappropriate to use ideal standards of justice and moral action in a system that is not ideal;
thus people should do all they can to get ahead, even unethi-
cally. Eugene Santaguida, earlier quoted as arguing the need
for classes, has no illusions about equal opportunity and
virtue in creating wealth. He explains the existence of the
rich by saying:

> They outsmarted other rich men, and other smart men, to get
> that money. They know how to *maneuver* their money. I think
> they deserve it, anyone who knows how to manipulate with
> money. An honest man never makes it, have to be a *thief.* If *I*
> steal $20, I'll have to confess it or they'll make me go to jail.
> *They* can steal $20,000, $20,000,000. He has the money to
> manipulate people. Money is power. That's how you get the big
> money, by manipulating, gyping *some*body. Above the law or
> within the law.

But society should not confiscate these ill-gotten holdings:

> It's their money—do as they please. If I was rich, I wouldn't want
> anybody telling me what to do with *my* money. Do what *I* want
> with it. I earned it, I maneuvered, I stole it, I did everything to
> get it. Well, if a guy got rich, just robbed banks, and he had
> people working for him, just robbin' them banks of all that
> money, that's *his. He* took all these chances. It belongs to *him.*

Besides, the poor are just as dishonest; they are simply less
successful manipulators. "The fella working in the shop, he's

trying to gyp his boss out of a day's work, and he's dishonest. Everybody's out to beat everybody, and it's just human nature to try to get away with everything you can."

Acquiescents. Acquiescents are epitomized by the post-1960's New Leftists, now uneasily embedded in the structures they formerly protested:

> The basic thing that Harvard runs on is that people here deserve to earn a lot of money. And so a lot of my classmates will go on to perpetuate the system; they'll be doctors and lawyers, and they'll say, "I'm going to do a lot of good things for other people, radical things, but I must be well paid for it." Lots of people live with accepted schizophrenia; they know the system is shit, but the sugar at the end of the trail is just sweet: the promise of jobs and money [Sayre, 1973: 146].

This uneasy acquiescence, among either former radicals or the poor, has received little systematic attention. The less educated are much more cynical about the political system and other people than the highly educated; controlling for education, low-income respondents are more politically and personally cynical than high-income respondents. People who feel politically powerless are "considerably more cynical than the more potent . . . . Feelings of potency increase sharply with higher education . . . [but] at every educational level, the more potent are more trusting of politics and politicians than the less potent". Finally, there is a negative relationship for the less educated between political participation and both cynicism and impotence. In other words, poor and less educated people trust government and other people less than does the rest of the population; those who distrust the government also feel unable to affect it and do not try to do so. Many of the poor, then, oppose the political system but make no effort to change it (Agger, Goldstein, and Pearl, 1961).

The acquiescent may demonstrate learned helplessness. A person is helpless "with respect to some outcome when the outcome occurs independently of all his [or her] voluntary responses". People respond to an uncontrollable noxious event with passivity, somatic symptoms, decreased competitiveness, inability to perceive success, and inability to learn (including learning that some events *are* controllable). These symptoms disappear if the person believes that he or she can control the situation. However, helplessness may generalize from a state to a trait; isolated habits or responses to specific situations become a deeply embedded mode of dealing with the world. Urban stress produces responses of learned helplessness, as do failure in work, school, or financial delaings, insoluble problems, and/or old age (Seligman, 1975). Thus, the helplessly acquiescent can be distinguished from the Radicals by the fact that, in similar circumstances, the former have learned to give up and the latter have not.

This response was particularly marked in one interviewee named Jane Sennett. She is 60 years old, ill, and lives on a $3,000 annual disability pension. Jane is extremely unhappy but completely passive. She can barely imagine how things might be different, and she rejects all concrete suggestions for change. When it is explained, she supports the idea of redistribution because "everybody would be equal then . . . . Oh, that would be wonderful! Sure! Like I told you, I don't even make 3,000 a year.". But when asked how the country should be different, she says: "I don't know, what are they doing? I don't know what you mean. I can't answer you that . . . . How different? You go in certain sections, the houses are nice, you go in another section, they're worse. So you pick on the better part. Maybe the whole world should be like the better part. That's impossible. When they throw down buildings, what do they do with all that stuff? Burn it? It's got to be someplace.".

THE ALIENATED

The alienated are satisfied with their position only because they do not believe any change is possible. They are frustrated and disappointed, rather than manipulative or depressed, in the face of an unfair system. They have, however, established a livable niche for themselves within the system, and will not jeopardize it by even entertaining radical ideas. As Mike Lefevre tells Studs Terkel, "Who you gonna sock? You can't sock General Motors, you can't sock anybody in Washington, you can't sock a system . . . . It isn't that the average working guy is dumb. He's tired, that's all" (Turkel, 1972: 27).

The young, blacks, women, Southerners, the less educated, and the poor are more politically alienated than are others, although rejection is rising in all segments of the population. In particular, low socioeconomic status respondents feel incapable politically, compared with high socioeconomic status respondents, who feel actively but negatively involved wth the political system. Perhaps for this reason, the low-income alienated are the least politically active of all segments of the population, as opposed to some high-income alienated who become politically radicalized and extremely active (Yinger, 1973; Keniston, 1968).

Hansen argues that "persons who distrust government officials or who think tax dollars are wasted, still favor governmental efforts to change the distribution of income in the United States. Such persons (most likely of low socioeconomic status) support redistributive goals in principle but (perhaps realistically) may doubt the sincerity or the ability of the federal government to implement effective tax or welfare reforms" (1976: 17). This corresponds with some interview responses. One man, Vincent Sandusky, accepted his own poverty because he was convinced that any effort at change would only put more money in the hands of big business and politicians. When asked if he would like incomes to be equalized, he answered, "boy, I tell you, this country would be really something . . . . Because, you know, you're the owner, you're still makin' your money. So why not have the person that's working for you have a fairly decent pay too?''. But he opposes increased taxation of the rich because:

> even if they do lose it, who's gonna wind up with it? The government. That's why I say, it's all just one big piece of pie, you know, and more than three quarters of it is the government. I don't have it word for word, like Lincoln said, in *those* days, "the government," like when he made that statement, "was *for* the people," and all that. The government today is just for the government. They work out these deals with these big companies, they're making their money. You know, it's people like us that don't have it, that really gotta struggle.

Thus more people than we have previously realized may believe in equalization of holdings, but not support it on pragmatic grounds. The effect of this view, however, is just as antiredistributive as the first two views. Acceptors may be hurt by the given structures but are resigned to, or even happy with, them. The Ambitious hope to improve their own place within the given structures. Inconsistents reject the structures, but diffuse this potentially radical view by accepting their own situation. Few, of course, have worked out these arguments; the overwhelming public response to redistributive ideas is massive ignorance. But a combination of these dynamics may best explain why the dog does not bark.

RADICALS

Two additional explanations for nondemand of redistribution differ from those above. Rather than calculations and perceptions, they focus on values and desires; the merits of these views are better debated from a normative than from a cognitive or emotional standpoint. They exceed demands for redistribution in that they seek even broader changes in the economic-political structure; a Nonmaterialist may not oppose redistribution so much as ignore it until more important values or goals are met. In other words, the dimension has changed from support or opposition to one of salience. Low salience is not the same as opposition, but it has the same effect on possible political demands.

What do Radicals want from the polity, if not redistribution? Some want to change the structure of positions, so that everyone is assured of a decent job. Others want to detach payments from positions, so that everyone, regardless of his or her employment status, has enough resources to live decently and an equal chance to seek limitless wealth. Finally, some want to conflate positions and payments so that intrinsic enjoyment of the job and nonmonetary rewards are increased—the content of the position becomes part of the payment. Some redistribution may in fact be needed to implement these changes, but it would be as much a means or a byproduct as a goal.

Jobs, not a handout. First, some Radicals want the polity to provide work, not income. In 1969, for example, 77% of those with incomes below $5,000 and 75% with incomes over $10,000 favored federally guaranteed jobs yielding $3,200 a year. However, only 40% below $5,000 and 24% above $10,000 favored a guaranteed annual income of the same amount (Gallup Opinion Index, 1969).

Even long-term welfare recipients would choose a regular, well-paying, enjoyable job to a comfortable life on welfare; they would accept, albeit reluctantly, menial jobs rather than no job and welfare payments. In 1977, 70% of the very poor were willing to move to areas with better job opportunities (Gallup Opinion Index, July 1977). Similarly most poor favor mandatory work requirements for welfare recipients if jobs are available. In 1976, 87% of those with incomes below $5,000 (compared with only 74% of those with incomes over $20,000) supported the creation of "youth camps, such as the CCC camps of the 1930's" (Gallup Opinion Index, Jan. 1977). Self-reports on happiness are very closely related to employment status for men of all classes (Goodwin, 1972; Gallup Opinion Index, 1965, 1971, 1975a, 1975b; Bradburn and Caplowitz, 1965).

Both rich and poor among my interviewees favor federally guaranteed jobs, even as public works programs that might require higher taxes. Some support is punitive; the recipients of a dole ought at least do some work. In many cases, however, they see it as a matter of human dignity; everyone has a right to be productive and self-respecting by not being forced to accept chairty. Almost none supported a guaranteed annual income except for those who could not work.

A floor, but no ceiling. However, a sizable minority of the population *does* favor a guaranteed annual income, regardless of employment status or personal characteristics of the recipients. Similarly, support for various forms of redistribution in kind—such as social security, unemployment compensation, a minimum wage, food stamps, and national health insurance—has been strong and steady since the 1930's. Some people, then, agree with one wealthy respondent who believed "that there should be a level beneath which people should not be allowed to drop". Even those with no occupational position deserve some payment, "enough of a subsidy so that people could live with reasonable dignity and the respect of other people . . . . They're entitled to be free from the anxiety of a pauper state, a dependent state".

Detaching payments from positions is the first step toward a demand for the downward redistribution of wealth. However, Radicals are distinguished from Redistributionists by the fact that they oppose any structural barriers to one's efforts to advance economically, no matter how tiny the probability of acquiring wealth. Rather than restrict efforts to advance, Radicals want to open up opportunities so that everyone has an equal, if tiny, probability of acquiring wealth (Parkin, 1971). This may require affirmative action programs, which change the nature of the assignment of persons to positions. It may also require large subsidies to previously disadvantaged groups such as black capitalists or neighborhood corporations—again detaching payments from positions, but not for egalitarian purposes. In their eyes, downward redistribution would simply constrain further the hopes of already deprived people. As Esther McLean said: "I think there will always be rich people. I don't mind that there is . . . . It's not any goal I care to reach, but I'm sure it's a lot of incentive for many other people. If they don't like the particular circumstances they find themselves in, I like that there's something that they can change to. You know, I would hate for us all to be the same, and just vegetate in that one area".

Providing a floor but no ceiling has, in the eyes of the stability-seeking polity, several desired effects. It gives security and dignity to all but the few who slip through the cracks, it fosters a belief in an open society and individual opportunity for all, and it permits competitive and aggressive impulses to flourish. It also, of course, denies the value of substantive equality.

Making jobs more desirable. Finally, some Radicals want nonmonetary payments and intrinsic rewards to be part of all positions, if necessary at the expense of monetary payment. A majority of all income groups—81% in 1949—choose job security over high pay (Strunk, 1949). Some workers are demanding more varied and interesting jobs, or more control over production decisions, even at the cost of efficiency and perhaps their income. Two points about the complex issue of job satisfaction are relevant here. Some workers choose security, independence, or meaningful work over monetary rewards; redistribution will not have high priority for them. Others choose high pay over all other intrinsic or extrinsic rewards; they also will reject redistributive policies that would place a ceiling on their ambitions. Studies of job satisfaction never include substantive equality as a possible goal, so these conclusions must be tentative. But to the degree that Radicals seek nonmonetary payments as part of the content of positions, to that degree they will not focus on the redistribution of monetary payments to positions.

NONMATERIALISTS

Finally, some people believe that the concern over economic positions and payments is passé. Most Americans are comfortable materially and feel gratified in comparison with their past and the rest of the world. Once pressing material needs are met and some security assured, people develop concerns that are not reducible to economic demands and would be touched only tangentially by economic equalization. Examples are desires for cultural roots, religious or ethical values, family problems, and meaningful political participation. From this perspective, false consciousness is not a misperception of one's place in the objective class struggle, but rather is an expectation that material gain or equality could bring contentment.

This proposition is hard to test, particularly in light of the Nonmaterialists' claim that our society is preoccupied with material matters to the exclusion of other needs. Furthermore, problems and pathologies are studied more than desires or ideals. Much theorizing and rhetoric, but little research, has been the result.

Worries and concerns. Nevertheless, surveys do suggest the relative importance of material and nonmaterial concerns. Between 20% and 40% of all classes cite economic problems when asked what worries them most. About the same proportion cite their own or family ill health; the third greatest concern until recently has been war (Erskine, 1973; Cantril and Roll, 1971; Watts and Free, 1974). Certainly economic issues matter, but they do not outweigh all others. Even this may be overstating the primacy of economics, since polls tend to tap only the most accessible attitude of the moment.

New Leftist political activism and immediate awareness has certainly diminished, but the nonmaterialist—even antimaterialist—critique of American society remains.

Hopes and wishes. People respond differently when asked about "what really matters in your life . . . your hopes and wishes for the future". Here material desires take second place to psychological well-being. Between 1959 and 1974, economic desires declined from 36% to 30% of the expressed wishes of the population; political and social desires increased from 4% to 20% and personal desires declined from 60% to 50% (Hochschild, 1977). Thus, nonegocentric hopes increased at the expense of both egocentric ones, but political and personal desires combined were expressed twice as often as economic wishes.

Low-income respondents do not equate happiness and economic well-being any more than high-income respondents do. In fact, in 1971, about 38% of the respondents with incomes between $4,000 and $14,000 expressed economic desires; only 31% of those with incomes below $4,000 and above $15,000 did so. The lowest and highest categories had personal wishes almost twice as often as economic ones, whereas for the middle categories, personal wishes exceeded economic ones only one and one-half times as often (Hochschild, 1977).

Thus the importance of economic issues depends on the question asked. Material concerns—and ill-health, which is closely related—present the greatest immediate problems to people. But the converse is not true; most people do not look to material success for happiness. In fact, all income levels believe that an improved standard of living has psychologically hurt our nation. In a 1967 sample, 36% of the upper class and 29% of the lower class thought Americans are more concerned about others as a result of increased affluence. However, 35% of the upper and 49% of the lower classes thought Americans were *less* concerned for others as a result of affluence. The same results hold for happiness; 23% of the sample, evenly divided among the classes, thought Americans were happier because of the higher standard of living. There were 41% of the upper class and 47% of the lower class who thought we were less happy (Erskine, 1969).

Thus, Nonmaterialists who do not necessarily oppose redistribution may see it as, at best, a side issue and, at worst, as a way of reinforcing materialistic concerns at the expense of more important psychological and political problems. Beyond a certain point, money does not buy happiness for a society, and a drive toward redistribution merely keeps us on an increasingly frustrating "hedonic treadmill" (Easterlin, 1970).

A fair, not an equal distribution. My research shows that some people want wealth to be distributed fairly, not equally, although definitions of fairness vary. For example, some think that any amount of earned wealth is legitimate, but all inherited or illegally gained wealth is not. Others argue that individuals and small businesses deserve large profits, but not large corporations. Equal opportunity and rights are fair for blacks; affirmative action is not because it hurts innocent whites. Fairness can be defined in terms of need, ascriptive characteristics, contribution to society, market value, survival of the fittest, and so on—all of which mitigate against seeing strict equality as fair. Thus an egalitarian redistribution seems morally wrong to many who are most concerned with creating a just society.

IMPLICATIONS OF THE SILENT DOG

Now that we understand why the dog does not bark, we can return to the original typology, abstracted again from its empirical manifestations.

First, the typological categories are mutually exclusive in logic, but entwined in actuality. We cannot state which strand is the most important in particular segments of the population; each exists in all demographic categories. Similarly, it is irrelevant which strand motivates any single individual or how many people remain consistently within one category. Attitudes are overdetermined and contradictory; but here interactions are more important than main effects. The point is that the combination of these views across or within individuals prevents redistributive demands. To maintain an inegalitarian distribution, it is necessary only that all or most of these strands exist, regardless of their distribution.

However, two distinctions *are* important for redistributive efforts. First, the categories of Acceptors, Ambitious, and Inconsistents are mainly cognitive. They rest on misperceptions, constrained awareness of alternatives, calculations of personal advantage, and judgments of feasibility of change. The categories of Radicals and Nonmaterialists, however, are mainly evaluative. They rest on goals other than economic equality. They do not oppose redistribution; they simply do not strongly support it.

Second, Acceptors and Ambitious are deeply conservative. They prescribe more of the same structurally and marginal change for the most energetic or lucky individuals. Radicals and Nonmaterialists seek change both generally and individually. Inconsistents are ambiguous, with change-oriented general views and conservative individual ones.

If we anticipate a decrease in the rate of economic growth, the policy implications of these distinctions are clear. For those with incomes below the mean, the polity can choose among four responses. It can do nothing different and hope to weather the storm of relative deprivation. It can foster conservatizing perceptions by emphasizing traditional values and explanations of the world, perhaps with marginal aid for the worst-off. It can defuse redistributive sentiments by emphasizing nonmaterial goals. Or, it can redistribute.

A final implication should be noted. The United States can change three basic orderings: (1) defining the nature and hierarchy of positions, (2) assigning persons to positions, and (3) assigning payments to positions. We have always been willing to manipulate the second ordering—of persons to positions—through the principle of equal opportunity, manifested in free compulsory education, civil service examinations, affirmative action, and so on. We sometimes manipulate the first ordering—the nature of positions—through concern for working conditions, the quality of life, workers' participation, and so on. But the United States has seldom chosen to change the third ordering, of payments to positions. After marginally adjusting the top and bottom of the economic distribution, we have taken for granted the justice of holdings resulting from the operation of the marketplace. The government has certainly manipulated the market, but never with the intention of fundamentally changing the way it allocates payments to positions.

This is precisely what a redistributive program seeks—the divorce of payments from positions in order to equalize the former but not the latter. Although we have tried to divorce the nature of persons from their assignment to positions, the next step seems foreign to our political culture and economic institutions. Basically, people do not seek redistribution because the United States has an underlying, unexamined set of norms and structures that lead to manipulation of persons and positions, but not payments. The dog that does not bark is a clue to political norms as it was a clue to murder; it is a trivial indication of a fundamental tragedy.

NOTES

1. The two structures—of positions and payments—are logically separate; positions are defined, persons are assigned to positions, and payments are assigned to positions in ways that can vary independently of the other two elements. A society could have, for example, equality of payments and a hierarchy of control or, less likely, it could have

equality of control and unequal payments. (This article is not concerned with assignment of persons to positions.) Empirically, of course, the structures are closely and complexly related.

2. There are 16 possible combinations of these elements. Most, however, are theoretically uninteresting or empirically uncommon. For example, a person who accepts the two general structures, and his or her position would simply be seeking a raise; a person seeking strict equality of control but inequality of payments seems unlikely.

3. No explanation is given for the discrepancy between the summed totals and 100%.

4. This is not necessary a leftist view. One of the most conservative and entrepreneurial of my interviewees saw the welfare system as a necessary evil in a desirable, if harsh, capitalist economy.

5. In the British sample, 60% agreed; the belief in contest mobility is not peculiarly American.

REFERENCES

ABEL-SMITH, B. (1958) "Whose welfare state?" pp. 55-73 in N. MacKenzie (ed.) Conviction. London: MacGibbon and Kee.

ADAMS, J. (1850) The Works of John Adams (vol. 6) C.F. Adams (ed.). Boston: Little, Brown.

AGGER, R., M. GOLDSTEIN and S. PEARL (1961) "Political cynicism: measurement and meaning." J. of Politics 23:477-506.

ARISTOTLE (1946) The Politics of Aristotle, trans. by E. Barker. Oxford: Clarendon Press.

BAGEHOT, W. (n.d., first pub. 1867) The English Constitution. Garden City, NY: Doubleday.

BOULDING, K. and M. PFAFF [eds.] (1972) Redistribution to the Rich and the Poor. Belmont, CA: Wadsworth.

BOWLES, S. and H. GINTIS (1976) Schooling in Capitalist America. New York: Basic Books.

BRADBURN, N. and D. CAPLOVITZ (1965) Reports on Happiness. Chicago: Aldine.

BUDD, E. (1970) "Postwar changes in the size distribution of income in the U.S." Amer. Econ. Rev. 60:247-260.

CANTRIL, A. and C. ROLL (1971) Hopes and Fears of the American People. New York: Universe Books.

CENTERS, R. (1949) The Psychology of Social Classes. Princeton: Princeton Univ. Press.

CHINOY, E. (1955) Automobile Workers and the American Dream. New York: Random House.

CHRISTLE, R., et al. (1970) Studies in Machiavellianism. New York: Academic Press.

COLES, R. (1971) The Middle Americans. Boston: Little, Brown.

DAHL, R. and D. RAE (1975) Debate on demands for the redistribution of wealth (mimeo). Project on American Democratic Institutions, Yale University, New Haven, CT.

DAVIS, A., B. GARDNER and M. GARDNER (1965) "The class system of the white caste," pp. 318-326 in H. Proshansky and B. Seidenberg (eds.) Basic Studies in Social Psychology. New York: Holt, Rinehart and Winston.

DEUTSCH, H.B. (1935) "Huey Long, the last phase." Saturday Evening Post 12:27.

DOYLE, A.C. (n.d.) "Silver Blaze," in The Complete Sherlock Holmes (vol 1). New York: Doubleday.

EASTERLIN, R. (1973) "Does money buy happiness?" The Public Interest 30: 3-10.

ERSKINE, H. (1969a) "The polls: Negro philosophies of life." Public Opinion Q. 33: 147-158.

――― (1969b) "The polls: Negro finances." Public Opinion Q. 33: 272-282.

――― (1973) "The polls: hopes, fears, and regrets." Public Opinion Q. 37: 132-145.

――― (1973-1974) "The polls: corruption in government." Public Opinion Q. 37: 628-644.

FARLEY, J. (1938) Behind the Ballots. New York: Harcourt, Brace.

FEAGIN, J. (1972) "Poverty: we still believe that God helps those who help themselves." Psychology Today 6:101ff.

FESTINGER, L. (1954) "A theory of social comparison processes." Human Relations 7: 117-140.

FOGARTY, R. [ed.] (1972) American Utopianism. Itasca, IL: F.E. Peacock.

"The Fortune quarterly survey: X" (1937) Fortune Magazine 16: 108ff.

"The Fortune Survey: XXII" (1939) Fortune Magazine 19: 68ff.

Gallup Opinion Index, Princeton: American Institute of Public Opinion, Gallup International. numbers 1 (June 1965); 22 (April 1967); 43 (Jan. 1969); 54 (Dec. 1969); 59 (May 1970); 73 (July 1971); 97 (July 1973); 101 (Nov. 1973); 102 (Dec. 1973); 111 (Sept. 1974); 117 (March 1975); 134 (Sept. 1976); 138 (Jan. 1977); 140 (March 1977); 142 (May 1977); 144 (July 1977); 150 (Jan. 1978); 157 (Aug. 1978)

Gallup Poll, Princeton: Field Enterprises. 20 July 1978, 12 October 1978.

GANS, H. (1973) More Equality. New York: Random House, Pantheon Books.

GEORGE, H. (1960, first pub. 1879) Progress and Poverty. New York: Robert Schalkenbach Foundation.

GILLESPIE, W.I. (1965) "Effect of public expenditures on distribution of income," pp. 122-186 of R. Musgrave (ed.), Essays in Fiscal Federalism. Washington, DC: Brookings.

GITLIN, T. and N. HOLLANDER (1971) Uptown: Poor Whites in Chicago. New York: Harper and Row.

GOODWIN, L. (1972) Do the Poor Want to Work? Washington, DC: Brookings.

GRAHAM, H. [ed.] (1970) Huey Long. Englewood Cliffs, NJ: Prentice Hall.

HANSEN, S. (1976) "Public opinion and the politics of redistribution" paper presented at the American Political Science Association meeting, Chicago.

HANSEN, W.L. and B. ELSBROD, (1969) "The distribution of costs and direct benefits of public higher education: the case of California." J. of Human Resources 4:176-191.

HARRINGTON, M. (1972) Socialism. New York: Saturday Review Press.

HARTZ, L. (1955) The Liberal Tradition in America. New York: Harcourt, Brace, and World.

HIRSCHMAN, A. and M. ROTHSCHILD (1973) "The changing tolerance for income inequality in the course of economic development." Q. J. of Econ. 87:544-566.

HOCHSCHILD, J.L. (1977) "Why the dog doesn't bark: income, attitudes, and the redistribution of wealth." New Haven, CT: Yale Univ., Institution for Social and Policy Studies, Working Paper #791.

HOXIE, R.F. (1920) Trade Unionism in the United States. New York: Appleton.

HUBER, J. and W. FORM (1973) Income and Ideology. New York: Free Press.

JACKER, C. (1968) The Black Flag of Anarchy. New York: Scribner.

JENCKS, C., et al. (1972) Inequality. New York: Basic Books.

JONES, E.E., et al. (1971) Attribution: Perceiving the Causes of Behavior. Morristown, NJ: General Learning Press.

KATZ, D., B. GUTEK, R. KAHN and E. BARTON (1975) Bureaucratic Encounters. Ann Arbor, MI: Institute for Social Research.

KENISTON, K. (1968) Young Radicals. New York: Harcourt, Brace, and World.

KOLKO, G. (1964) Wealth and Power in America. New York: Praeger.

LAMPMAN, R. (1959) "Changes in the share of wealth held by top wealth holders, 1922-1956." Rev. of Econ. and Statistics 41:379-392.

——— (1974) "What does it do for the poor?" Public Interest 34:66-82.

LANE, R. (1962) Political Ideology. New York: Free Press.

LASLETT, J. and S.M. LIPSET [eds.] (1974) Failure of a Dream? Garden City, NY: Anchor Press.

LAWLER, E.E. (1977) "Reward systems," in J.R. Hackman and J.L. Suttle (eds.) Improving Life at Work. Santa Monica, CA: Goodyear.

LEBERGOTT, S. (1976) The American Economy: Income, Welath, and Want. Princeton: Princeton Univ. Press.

LERNER, M. and L. ELKINTON (1976) "Perception of justice: an initial look." Waterloo, Canada: Univ. of Waterloo, mimeo.

LIPSET, S.M. (1963) Political Man. Garden City, NY: Doubleday.

——— and H. ZETTERBERG (1959) "Social mobility in industrial societies." pp. 11-75 in S.M. Lipset and R. Bendix, Social Mobility in Industrial Society. Berkeley: Univ. of California Press.

LITWAK, E., N. HOOYMAN and D. WARREN (1973) "Ideological complexity and middle-American rationality." Public Opinion Q. 37:317-332.

LOCKE, J. (1967) Two Treatises of Government. P. Laslett (ed.). London: Cambridge Univ. Press.

LONG, H. (1933) Every Man a King. New Orleans: National Book Co.

LOPREATO, J. (1967) "Upward social mobility and political orientation." Amer. Soc. Rev. 32:586-592.

MACAULAY, J. and L. BERKOWITZ [eds.] (1970) Altruism and Helping Behavior. New York: Academic Press.

MACAULAY, T.B. (1877) "Lord Macaulay on American Institutions." Harper's New Monthly Magazine 54:460-463.

MANN, M. (1973) Consciousness and Action among the Western Working Class. London: Macmillan.

MERTON, R. (1957) Social Theory and Social Structure. Glencoe, IL: Free Press.

MILLER, H. (1966) Income Distribution in the United States (a 1960 Census Monograph). Washington, DC: U.S. Government Printing Office.

MILLER, S.M. and P. ROBY (1970) The Future of Inequality. New York: Basic Books.

MYERS, H.A. (1945) Are Men Equal? Ithaca, NY: Cornell Univ. Press, Great Seal Books.

New Haven Journal Courier (1977) "Legally poor in U.S. increase by 10%." July 14: 1.

NORDHOFF, C. (1965) The Communistic Societies of the United States. New York: Schocken Books.

NOYES, J.H. (1966) History of American Socialisms. New York: Dover.

NOZICK, R. (1974) Anarchy, State, and Utopia. New York: Basic Books.

OLSON, M. (1965) The Logic of Collective Action.: Cambridge, MA: Harvard Univ. Press.

PARKIN, F. (1971) Class Inequality and Political Order. New York: Praeger.

PECHMAN, J. and B. OKNER (1974) Who Bears the Tax Burden? Washington, DC: Brookings.

PEN, J. (1971) Income Distribution. London: Penguin Press.

PERLMAN, S. (1970) A Theory of the Labor Movement. New York: Augustus M. Kelley.

PETTIGREW, T. (1967) "Social Evaluation theory: convergences and applications," pp. 241-318 in D. Levine (ed.) Nebraska Symposium on Motivation (vol. 15). Lincoln: Univ. of Nebraska Press.

PLOTNICK, R. (1977) "The real cost and net redistributive impact of cash transfers." Institute for Research on Poverty, Univ. of Wisconsin—Madison, Discussion Paper #398-77.

POTTER, D. (1954) People of Plenty. Chicago: Univ. of Chicago Press.

PROJECTOR, D. (1964) "Survey of financial characteristics of consumers." Federal Reserve Bulletin 50:285-293.

Public Opinion Q. (1946) "The quarter's polls" 10:104-139.

RAINWATER, L. (1974) What Money Buys. New York: Basic Books.

REYNOLDS, M. and E. SMOLENSKY (1974) "The post FISC distribution: 1961 and 1970 compared." National Tax J. 27:515-530.

——— (1975) "Post-FISC distribution of income: 1950, 1961, and 1970." Institute for Research on Poverty, Univ. of Wisconsin—Madison. Discussion Paper 270-75.

ROSENBAUM, J. (1976) Making Inequality: the Hidden Curriculum of High School Tracking. New York: Wiley/Interscience.

ROSENBERG, M. (1953) "Perceptual obstacles to class consciousness." Social Forces 32:22-27.

RUBENSTEIN, R. (1970) Rebels in Eden. Boston: Little, Brown.

RUBIN, Z. and L.A. PEPLAU, "Who believes in a just world?" J. of Social Issues 31:165-189.

RUNCIMAN, W.G. (1966) Relative Deprivation and Social Justice. Berkeley: Univ. of California Press.

SAMSON, L. (1935) Toward a United Front. New York: Farrer and Rinehart.

SAYRE, N. (1973) Sixties Going on Seventies. New York: Arbor House.

SCHAAR, J. (1967) "Equality of opportunity, and beyond," pp. 228-249 in J.R. Pennock and J.W. Chapman (eds.) Equality: Nomos IX. New York: Atherton Press.

SCHREIBER, E.M. and G.T. NYGREEN (1970) "Subjective social class in America: 1945-1968." Social Forces 48:348-356.

SELIGMAN, M. (1975) Helplessness. San Francisco: W.H. Freeman.

SENNETT, R. and J. COBB (1972) The Hidden Injuries of Class. New York: Alfred Knopf.

SHANNON, D. (1955) The Socialist Party of America. New York: Macmillan.

SILVERMAN, H. [ed.] (1970) American Radical Thought: The Libertarian Tradition. Lexington, MA: D. C. Heath.

SIMPSON, S. (1954) "Political economy and the workers," pp. 137-162 in J.L. Blau (ed.) Social Theories of Jacksonian Democracy. Indianapolis: Bobbs-Merrill.

SINCLAIR, U. (n.d.) I, Governor of California and how I ended Poverty. Los Angeles: n.p.

SMEEDING, T. (1977) "The antipoverty effectiveness of in-kind transfers." J. of Human Resources 12:360-378.

SMITH, G. L. K. (1935) "How come Huey Long? (2. or Superman?)." New Republic 82: 13 February, 14-15.

SMITH, J. and S. FRANKLIN (1974) "The concentration of personal wealth, 1922-1969." Amer. Econ. Rev. 64:162-167.

SOMBART, W. (1976) Why is There No Socialism in the United States? trans. P.M. Hocking and C.T. Husbands. White Plains, NY: M.E. Sharpe.

SPENGLER, J. (1953) "Changes in income distribution and social stratification: a note." Amer. J. of Soc. 59:247-259.

STEPHANSON, R.M. (1957) "Mobility orientation and stratification of 1000 ninth graders." Amer. Soc. Rev. 22:204-212.

STIGLER, G. (1970) "Director's law of public income redistribution." J. of Law and Economics 13:1-10.

STOUFFER, S., et. al. (1949) The American Soldier: Adjustment During Army Life. Princeton: Princeton Univ. Press.

STRUNK, M. ed. (1949) "The quarter's polls." Public Opinion Q. 13:537-561.

––– (1950) "The quarter's polls." Public Opinion Q. 14:174-192.

TERKEL, S. (1974) Working. New York: Pantheon.

THUROW, L. (1975) Generating Inequality. New York: Basic Books.
TOCQUEVILLE, A. de (1969) Democracy in America, J.P. Mayer (ed.) and G. Lawrence (trans). New York: Doubleday.
TUMIN, M. (1957) "Some unapplauded consequences of social mobility in a mass society." Social Forces 36:32-37.
TURNER, R. (1966) "Acceptance of irregular mobility in Britain and the United States." Sociometry 29:334-352.
U.S. Bureau of the Census (1976) Current Population Reports, P-60, No. 101, "Money income in 1974 of families and persons in the United States." Washington, DC: U.S. Government Printing Office.
——— (1978) Current Population Reports, P-60, No. 109, "Household money income in 1976 and selected social and economic characteristics of households." Washington, DC: U.S. Government Printing Office.
U.S. Congress. Joint Economic Committee (1972). The American Distribution of Income: a Structural Problem, by L. Thurow and R. Lucas. Joint Committee Print, 92nd Cong., 2d sess. Washington, DC: U.S. Government Printing Office.
VERBA, S. and K. SCHLOZMAN, (1977) "Unemployment, class consciousness, and radical politics: what didn't happen in the thirties." J. of Politics 39:291-323.
WATTS, W. and L. FREE (1974) State of the Nation 1974. Washington, DC: Potomac Associates.
WILENSKY, H. and H. EDWARDS, (1959) "The Skidder: ideological adjustments of downward mobile workers." Am. Soc. Rev. 24:215-230.
YINGER, J.M. (1973) "Anomie, alienation, and political behavior," pp. 171-202 in J. Knutson (ed.) Handbook of Political Psychology. San Francisco: Jossey-Bass.

3

ECONOMIC AND FISCAL EFFECTS ON THE POPULAR VOTE FOR THE PRESIDENT

WILLIAM A. NISKANEN

Director-Economics The Ford Motor Company

THE CONFUSED POLITICS OF ECONOMICS

One of the central perceptions of social science is that the behavior of a person in a specific role is strongly determined by the conditions affecting his survival in that role. Accordingly, one would expect federal economic and fiscal policy to be influenced by the relation between voting behavior and economic conditions. This relation, however, is not well understood, and the academic literature has only confused the issue.

The "party" hypothesis, most favored by political scientists, states that the vote for the conservative party will increase with improvements in economic conditions, regardless of the party of the incumbent President. Scammon and

Wattenberg, for example, write: "As Democrats see it, Democratic prosperity tends to be counterproductive to what had become the Democratic Issue: middle-class poverty. As middle-class poverty disappeared, so did some of the Democratic appeal" (1970: 33). A confirmation of this hypothesis, of course, would have most serious implications for economic policy by a Democratic administration. The theory from which the hypothesis is derived, however, is not clear. If voters believe that economic policy can change economic conditions, why would people vote Republican if the economic policy of a Democratic administration has been unusually successful, and why would they vote for the Democratic candidate if the consequences of Democratic economic policy have been disastrous? One plausible theory that would lead to the party hypothesis is that voters believe that changes in economic conditions are random, that is, independent of economic policy, but that a Democratic administration is more likely to provide relief for whatever poverty, unemployment, or other problem that occurs. Maybe so. Several recent empirical studies of voting behavior are based on this party hypothesis, but these studies neither develop the theory that would lead to this hypothesis nor do they test this hypothesis against the major competing hypotheses (Arcellus and Meltzer, 1975; Meltzer and Vellrath, 1975).

The "incumbency" hypothesis has been most carefully stated by Kramer:

> If the performance of the incumbent party is "satisfactory" according to some simple standard, the voter votes to retain the incumbent party in office to enable it to continue its present policies; while if the incumbent's performance is not "satisfactory," the voter votes against the incumbent, to give the opposition party a chance to govern [1971: 134].

Scammon and Wattenberg, perhaps unknowingly, also endorse the incumbency hypothesis:

> Politically, the Economic Issue tends to be a "Ping-Pong" issue—
> that is, when conditions are bad it is the fault of the people in
> power (a "Ping") and works for the people out of power (a
> "Pong") [1970: 282-283].

A confirmation of this hypothesis, at least, suggests that the
political incentives of an administration of either party work
in the right direction. Several recent studies of the vote for
congressional candidates are based on this hypothesis (Kramer, 1971; Lepper, 1974).

Stigler has recently questioned both the existence and the
rationality of any relation of voting behavior to aggregate
economic conditions, stating:

> It is foolish to sell one's stock in a corporation simply because
> that corporation has had recent reverses, and it is equally foolish
> to assume that the political fire is always more pleasant than the
> political frying pan [1973: 165].

Economic conditions and economic policy, of course, are not
perfectly correlated. It is, in some sense, unfair to vote
against an administration that makes the best of bad circumstances, but it is not necessarily foolish. Stigler may be able
to identify and directly evaluate past and prospective economic policy, but it seems implausible to attribute such
information and expertise to most voters. Given the cost of
acquiring information about economic policy and an understanding of the relation between economic conditions and
economic policy, it may be rational for most voters to use a
simple decision rule based on economic conditions. In any
case, theory should not be judged by its plausibility; "the
proof is in the pudding." Stigler's hypothesis is that there will
be no observed relation between voting behavior and economic conditions and this can be tested.

The combination of abundant argument and scanty evidence, unfortunately, has not achieved any consensus on the

relation between voting behavior and economic conditions. As a consequence, the administration has an understandable but unfortunate incentive to try everything, an incentive that increases as the election nears. Federal economic and budget analysts have had no counter to the assertions that arise from every quarter that the proposed policy or program is "necessary for political reasons." Our understanding of the relations of economic conditions to economic policies is confused enough, but we do not appear to have the minimal understanding of the politics of economic conditions that is necessary to close a theory of economic policy.

APPROACH

For several years, I have been formulating and testing crude economic models of government organizations, starting with the characteristic production unit, the bureau (Niskanen, 1971, 1975). More recently, I have been trying to understand the behavior of the U.S. Presidency in terms of the conditions necessary to achieve and retain that position. This approach avoids speculation about the utility function or the psychohistory of specific Presidents. As such, this approach does not address the difference in the behavior among Presidents, a topic that has been the focus of popular and sometimes academic fascination. In contrast, this approach focuses on the common behavior of different men and "teams" in the same position. An understanding of the Presidency, as distinct from the President, I contend, must be based on an explanation of this common behavior.

The immediate objective of this article is to identify the primary economic and fiscal conditions that affect the popular vote for the President, as a first step toward constructing a model of the behavior of the Presidency. In other words, I am trying to estimate a function that would be the maximand in a model of a vote-maximizing Presidency or the reelection constraint in a model, such as suggested by Frey and Lau (1941), with a utility maximand. My own experience in the federal government suggests that a President has a large amount of discretion on economic policy that is consistent with his reelection. A vote-maximizing assumption, however, may still be sufficient to explain a President's behavior. Popular approval may be an element in a President's utility function as well as in the reelection constraint. And the interests of other groups on which a President is dependent—members of his administration, members of his own party in Congress, and so on—are correlated with the popular vote for the President or the successor candidate of his party. For the time being, however, the choice between these two types of models can be deferred.

The seminal article by Kramer shaped the analysis presented in this article, although Kramer's work focused on the vote for Congress. My basic hypothesis, following Kramer, is that the popular vote for the President, among other things, is a referendum on the economic *performance* of the governing party. In effect, this hypothesis assumes that voter expectations about future performance are positively correlated with the recent performance. The popular vote for the candidate of the incumbent party in the next election, thus, should increase with an improvement in economic conditions.

A more specific formulation of the incumbency hypothesis can be developed from a model suggested by Lepper (1974). Consider an individual voter with a utility function of the following form:

$$U = a(Y\text{-}tX)^b X^c , \qquad [1]$$

in which Y is total real family income, X is total real federal expenditures, and t is the family share of the (present and future) taxes necessary to finance current federal expenditures. The marginal value of after-tax income and of total federal expenditures is assumed to be positive over the whole range of the variables.

Second, assume that the voter uses the following voting rule: vote for the candidate of the incumbent part if

$$\frac{U}{U_{-1}} \geqslant R \qquad\qquad [2]$$

and vote for the candidate of the major opposition party if

$$\frac{U}{U_{-1}} < R. \qquad\qquad [3]$$

The rationale for this voting rule follows. The voter believes that economic conditions are correlated with economic policy. The costs of acquiring information and expertise on economic policy, however, are higher than the benefits to him of using a more discriminating voting rule based directly on economic policy. The voter, thus, believes that the best indicator of future economic policy is some set of recent economic conditions. Moreover, the voter faces a binary choice, that is, he has the opportunity to vote for or against the candidate of the incumbent party but does not have the opportunity to register his degree of approval of the expected economic policies. For these conditions, he will vote for the candidate of the incumbent party if the recent changes in his utility are equal to or greater than could reasonably have been expected, and the value of R will reflect this threshold. This type of behavior is best described, I believe, as utility-maximizing behavior under binary-choice conditions rather than, as has been suggested by Kramer and Lepper, as "satisficing" behavior.

All voters are assumed to have the same general form of utility functions and to use the same type of voting rule.

Voters differ in terms of their preferences for after-tax income and federal spending, their tax share, their expectations of feasible increases in their utility, and the strength of their party identification. A strong partisan of the incumbent party, for example, will have a lower value of R for any given expectation of economic conditions.

For each voter, then, Equations 1, 2, and 3 define a boundary of Y and X values in the election year that are just sufficient to induce him to vote for the candidate of the incumbent party. Other terms in these boundary functions include values of Y and X in some prior year, the current and prior tax shares, the voter's preferences, and the value of R. The general forms of these implicit boundary functions for each voter, thus, are represented as follows:

$$v_i(Y \, X : Y_{-1}, X_{-1}, t, t_{-1}, b, c, R) \qquad [4]$$

These functions will be concave from below in the Y,X plane.[1] Figure 1 illustrates a set of boundary functions for a community of five voters. Voters 1,2, and 3, for example, might be partisans of the incumbent party who differ primarily in terms of their preferences and/or tax shares. Voters 4 and 5 demand a higher performance as a condition for voting for the candidate of the incumbent party. The numbers in Figure 1 indicate the number of votes a candidate of the incumbent party would receive for different combinations of Y and X. An incumbent party, for example, must generate Y, X combinations above the left section of the V_3 function and the right section of the V_1 function, given majority rule, to be returned to office. The aggregate equal vote functions are the lower bounds of those Y, X combinations that yield an equal number of votes. For a small number of voters with significantly different preferences and/or tax shares, the aggregate equal vote functions are not necessarily continuously concave, but a concave function

Figure 1

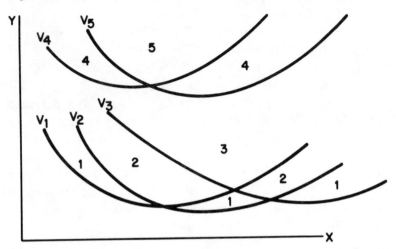

should be a sufficient approximation for a large number of voters.

Figure 2 illustrates the conditions that would generate an observed relation between votes and economic conditions. The V functions are aggregate equal vote functions for different percentages of the popular vote for the candidate of the incumbent party. The F function represents the feasible combinations of Y and X in a given election year. This F function will be convex from below if federal spending has a net stimulative effect at low levels and a net disincentive effect at higher levels; in the absence of these two effects, the F function would be horizontal.

If the V and F functions are stable over elections and incumbent parties always maximize votes, only one combination of V, Y, X would be observed. In the case illustrated, the candidate of the incumbent party would always receive 60% of the popular vote by a Y,X combination at the tangency of the V_{60} and F functions. For such a case, there would be no possibility of observing a relation between votes and economic conditions.

If the V and F functions are stable over elections and incumbent parties do not maximize votes, all of the observable combinations would be along the F function. A linear regression would yield the dashed lines connecting the intersection of the V functions with the F function, rather than the true concave V functions.

If the V functions are stable over elections and the incumbent party does not maximize votes, then shifts in the F function generate observations on the V functions. Only in this case would a single-equation estimate of the V, Y, X relation identify the aggregate relation between votes and economic conditions. For this article, no attempt is made to estimate the F function, and the characteristics of the full simultaneous equations system are not defined. It is important to identify other conditions that might shift the V function over elections, however, in order to stabilize this function relative to shifts in the F function. The single-equation estimates presented in the next section, thus, can be

Figure 2

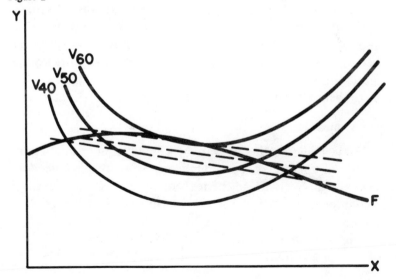

interpreted as approximations of the aggregate relation between votes and economic conditions only if the V function is stable relative to the F function *and* the administration either does not try or is not fully successful in achieving a Y, X combination that maximizes votes.

EMPIRICAL ANALYSIS[2]

THE SAMPLE

The full sample consists of observations for the 20 Presidential election years from 1896 through 1972. The available economic data do not permit expansion of the sample to include elections prior to 1896, and the assumption of stable voting behavior might be increasingly tenuous. In addition, a restricted set of estimates are made for two pairs of subsamples. One pair of estimates is made for the 10 elections from 1896 through 1932 and for the 10 elections from 1936 through 1972 in order to test the stability of voting behavior over time. Another pair of estimates is made for the 10 elections for which the incumbent President was a Republican and for the 10 elections in which the incumbent President was a Democrat in order to test the stability of voting behavior over parties of the incumbent President; these estimates provide a crude test of the relative strength of the incumbency and party hypotheses.

THE VARIABLES

Table 1 summarizes the variables included in test equations based on the full sample. Only a few of the independent variables are included in the test equations based on the small subsamples. A more complete description of the basic data is presented in the Appendix.

The Dependent Variable. Statistical criteria suggest the use of the logit transformation $\ln(I/1\text{-}I)$ rather than I as the

Table 1: Test Equation Variables

Test Variable		Basic Variables
Dependent		
$V = \ln\left(\frac{I}{1-I}\right)$	$I =$	fraction of major party popular vote for candidate of the incumbent party
Economic		
$DNP = (\ln NP - \ln NP_{-4})$	$NP =$	real per capita net national product
$DER = [\ln(1-U) - \ln(1-U_{-4})]$	$U =$	unemployment rate, expressed as a fraction
$DCP = (\ln CP - \ln CP_{-4})$	$CP =$	index of consumer prices
$DSP = (\ln SP - \ln SP_{-4})$	$SP =$	real stock price index
$CBR =$ corporate bond rate		
Fiscal		
$DFX = (\ln FX - \ln FX_{-4})$	$FX =$	real per capita total federal expenditures
$DFR = (\ln FR - \ln FR_{-4})$	$FR =$	real per capita total federal revenues
Political		
$LVR = \ln\left(\frac{I_{-4}}{1-I_{-4}}\right)$	$I_{-4} =$	fraction of major party popular vote in prior election for candidate of current incumbent party
$ID =$ 1 if incumbent President is candidate, 0 otherwise		
Other		
$WD =$ 1 if election in war year, 0 otherwise		

dependent variable. The logit form is unbounded, and the variance of the residuals is expected to be symmetrical and constant. Use of this form of the dependent variable has two other effects: Elections for which I is unusually low or high have a greater effect on the regression results. In addition, for

$$\ln(I/1-I) = a+bX+\cdots+u$$

$$\varphi I/\varphi X = I(1-I)b.$$

The differential effect of X on I, thus, is largest for close elections; where I = (1-I) = .5, the effect is equal to .25 times the coefficient b. As the range of observed values of I is from 0.4 to 0.6, these several effects are not substantial, and the estimated partial derivatives are probably not much different from those from a test equation using I as the dependent variable.[3]

The dependent variable, with the exception of one election year, does not reflect the popular votes for candidates of minor parties. I do not know how to interpret these votes, for example, whether they should be regarded as part of the vote against the candidate of the incumbent party or as a vote against both major parties; my implicit assumption, by omitting these votes, is that they reflect a vote against both major parties. For the 1912 election, however, I included the votes for both Taft and Roosevelt as votes for the candidate of the incumbent party (Taft). My treatment of minor party votes, thus, is neither consistent nor entirely satisfactory. One would have to sort out the issues in each election to interpret the preferences revealed by these minor party votes.

The Economic Variables. Economic conditions are represented by five variables—real per capita net national product, the employment rate, the level of consumer prices, the level of real stock prices, and the corporate bond rate—the first four of these variables expressed as the percent change from the prior election year to the current election year. Although there is no a priori reason to choose a four-year interval to evaluate the economic performance of the incumbent party, this seemed to be the most obvious simple approach without exploring complex lag relations. One might expect voters to weight recent economic conditions more than earlier conditions, but a prior test using one-year changes produced much weaker results.

Real per capita net national product is the broadest definition of average real output and is the best available approximation of the total real income of the median voter. The coefficient on this variable should be positive.

The *employment* rate, rather than the unemployment rate, is used to reflect an increasing effect at higher levels of unemployment. An increase in the employment rate from .88 to .94, for example, is a larger proportionate increase than from .94 to .97, although it represents the same proportionate reduction in the unemployment rate. Although those voters directly affected by unemployment are a small fraction of the electorate, the coefficient on the change in employment rate should be positive if some of the swing voters are unemployed or expect to be unemployed and/or if voters are benevolently concerned about the unemployed. This variable presents a substantial statistical problem, as it is highly correlated with the change in real per capita net national product ($r = 0.9$). For this reason, the estimated coefficents on these variables may be highly unstable in any test equation using both variables, and most of the test equations use only one or the other of these variables.

A change of consumer prices also represents a distributional effect, most strongly affecting those on fixed nominal incomes. Although those voters most strongly affected by a change in consumer prices also represent a small part of the electorate, the coefficient on this variable should be negative if some of those affected are swing voters and/or if other voters are benevolently concerned about their status.

The change of real stock prices is included to reflect two effects—a change in wealth and expectations about future economic conditions. Although a change in wealth may be concentrated among a few voters, stock prices also reflect more general expectations about future real conditions. The coefficient on this variable should be positive.

The corporate bond rate is included as an index of expected inflation. If voters are concerned about expected inflation, the coefficient on this variable should be negative.

The Fiscal Variables. Federal fiscal conditions are represented by two variables—real per capita federal expenditures and real per capita tax revenues—both expressed as percent changes from the prior election year. The structural relation between the popular vote for the candidate of the incumbent party and federal spending is convex from below: if most voters prefer an increase in federal spending, the popular vote for the candidate of the incumbent party should increase in response to a spending increase within this range. Conversely, if most voters would prefer a reduction in federal spending, the popular vote for the candidate of the incumbent party should decrease in response to an increase in federal spending. The test equations used in this analysis yield an estimate of the average relation between votes and the changes in federal spending in the observed range but do not permit an estimate of the aggregate vote-spending relation over a range in which the sign of the partial effect should change from positive to negative as federal spending increases. Conventional democratic theory suggests that the federal budget would be set at a level equal that maximizes the net benefits to the median voter, in which case the coefficient on the change in federal spending should not be significantly different from zero. My own work suggests that the combination of bureaucratic and legislative processes leads to a budget that is larger than that desired by the median voter, in which case the coefficient on this variable within the observed range should be negative (Niskanen, 1975). This analysis provides a crude but important test of the general argument of my theory of bureaucracy and representative government.

If the federal budget was always balanced and/or voters perceived the total opportunity cost of deficits (in displaced investment and future taxes), the vote effect of federal fiscal conditions could be sufficiently represented by the effect of federal spending. The federal budget is never exactly balanced, of course, and voters may not perceive the opportunity cost of deficits. In this case, per capita federal tax revenues may be a better index of the perceived cost of federal activities. The test equations should probably include both the change in federal spending and the change in federal tax revenues, but the correlation of these two variables is too high to include both in the same regression. As a consequence, all of the test equations use only one or the other of these two variables, and the difference in the coefficients can be interpreted as an estimate of the amount of "debt illusion" by voters.

The Political Variables. Two variables are included to reflect political conditions. The vote ratio in the prior election is intended to reflect any residual net approval of the incumbent party. A coefficient on this variable that is not significantly different from zero suggests that each election is a new event, that is, there is complete depreciation of the prior vote ratio. A positive coefficient would indicate some residual net approval in the current election based on the prior vote ratio.

The incumbent dummy (no pun intended) provides for a crude test of the net advantage accruing to the incumbent as a candidate, as distinct from any advantage that accrues to another candidate of the incumbent party. This advantage probably derives from name recognition, sustained free access to the media, reduced uncertainty about personal behavior, and so on. The cost of promoting a different candidate suggests that the sign of the coefficient on this dummy should be positive.

The War Dummy. A war dummy is included to test for voter response to a current war. One popular hypothesis is that voters rally around the flag, in which case the coefficient on this dummy should be positive. My own views are that wars gain a momentum that goes beyond the preferences of the median voter, in which case the coefficient on this dummy should be negative. It is important to recognize that the three Presidential elections in war years—1944, 1952, 1968—were each in late years of the respective wars, and the findings may not apply to elections in an early year of a war.

TEST PROCEDURE

All of the test equations were estimated by ordinary least squares by a manual form of a backward step-wise procedure. The largest set of variables were included, and those for which the coefficients had the wrong sign or were insignificant were stepped-out.

RESULTS FROM THE FULL SAMPLE

Table 2 summarizes the regression estimates based on the full sample. The results for five pairs of equations are presented; the second equation in each pair differs from the first only in the substitution of DFR for DFX.

Economic Conditions. Changes in real per capita net national product have a strong, positive, and significant effect on the popular vote for the candidate of the incumbent party. This effect is consistently stronger and more significant in equations in which federal fiscal changes are represented by DFR. From the E10 column of Table 2, for example, a 10% increase in real per capita net national product between election years appears to increase the popular vote for the candidate of the incumbent party by around 5.6% of the total vote.

Controlling for DNP, the partial effects of changes in the employment rate are negative and insignificant. This result is consistent with Kramer's result that unemployment has no significant effect on the popular vote for Congress. The partial effects of changes in the consumer price level are inconsistent and insignificant; this result is not consistent with Stigler's estimate, based on a reworking of Kramer's data, that inflation has a small negative and significant effect.

Table 2: Summary of Full-Sample Estimates

	E1	E2	E3	E4	E5	E6	E7	E8	E9	E10
Variables										
C	.068	.009	.048	.068	-.433*	-.168	-.006	.054	.020	.077
DNP	2.006*	2.349*			-.926*	1.652*	.968*	1.813*	1.511*	2.220*
DER	-.842	-.127	1.052	1.447						
DCP	-.438	.338	-.307	-.194						
DSP			.328*	.322*	.300*	.189	.248*	.135		
CBR					.063*	.032				
DFX	-.316*	-.645*	-.077	-.146	-.185*	-.416	-.206*	-.474*	-.313*	-.572*
DFR	.073	.110	.201	.188	.279*	.162	.185*	.110	.143	.077
ID	.039	.155			.273	.129				
LVR										
WD	-.215	-.347*	-.122	-.158	-.104	-.266	-.166	-.309*	-.190	-.351*
Test Statistics										
R²	.795	.873	.721	.725	.854	.888	.796	.881	.732	.864
S.E.	.173	.136	1.94	1.92	1.46	.128	.160	.122	.176	.126
D.W.	1.804	2.212	1.639	1.655	2.309	1.961	1.738	1.741	1.885	2.077

*Indicates coefficients with "t" of 2 or higher.

The apparent absence of distributional effects on the popular vote for the President suggests that a standard benefit-cost model may be sufficient to explain most decisions by the Presidency, except when other groups, such as Congress, on which the President is dependent are concerned about these effects.

Deleting DNP, the effects of an increase in the employment rate are positive and the effects of an increase in consumer prices are negative. These results are consistent with Lepper's results, which also do not control for income changes, on the popular vote for Congress. In columns E3 and E4 of Table 2, however, DER serves only as a weak proxy for DNP. The effects of both DER and DCP are insignificant, and the significance of other coefficients and the regression are all reduced.

For about a decade, the standard example of the theory of economic policy has been the unemployment-inflation trade-off. Subsequent analysis suggests that this example has no empirical content: not only has the Phillips curve proved to be unstable but it now appears that there are no partial effects of unemployment and inflation on the primary signals to which politicians respond, given the level of average real output. For whatever reasons, politicans may be compelled to act to reduce unemployment and/or inflation, but there do not appear to be any pressures operating through the popular vote to achieve results. Yet to be explained is why they express concern over these conditions.

An increase in real stock prices has a positive and generally significant effect on the popular vote for the candidate of the incumbent party. The extent to which this reflects a wealth effect and/or expectations of real conditions is not clear. The corporate bond rate has a small, positive, and sometimes significant effect; the sign of this effect is different from that expected, however, so it is not clear what it reflects.

Fiscal Conditions. Changes in real per capita federal spending have a negative and highly significant effect on the popular vote for the candidate of the incumbent party. From column E9 of Table 2, for example, a 10% increase in real per capita federal spending between election years appears to reduce the popular vote for the candidate of the incumbent party by around 0.8% of the total vote. Changes in real per capita federal tax revenues has a stronger negative and highly significant effect. From E10, a 10% increase in real per capita federal tax revenues appears to reduce the popular vote for the candidate of the incumbent party by around 1.4% of the total vote. For each pair of test equations, the equation using DFR is more significant than that using DFX to represent federal fiscal conditions.

These fiscal effects have several interesting implications. Most important, federal budgets appear to have been significantly larger than the vote-maximizing level. An estimate of the *amount* of overspending can be derived by using both the DNP coefficient and the DFX (or DFR) coefficient. From E9, at the margin of 1974 conditions, an $8.86 billion increase in real net national product would be necessary to offset the votes lost by a $10 billion increase in real federal expenditures. This suggests that voters are willing to forego only $1.14 billion of other uses of national output for federal services which cost $10 billion. From E10, an $11.3 billion increase in real net national product would be necessary to offset the votes lost by a $10 billion increase in real federal tax revenues. This suggests a negative value of $1.3 billion of the services financed by an additional $10 billion of federal tax revenues. Voters appear to be roughly indifferent to an increase in federal spending on revenues only if there is no reduction in the revenues available for other uses, and the marginal value of the aggregate package of federal services appears to be nearly zero. This result is most disturbing but should not be considered conclusive, without support from other forms of evidence. In addition, the significant difference between the DFX and DFR coefficients suggests that there is considerable "debt illusion"; voters appear to be substantially more affected by changes in taxes than by changes in the total resource costs of federal services.

Political Conditions. Any vote advantage accruing to a candidate of the incumbent party who is not the incumbent President, for zero levels of other variables, is indicated by the constant term in each of the test equations. This effect appears to be consistenly small and insignificant. An incumbent *party,* thus, does not appear to have any advantage in addition to that deriving from other conditions.

An incumbent *President* running for reelection, in contrast, appears to have a positive and sometimes significant advantage amounting to 3% to 6% of the total vote.

Finally, there appears to be a small positive residual effect of the vote ratio in the prior election, but this effect is insignificant. This suggests that each election is essentially a new event that is determined by conditions since the prior election.

War. A war appears to have a negative and marginally significant effect on the popular vote for the candidate of the incumbent party. This conclusion may apply only to those elections held in late years of a war. The magnitude of this effect appears to be 5% to 9% of the total vote.

General. All in all, the pattern that emerges is that of quite rational voters who vote for or against the candidate of the incumbent party based on a few objective conditions. Only three or four variables explain 80% to 90% of the variance in the aggregate popular vote. A President is almost assured reelection if a moderate growth of real output can be maintained, if the growth of federal spending is restrained, and a war can be avoided or ended. Another candidate of the incumbent party would do almost as well. This conclusion is consistent with the long periods of one-party dominance of the Presidency. Such vote behavior should produce moderately responsive government as long as a President is concerned about reelection or the future of his party. The evidence suggests, however, that Presidents do not maximize votes, and this can lead to nonoptimal levels of some major federal instruments. As long as general economic conditions are improving and wars avoided, a package of conditions that includes an overly large federal budget is probably sufficient for reelection. The major changes in the American Presidency that are suggested by this analysis are to strengthen the incentives for the President to maximize the votes for himself or another candidate of his party in the next election and to reduce the vote advantage of the incumbent.

SUBSAMPLE RESULTS

Table 3 presents the results based on two pair of subsamples. The small number of observations (n=10) in each of the subsamples requires use of only the smallest set of variables. The subsample test equations use only those variables included in column E10 of Table 2, and this full-sample test equation is also presented for comparison.

Time. Many people share a perception that voting behavior has changed substantially since the first years of the New Deal. According to this perception, voters now demand better economic performance and higher federal spending. And the Presidency has become more personalized. Only the last of these hypotheses appears consistent with the results presented in Table 3.

The vote effects of changes in real per capita net national product and in real per capita federal tax revenues are almost identical in the 1896-1932 period and in the 1936-1972 period, although the variance of these effects is somewhat higher in the later period. Voters appear to have reacted to general economic and fiscal changes in much the same way for 80 years.

The primary difference in vote behavior between these two periods appears to be the role of the party and the President. In the early period, any candidate of the incumbent party

Table 3:   Summary of Sub-Sample Estimates

	Total	96–32	36–72	Republican	Democratic
Variables					
C	.077	.080	.047	.105	.104
	(.055)	(.031)	(.089)	(.056)	(.072)
DNP	2.220	2.131	2.190	2.169	2.453
	(.273)	(.231)	(.809)	(.441)	(.368)
DFR	−.572	−.614	−.619	−.590	−.660
	(.084)	(.064)	(.285)	(.226)	(.097)
ID	.077	−	.207	−	.119
	(.066)		(.102)		(.079)
WD	−.351	NA	−.327	NA	−.399
	(.093)		(.113)		(.095)
Test Statistics					
R^2	.864	.943	.889	.784	.963
S.E.	.126	.097	.109	.152	.082
D.W.	2.077	2.740	1.158	1.673	3.002
n	20	10	10	10	10

(figures in parentheses are standard errors of the coefficients)

appears to have had a significant advantage equal to around 2% of the total vote, and the President did not have a significant incremental advantage as a candidate. In this period, people seemed to be voting for or against the incumbent party rather than for a specific candidate.

In the later period, a candidate of the incumbent party other than the President does not seem to have a significant advantage, but the President as a candidate appears to have a significant advantage equal to around 6% of the total vote. One important effect of this advantage of the President as a candidate is that it substantially increases a President's discretion on economic and fiscal policies consistent with his reelection. The Presidency appears to have been personalized in the last 40 years. It is plausible to attribute this effect to the increasing role of radio and television in communicating the President's voice and image; these media probably favor the President, relative to another candidate, because of the President's sustained free access to the media prior to the formal campaign.

It is not possible to test any difference in voter response to wars between these two periods because there were no wars during a Presidential election year in the early period.

Party. A crude test of the party hypothesis is provided by comparing voter behavior in the 10 elections for which the incumbent President was a Republican with voter behavior in the 10 elections in which the President was a Democrat. The party hypothesis suggests that the effect of increasing real per capita net national product on the popular vote for the candidate of the incumbent party is *negative* if the incumbent President is a Democrat. This test is crude because it is not possible to separate changes in voter behavior over time from any effects of party. A Republican was President in 7 out of the 10 election years in the early period, and a Democrat was President in 7 out of the 10 years in the later period.

The results presented in Table 3 are strongly inconsistent with the party hypothesis. Again, the vote effects of changes in real per capita net national product and in real per capita federal tax revenues are almost identical between the two-party subsample test equations, and the effects are somewhat more significant in the Democratic subsample. These results should allay any concern that a Democratic President has a political incentive to promote a recession.

Several minor effects deserve mention: the incumbency effect appears to be specific to the late period rather than to Democratic candidates; the size and significance of the incumbency effect is much lower in the Democratic subsample than in the late period subsample. Again, it is not possible to test any party difference on the vote effect of a war, as there were no wars during election years in which the incumbent President was a Republican.

It may still be worthwhile to make other tests of the relative strength of the incumbency hypothesis and the party hypothesis. These results, however, suggest that the explanatory power of the party hypothesis is as weak as its plausibility.

NOTES

1. For given values of the other variables, the explicit iso-utility relation between Y and X, from equation 1, is the following:

$$Y = C(X)^{\frac{-c}{b}} + tX.$$

2. Seymour Neustein aided me with the empirical work for this article. Robert Raynsford, Thomas Linn, Robert Berry, and Joe Litten contributed to earlier incarnations of this study. Their several contributions are gratefully acknowledged.

3. Lepper (1974) made estimates using both types of dependent variables and found that the estimated partial derivatives are almost identical.

REFERENCES

ARCELLUS, F. and A.H. MELTZER (1975) "The effect of aggregate economic variables on congressional elections." American Political Science Review 69: 1,232-1,239.

FREY, B. and L. LAU (1941) "Ideology, public approval, and government behavior." Public Choice 10: 21-39.

KRAMER, G. (1971) "Short-term fluctuations in U.S. voting behavior 1896-1964." American Political Science Review 65: 131-143.

LEPPER, S.J. (1974) "Voting behavior and aggregate policy targets." Public Choice 18: 67-81.

MELTZER, A.H. and M. VELLRATH (1975) "The effects of economic policies on votes for the presidency: some evidence from recent elections." Paper read at the National Bureau of Economic Research Conference on Economic Analysis of Political Behavior, April.

NISKANEN, W.A. (1975) "Bureaucracy and the interests of bureau-
    crats." Paper read at the National Bureau of Economic Research
    Conference on Economic Analysis of Political Behavior, April.
——— (1971) Bureaucracy and Representative Government. Chicago:
    Aldine.
SCAMMON, R.M. and B.J. WATTENBERG (1970) The Real Majority.
    New York: Coward McCann.
STIGLER, G. (1973) "General economic conditions and national elec-
    tions." American Economic Review 63: 160-171.

APPENDIX
DESCRIPTION OF VARIABLES AND DATA SOURCES

I   Popular vote for Presidential candidate of incumbent party ÷ total popular vote for Presidential candidates of major parties

1892-1896 Historical Statistics P-31
1900-1972 Statistical Abstract 1974 No. 680

NP   Net national product ÷ (estimated resident population x index of consumer prices)

Net national product

1892-1928 Kendrick, Productivity Trends in the U.S. A-III
1932-1972 1975 Economic Report of the President C-14

Estimated resident population

1892-1896 Historical Statistics B-31
1900-1972 Statistical Abstract 1974 No. 2

Consumer Prices

1892-1912 Historical Statistics L-36
1916-1928 Historical Statistics L-41
1932-1972 1975 Economic Report of the President C-44

U   Unemployment ÷ total civilian labor force

1892-1896 Lebergott, Manpower in Economic Growth, P. 522

1900-1928 Historical Statistics D-47
1932-1972 1975 Economic Report of the President
C-24

SP   Stock price index ÷ index of consumer prices

Stock prices Standard and Poor's 500 Stock Index

1892-1936 Historical Statistics N-215
1940-1972 1975 Economic Report of the President
C-81

CBR   Moody's Aaa Corporate Bond Yield

1892-1916 Historical Statistics (railroad bond rates)
1920-1928 Historical Statistics
1932-1972 1975 Economic Report of the President
C-58

FX   Total federal expenditures ÷ (estimated resident population x index of consumer prices)

Federal expenditures

1892-1972 1972 Report of the Secretary of the Treasury

FR   Total federal tax revenues ÷ (estimated resident population ÷ index of consumer prices)

Federal Revenues

1892-1972 1972 Report of the Secretary of the Treasury

4

BUDGETS AND BALLOTS:
THE POLITICAL CONSEQUENCES OF FISCAL CHOICE

THEODORE J. EISMEIER

Hamilton College

Government has grown at a rapid pace in this century. Both as a regulator of the market and as a supplier of goods and services, the public sector has assumed a vastly expanded role. But building the American welfare state has not been accomplished without political growing pains. More government has meant higher taxes, and there have been signs of public hostility to rising tax bills. Many fear that this portends a serious and widespread taxpayers' revolt in the United States.

Of course, citizens have never been happy about paying taxes. In the past, opposition to taxes has been strong and often violent, as Sabine's description of the plight of the nineteenth century British tax collector illustrates:

But in some areas the hated commissioners were set upon and stoned. The Chief Justice of the Common Pleas was met by an

armed mob, three of his clerks seized and executed and their
heads mounted on poles. The unhappy judge was lucky to escape
with his life [1966: 12].

Today's tax protests seem tame in comparison. Some citizens
simply grumble about high taxes; others relieve their own tax
burdens by evasion. Recently, opposition to tax increases has
taken more organized forms such as taxpayer strikes, campaigns against bond issues, and efforts to impose statutory
limits on government spending. I am interested here in another expression of popular sentiment—voting. In both its
normative and positive versions, democratic theory presumes
that citizen electoral judgments reflect a weighing of the
costs and benefits of public policies. If citizens are dissatis-
fied with "big spending," we might expect them simply to
turn the culprits out of office at the next election. My
purpose here is to gauge citizen reaction to the rising cost of
American government, to examine the relationship between
tax decision and electoral choice.

Political wisdom about the electoral consequences of tax
increases is ambiguous. Politicians certainly have a healthy
fear of taxpayers and many believe that tax issues can put an
untimely end to promising political careers. Former Governor
John Anderson (quoted in Reuss) expresses this fear of the
hostile electorate:

> The rate of "tax mortality" among state and local political
> leaders is very high. A governor or mayor must raise taxes to meet
> his increasing responsibilities—but he is often voted out of office
> for doing so [1970: 33-34].

In support of their beliefs about the riskiness of tax decisions, most politicians would probably point to one of their
colleagues who allegedly fell victim to the wrath of taxpayers.

Voters may not like new taxes, but they apparently do like
new programs. According to another piece of political folk-

lore, the affection of voters can be "bought" with new spending programs, even if this requires new taxes. This idea that there is political capital to be made by a judicious mix of new spending and new taxes is behind the famous electoral strategy attributed to Harry Hopkins: "We shall tax and tax, and spend and spend, and elect and elect" (Sherwood, 1950: 102-103). At least on its face, this buy-the-vote strategy appears to be at odds with the fear-the-taxpayer strategy.

What systematic evidence there is about taxpayer retribution at the polls is inconclusive. To support his argument that the behavior of government bureaus produces an oversupply of public goods, Niskanen (1975) has looked at the effect of tax increases in 20 Presidential elections from 1896 to 1972.[1] He finds that the partial effect of tax increases on the popular vote for the candidate of the incumbent party is negative. A 10% increase in real per capita federal revenues costs the candidate of the incumbent party about 1.4% of the popular vote.

In his analysis of short-term fluctuations in voting behavior, Li (1976) has estimated the electoral consequences of changes in the fraction of total federal tax revenues accounted for by the federal income tax. He reasons that changes in this fraction are a measure of policy choice about income redistribution—if the fraction grows larger, this presumably measures a policy decision to rely on more progressive, "redistributive" taxes. Li finds that this measure reveals a consistent lack of association with fluctuations in congressional elections. He notes, however, that since the income tax variable is sensitive to income trends as well as to fiscal policy decision, the apparent absence of effect may reflect a measurement problem.

Pomper (1968) has examined the effects of tax increases in gubernatorial elections. He develops several ordinal measures of political success and of change in aggregate tax burden. Among the latter are the increase in per capita spending since the last election and the increase in per capita spending as a fraction of per capita personal income. From the results of a cross-sectional correlational analysis, Pomper concludes that governors who lead in passing taxes do not suffer at the polls.

It is difficult to draw any firm conclusions from this evidence. Niskanen finds that taxes have a significant effect in Presidential elections; Li and Pomper find no such effect in congressional or gubernatorial elections. Part of the problem may be the use in each of the studies of aggregate policy measures such as per capita tax burden. The politics of taxation is often dominated by battles over specific policy decisions—whether or not to raise particular and sometimes obscure tax rates, whether or not to close a tax loophole. A more appropriate test of the taxpayer retribution thesis might focus on voter response not to changes in aggregate tax burdens but to specific tax policy decisions.

This study examines the electoral consequences of legislated increases in tax rates in gubernatorial elections between 1948 and 1974. This is the period in which the American welfare state came of age, and the tax bills of most Americans rose sharply. Since 1948, real per capita federal revenues have risen by more than 230%, state revenues by more than 250%, and local revenues by more than 200%. Economic growth and inflation have vastly increased the take of the federal tax system, even as national policymakers have lowered the nominal rates. But state policymakers have enjoyed no such political luxury. The U.S. Advisory Commission on Intergovernmental Relations (1974) estimates that between 1959 and 1973, for example, state governments enacted 40 new taxes and 525 rate increases. Since my interest is in the electoral consequences of tax *decisions,* this recent necessity for state policymakers to bite the fiscal bullet has produced a fertile source of data.

DATA AND ANALYSIS

The set of observations used in this analysis consists of 320 gubernatorial elections between 1948 and 1974. This does not represent all gubernatorial elections during the period; a list of excluded elections with the reasons for their exclusion is contained in Appendix I. The set of observations does include almost all elections held in 35 states with at least nominal two-party competition during the period.

My purpose is to estimate the effects of tax decisions on the electoral fortunes of incumbent gubernatorial parties, so the first step is to create a measure of electoral change. I chose a simple one. VOTE CHANGE was defined as the proportion of the two-party vote for the Democratic guber- natorial candidate in the election minus the proportion of the two-party vote for the Democratic candidate in the preceding election.[2] Thus, a change in the Democratic gubernatorial vote share from 35% to 45% or from 55% to 65% would yield a VOTE CHANGE score of +0.10. Alternatively, a change in the Democratic gubernatorial vote share from 45% to 35% or from 65% to 55% would yield a score of -0.10.

The next step is to define tax policy variables. I began with four simple dummy variable measures of tax activity during the term of the incumbent administration:

NEW TAX = 1, if a new tax was enacted during the term of the incumbent administration; 0, otherwise.

SALES TAX INCREASE = 1, if the rate of the retail sales tax was raised during the term of the incumbent administration; 0, other- wise.

INCOME TAX INCREASE = 1, if the rate of the state personal income tax was raised during the term of the incumbent administra- tion; 0, otherwise.

UNSUCCESSFUL TAX PROPOSAL = 1, if during the term of the incumbent administration the governor proposed a new tax or an increase in the rate of an existing broad based tax which was not enacted by the legislature; 0, otherwise.

Each of these variables was multipled by another variable, INCUMBENCY, which takes a value of 1 if the incumbent gubernatorial administration was Democratic and - 1 if the incumbent administration was Republican. For example, if the rate of the retail sales tax was raised during a Democratic administration, SALES TAX INCREASE has a value of 1; if the sales tax was increased during a Republican administration, the variable has a value of - 1.

Of course, the electoral fortunes of gubernatorial candidates are not influenced solely by tax decisions. Candidates for governor may also be the beneficiaries or victims of national swings toward one party or the other. In 1958, for example, Democratic gubernatorial candidates benefited from a national swing to the Democratic party. In 1966 the reverse was true; Democratic candidates suffered from a national swing to the Republican party. In order to estimate the electoral effects of tax increases, it is necessary to control for these national trends in party fortunes. Because governors in the various states serve terms of different lengths, the set of observations includes 27 different election periods. These elections periods are listed below:

1946-1948	1954-1958	1964-1966
1946-1950	1956-1958	1964-1968
1948-1950	1956-1960	1966-1968
1948-1952	1958-1960	1966-1970
1950-1952	1958-1962	1968-1970
1950-1954	1960-1962	1968-1972
1952-1954	1960-1964	1970-1972
1952-1956	1962-1964	1970-1974
1954-1956	1962-1966	1972-1974.

To measure the national trends for each of these election periods, 26 dummy variables were created (one for each election period except 1946-1948). In the regression equation the coefficients of these dummy variables—named TREND 46-50, TREND 48-50, and so on—when added to the intercept term provide estimates of the national trends in the Democratic gubernatorial vote share for these election periods. The intercept term provides an estimate of the national trend in the election period 1946-1948 (Johnston, 1963).

The results of a multiple regression of VOTE CHANGE on the party trend variables and the initial tax policy variables are presented in Table 1. As I have noted, the regression coefficients for the trend variables when added to the intercept term are estimates of the national swing in the proportion of the two-party vote given to Democratic gubernatorial candidates. Thus, the national trend for 1972-1974, for example, was (-0.029) + (+0.049) or 2% in the Democratic direction. Our primary interest here, however, is in the partial effect of tax decisions on changes in the vote. The first thing to note about the coefficients of the tax variables is that the signs are consistent and support political wisdom about taxpayer retribution—tax increases hurt the political fortunes of incumbent gubernatorial parties. Except for INCOME TAX INCREASE, each of the tax variables is significant at the .01 level. As we might expect, new taxes seem to do the most political damage. Enacting a new tax results in a drop of about 3.8% in the two-party vote share of the incumbent party, and trying to enact a new tax or tax increase but without success hurts about as much.

Implicit in the original specification of the tax variables is the idea that regardless of the circumstances of their enactment, tax increases will have the same electoral effects. It is possible, however, that the circumstances of a tax's enactment might influence its political impact. For example, an incumbent party might be able to avoid the wrath of taxpayers if it can successfully cast the blame for a tax increase on the previous administration. This apparently was the strategy of Vermont's incumbent governor, who had engineered the adoption of a retail sales tax, in the 1970 election:

Table 1:   Effects of National Trends and Tax Policy Decisions on
           Changes in the Vote Share of Incumbent Gubernatorial
           Parties

Independent Variable	Coefficient	Standard Error
Trend Variables		
TREND 46–50	– 0.078	0.029
TREND 48–50	– 0.084	0.021
TREND 48–52	– 0.100	0.028
TREND 50–52	– 0.074	0.022
TREND 50–54	– 0.021	0.025
TREND 52–54	0.014	0.022
TREND 52–56	– 0.057	0.029
TREND 54–56	– 0.052	0.021
TREND 54–58	0.031	0.026
TREND 56–58	– 0.018	0.022
TREND 56–60	– 0.034	0.029
TREND 58–60	– 0.080	0.022
TREND 58–62	– 0.119	0.024
TREND 60–62	– 0.029	0.023
TREND 60–64	– 0.012	0.028
TREND 62–64	0.002	0.024
TREND 62–66	– 0.083	0.024
TREND 64–66	– 0.136	0.024
TREND 64–68	– 0.042	0.026
TREND 66–68	– 0.070	0.027
TREND 66–70	– 0.018	0.023
TREND 68–70	– 0.027	0.026
TREND 68–72	– 0.080	0.026
TREND 70–72	0.001	0.033
TREND 70–74	0.017	0.022
TREND 72–74	– 0.029	0.033
Tax Variables		
NEW TAX	– 0.038	0.011
SALES TAX INCREASE	– 0.027	0.010
INCOME TAX INCREASE	– 0.018	0.009
UNSUCCESSFUL TAX PROPOSAL	– 0.037	0.011

$N = 320$
$R^2 = 0.418$
Intercept $= 0.049$

The Davis organization's answer to the odds was a masterpiece of advertising that meshed strategy with television. The governor's pants were rolled up, he was put in a rowboat half filled with water in the middle of the pond, and he was set to bailing. The audio hammered away at the theme that Davis had bailed the state out of economic disaster. The commercial was short and was broadcast incessantly around the state. With one theme the Republicans had justified the sales tax [Bryan, 1974: 120].

If such a strategy works, tax increases for which the blame can be shifted should have less severe electoral consequences.

The data here do not bear directly on questions about the extent to which incumbent parties do try to blame tax increases on their competitor or about the success of this strategy of blame shifting. It is, however, possible to obtain indirect evidence about such questions by comparing the electoral effects of tax initiatives taken under different political circumstances. To this end a new set of tax policy variables was created:

NEW TAX IN FIRST YEAR = 1, if a new tax was enacted during the first year in office of the incumbent administration and the previous administration was of the opposite party; 0, otherwise.

NEW TAX NOT IN FIRST YEAR = 1, if a new tax was enacted in a year other than the first year in office of the incumbent administration, or if a new tax was enacted in the first year in office of the incumbent administration but the previous administration was of the same party; 0, otherwise.

SALES TAX INCREASE IN FIRST YEAR = 1, if the rate of the retail sales tax was increased during the first year in office of the incumbent administration and the previous administration was of the opposite party; 0, otherwise.

SALES TAX INCREASE NOT IN FIRST YEAR = 1, if the rate of the retail sales tax was increased in a year other than the first year in office of the incumbent administration, or if the rate of the retail sales tax was increased during the first year in office of the incumbent administration but the previous administration was of the same party; 0, otherwise.

INCOME TAX INCREASE IN FIRST YEAR = 1, if the rate of the state personal income tax was increased during the first year in office of the incumbent administration and the previous administration was of the opposite party; 0, otherwise.

INCOME TAX INCREASE NOT IN FIRST YEAR = 1, if the rate of the state personal income tax was increased in a year other than the first year in office of the incumbent administration, or if the rate of the state personal income tax was raised during the first year in office of the incumbent administration but the previous administration was of the same party; 0, otherwise.

UNSUCCESSFUL TAX PROPOSAL IN FIRST YEAR = 1, if during the first year in office of the incumbent administration the governor proposed a new tax or an increase in the rate of an existing broad-based tax which was not enacted by the legislature and the previous administration was of the opposite party; 0, otherwise.

UNSUCCESSFUL TAX PROPOSAL NOT IN FIRST YEAR = 1, if during the term of the incumbent administration the governor proposed a new tax or an increase in the rate of an existing broad-based tax in a year other than the first year in office which was not enacted by the legislature, or if during the first year in office of the incumbent administration the governor proposed a new tax or an increase in the rate of an existing broad-based tax which was not enacted by the legislature but the previous administration was of the same party; 0, otherwise.

Again, the tax policy variables were multiplied by the variable INCUMBENCY. This seemingly intricate coding scheme has a simple purpose; it allows us to compare the electoral effects of tax initiatives taken when the party in power is in a position to blame the other party for the need for higher taxes with the effects of tax initiatives taken when the party in power is not in a position to blame the other party for a state's fiscal difficulties.

The results of a multiple regression of VOTE CHANGE on the party trend variables and the new set of tax policy variables are presented in Table 2. The coefficients for the trend variables differ very little from the previous equation, but some interesting differences do turn up in the tax variables. Let us look first at the effects of tax initiatives taken in the first year in office after one party wrested control of the governorship from the other and was therefore in a position to blame its competitor for the need for a tax increase. Of these "first-year" tax initiatives, only the coefficient for enacting a new tax is significant at the .05 level. Enacting a new tax is apparently harmful regardless of the circumstances of enactment. The coefficients for the other first-year tax initiatives are positive and small in magnitude relative to the size of the standard error. Now if we look at tax initiatives taken when the incumbent party was not in a position to blame its competitor, the electoral consequences are consistently adverse. The coefficients for these tax initiatives are all negative and each is significant at the .01 level. For example, enacting a rate increase in the state sales tax or the state income tax when the party in power is not in a position to blame the other party results in a drop of about 3% in the two-party vote share of the incumbent party.

The use of dummy variable measures of tax policy decision has allowed us to estimate the average effect of different kinds of tax initiatives. In effect, we have been comparing the electoral fate of incumbent parties which enact or propose tax increases—regardless of the magnitude of the increase— with those which do not. Another question we might ask is this: Given that a party is in power when a tax increase is enacted, what is the electoral effect of the *magnitude* of the increase? To explore this question, two subsamples of the original set of observations were isolated. To be included in Subsample 1, cases had to meet each of the following requirements:

(1) The rate of the retail sales tax was raised during the term of the incumbent administration.

Table 2: Effects of National Trends and Tax Policy Decisions on Changes in the Vote Share of Incumbent Gubernatorial Parties

Independent Variable	Coefficient	Standard Error
Trend Variables		
TREND 46–50	− 0.080	0.029
TREND 48–50	− 0.088	0.021
TREND 48–52	− 0.098	0.027
TREND 50–52	− 0.071	0.022
TREND 50–54	− 0.021	0.025
TREND 52–54	0.015	0.022
TREND 52–56	− 0.060	0.029
TREND 54–56	− 0.056	0.021
TREND 54–58	0.032	0.026
TREND 56–58	− 0.020	0.021
TREND 56–60	− 0.037	0.028
TREND 58–60	− 0.076	0.022
TREND 58–62	− 0.117	0.024
TREND 60–62	− 0.016	0.023
TREND 60–64	− 0.016	0.028
TREND 62–64	0.004	0.023
TREND 62–66	− 0.077	0.024
TREND 64–66	− 0.137	0.024
TREND 64–68	− 0.044	0.026
TREND 66–68	− 0.065	0.026
TREND 66–70	− 0.019	0.023
TREND 68–70	− 0.028	0.026
TREND 68–72	− 0.081	0.026
TREND 70–72	− 0.001	0.033
TREND 70–74	0.011	0.021
TREND 72–74	− 0.028	0.032
Tax Variables		
NEW TAX IN FIRST YEAR	− 0.044	0.020
NEW TAX NOT IN FIRST YEAR	− 0.035	0.012
SALES TAX INCREASE IN FIRST YEAR	0.001	0.024
SALES TAX INCREASE NOT IN FIRST YEAR	− 0.030	0.010
INCOME TAX INCREASE IN FIRST YEAR	0.010	0.017
INCOME TAX INCREASE NOT IN FIRST YEAR	− 0.030	0.010
UNSUCCESSFUL TAX PROPOSAL IN FIRST YEAR	0.055	0.032
UNSUCCESSFUL TAX PROPOSAL NOT IN FIRST YEAR	− 0.048	0.012

N = 320
R^2 = 0.447
Intercept = 0.049

[132]

(2) The rate increase did not occur in the first year in office after one party had wrested control of the governorship from the other party.

(3) No other tax increases were enacted or proposed during the term of the incumbent administration.

To be included in Subsample 2, cases had to meet each of the following requirements:

(1) The rate of the state personal income tax was raised during the term of the incumbent administration.

(2) The rate increase did not occur in the first year in office after one party had wrested control of the governorship from the other party.

(3) No other tax increases were enacted or proposed during the term of the incumbent administration.

These requirements drastically reduce the number of observations. Subsample 1 consists of 31 cases; Subsample 2 consists of 23 cases. There is, of course, no overlap between the two subsamples.

In order to estimate the electoral effects of the magnitude of tax increases, the following tax variables were then defined:

CHANGE IN RATE OF SALES TAX = the change in the rate of the retail sales tax during the term of the incumbent administration.

PERCENT CHANGE IN RATE OF SALES TAX = the percentage change in the rate of the retail sales tax during the term of the incumbent administration.

CHANGE IN RATE OF INCOME TAX = the estimated change in the rate of the state personal income tax for a family of four with an income 25% above the national median family income during the term of the incumbent administration.[3]

PERCENT CHANGE IN RATE OF INCOME TAX = the estimated percentage change in the rate of the state personal income tax for a family of four with an income 25% above the national median family income during the term of the incumbent administration.

Each of the variables was multiplied by the variable INCUM-BENCY. The sales tax variables are for use in Subsample 1, while the income tax variables are for use in Subsample 2.

Because the number of cases in these two subsamples is small, the use of a large set of dummy variables to control for national swings is impossible. Instead, a new variable, CONG-VOTE, was introduced. CONGVOTE was defined as the change in the Democrat's share of the state's two-party congressional vote during the election period in question. This measure has its problems, but it is at least a crude control for state party swings which affect the electoral fate of gubernatorial candidates.[4]

The results of four regression equations, two for each subsample, are presented in Tables 3 and 4. The equations in Table 3 address the following question: Given that a party is in power when a sales tax increase is enacted, what effect does the magnitude of the increase have on the change in the party's vote? Similarly, the equations in Table 4 address this question: Given that a party is in power when an increase in the state income tax is enacted, what effect does the magnitude of the increase have on the change in the party's vote? Regression coefficients of zero, for example, would suggest that the magnitude of a tax increase has no effect on electoral fortunes. The first thing to say about the results is that not too much stock should be put in the specific estimates of the effects of tax increases on VOTE CHANGE. The number of cases is small, the standard errors of the coefficients are relatively large, and the measure of party swings is a bit troublesome. Nevertheless, the fact that the coefficient for each of the tax variables is negative does suggest that the greater the magnitude of a sales or income tax increase, the more damaging its electoral consequences.

Table 3: Effects of the Magnitude of Sales Tax Increases on Changes in the Vote Share of Gubernatorial Parties

Variable	Equation 1		Variable	Equation 2	
	Coefficient	Standard Error		Coefficient	Standard Error
CONGVOTE	0.271	0.159	CONGVOTE	0.319	0.164
CHANGE IN RATE OF SALES TAX	-3.641	1.328	%CHANGE IN RATE OF SALES TAX	-0.065	0.031
N = 31			N = 31		
R² = 0.355			R² = 0.293		
Intercept = -0.005			Intercept = -0.003		

Table 4: Effects of the Magnitude of Income Tax Increases on Changes in the Vote Share of Gubernatorial Parties

Variable	Equation 1 Coefficient	Standard Error	Variable	Equation 2 Coefficient	Standard Error
CONGVOTE	0.603	0.258	CONGVOTE	0.609	0.241
CHANGE IN RATE OF INCOME TAX	−4.193	3.001	%CHANGE IN RATE OF INCOME TAX	−0.069	0.037
N = 23			N = 23		
R^2 = 0.361			R^2 = 0.403		
Intercept = −0.019			Intercept = −0.018		

Thus far, we have estimated the effects of tax increases on the two-party vote share of incumbent gubernatorial parties. Politicians, I expect, might be more interested in a question about the bottom line of all of this. Is an incumbent party more likely to be voted out of office if it enacts or proposes a tax increase than if it does not? Some evidence relevant to this question is presented in Table 5. This simple two by two table allows us to compare the proportion of incumbent parties enacting or proposing tax increases that were turned out of office against the proportion of incumbent parties not enacting or proposing tax increases that were turned out of office. The table shows that 45.1% of incumbent gubernatorial parties which enacted or proposed a tax increase were defeated in the next election, while only 27.5% of incumbent parties which held the line on higher taxes met such a fate. Put another way, the odds of an incumbent party which

Table 5: Comparison of the Electoral Fates of "Taxing" and "Non-Taxing" Incumbent Gubernatorial Parties

	TAX	NO TAX	
Incumbent Party Lost	45.1% (74)	27.6% (43)	117
Incumbent Party Won	54.9% (90)	72.4% (113)	203
	164	156	

N = 320
Odds Ratio = 2.15
LN Odds Ratio = 0.765
Standard Error = 0.237

Figure 1: Niskanen's Analysis of the Relation Between Popular Votes and Government Budgets

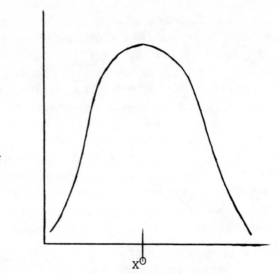

Government Spending and Revenues

enacted or proposed a tax increase being turned out of office were more than twice those of a party which did not.[5] Tax initiatives apparently cost not just votes but also elections.

IMPLICATIONS

There is, it seems, some truth in political wisdom about the damaging effects of tax decisions on electoral fortunes. But the phenomenon of taxpayer retribution at the polls has significance beyond the mere fate of individual politicians. It will be useful, therefore, to close with a brief discussion of two broader questions—What are the reasons behind the electoral rebelliousness of American taxpayers? What are its implications?

One explanation of the negative electoral consequences of tax increases is that government budgets are simply too large.

Larger, that is, than the preference of the median voter. Niskanen (1975), as I have shown in Figure 1, illustrates this "overspending" argument graphically.[6] If the government budget is *less* than the vote-maximizing level, X^0, the partial effect of an increase in government spending and taxing on the popular vote of the candidate of the incumbent party should be positive. If, on the other hand, the government budget is *greater* than the vote-maximizing level, the effect of an increase in government spending and taxing on the popular vote for the incumbent party should be negative. Thus, Niskanen interprets his data about the electoral consequences of tax increases as evidence that the public sector is too large. An important implication of this argument is that for a number of possible reasons (Niskanen thinks the reason is a perverse combination of bureaucratic and legislative processes) politicians do not follow vote-maximizing fiscal strategies.

The normative force of this overspending argument rests on several assumptions about the nature of citizen judgments about the fiscal performance of government. The most important of these assumptions are:

(1) That voters know what is good for them and what they want.
(2) That voters can make at least roughly accurate judgments about the costs and benefits of public activity.
(3) That voters judge the fiscal performance of government against some feasible set of alternatives.

These assumptions are by no means trivial, and each has been challenged. To challenge these assumptions is to challenge the thesis that taxpayer rebelliousness reflects the considered view that government budgets are too big.

The most famous case that citizens do not know what is good for them or even what they want is Galbraith's in *The Affluent Society*. His argument is straightforward—tradition and manipulation through advertising create a bias against public production as opposed to private production. Galbraith's main conclusion is that the public sector is therefore "starved," but an important corollary is that politicians who try to redress this social imbalance will suffer adverse public reaction:

> The scientist or engineer or advertising man who devotes himself to developing a new carburetor, cleanser, or depilatory for which the public recognizes no need and will feel none until an advertising campaign arouses it, is one of the valued members of our society. A politician or a public servant who dreams up a new public service is a wastrel. Few public offenses are more reprehensible [1958: 261].

Galbraith then rejects the idea that the unwillingness of taxpayers to pay for more public services means that government is spending more than people want or need because he rejects the idea that citizen tastes about the relative mix of public and private goods are independently determined. Whether they are, of course, is an empirical question, and others have taken issue with the Galbraith thesis (Hayek, 1961; Wallich, 1961; Amacher et al., 1975).

In his argument about the budget size in democracies, Downs (1960) challenges the assumption that voters make accurate judgments about the costs and benefits of public policies. Information is costly, Downs argues, and rational citizens therefore judge the performance of government on the basis of highly imperfect information. Moreover, citizens are more aware of the costs of government than of the benefits. Taxes, the most important costs of government, are highly visible. Wage earners see their income tax payments in their pay stubs; homeowners are sent property tax bills in the mail; consumers may notice their sales tax payments whenever they make a purchase. In contrast, the benefits of government are remote and uncertain. Government spending on education, for example, may have far-reaching spillover effects of which most of us are but dimly aware. We might fully appreciate the value of other public services—fire protection is a good example—only if government *did not* provide them. The implications of this alleged tendency for citizens to know more about the costs of government than about the benefits are important. First, people will demand levels of public spending lower than those they would demand if they were the possessors of perfect information. Second, politicians who give the public what it would want under conditions of perfect information will be regarded as spendthrifts.

Downs makes another argument about citizen fiscal judgments which bears on the third assumption of the overspending thesis. Niskanen's analysis of public fiscal choice is, of course, a simplification of reality. Political parties and candidates do not offer voters a choice simply about how much government should spend. Rather, they must engage in what Breton (1974) calls "full line supply," offering complex bundles of different programs to gain political support. The necessity of full line supply, Downs argues, means that citizens never reach equilibrium in their dealings with government. That is, for each citizen there is some reallocation of resources within the public sector or between the public and private sector which would be preferred. What this means is that citizens will always believe that the government budget is too large in relation to the benefits that they receive from it and that their taxes are therefore too high. Thus, the following situation is not unusual:

> Voter A believes in good schools but is willing to do without four lane highways in various sections of the state. If his desires were generally shared, increased and improved education could be bought with no increase in taxes. Voter B demands many four lane highways for his personal travel and as a requisite for his business. To satisfy the expenditure demands of both A and B, new and increased taxes are needed, yet A and B, who view

expenditure priorities differently, may pool their resources politically to oppose tax increases [Penniman, 1971: 521].

The important point here is that taxpayer discontent may
result from the fact that citizens judge government by some
ideal performance standard which, given the heterogeneity of
public tastes, is unattainable.

At issue here are fundamental questions about the nature
of citizen fiscal choice. Because he regards citizen-taxpayers
as fairly accurate assessors of the costs and benefits of public
activity, Niskanen interprets the fact that tax increases cost
votes as evidence that the public sector is too large. Because
they believe that citizen fiscal judgments are biased, based on
scanty and distorted information, or made against some
unattainable performance standard, Galbraith and Downs
would probably interpret the same fact as evidence that the
public sector is too small. Quite clearly, the evaluative weight
we attach to citizen fiscal judgments depends very much on
our view of the nature and quality of these judgments.

This speculation is not merely academic. In various forms
questions about citizen fiscal judgments play an important
part in public policy dialogue. The issue of revenue-sharing is
a case in point. Governors and mayors, in a style not unlike
Galbraith and Downs, argue passionately that political constraints and electoral hazards prevent them from developing
tax and expenditure policies adequate to meet the needs and
demands of citizens and that this situation should be
remedied by financing increased state and local spending
through the progressive federal tax system (Haider, 1974).
Some critics of revenue-sharing, on the other hand, argue that
states and especially localities are the last bastions of fiscal
accountability and that shifting the financing of these governments to the invisibly growing federal income tax only weakens the nexus between cost and benefit in public policy
choice. Our assessment of evidence about citizen fiscal choice

has an important bearing on our evaluation both of government policy performance and of alternative structures of public policy decision.

One final point. If Downs is right that taxpayers are chronically discontent, this would seem to put politicians in a precarious position. Is there anything they can do about it? Puviani considered such a question at the turn of the century.[7] The ruling class, he argued, will organize the fiscal system in such a way as to create "fiscal illusions" which minimize taxpayer resistance at any given level of taxation. He described a number of strategies which might be used to create such illusions—public debt, inflation, using excise taxes which are concealed in the price of goods, fragmenting the tax base into numerous small levies, employing taxes with unknown or uncertain incidence. Puviani wrote in a different era and in a different political setting, but the logic of his analysis remains remarkably intact. Indeed, as demands for increased public spending grow and opposition to tax increases stiffens, we might expect politicians to devise more ingenious strategies of easing the felt pain of taxpayers, of getting "the most feathers for the least squawking."

NOTES

1. For a somewhat different analysis of the effects of tax policies on Presidential elections, see Meltzer and Vellrath (1975).

2. All variables included in the analysis are capitalized in the text. Sources of data are described in Appendix II.

3. Several income levels were used originally to estimate the change in the rate of the personal income tax. These various measures were highly correlated. For example, for the entire set of observations, the simple correlation between a measure of the percentage change in the income tax rate for a family of four with a median income and a similar measure for a family of four with an income 25% above the median is

0.84. The higher income measure is used here simply because it slightly enlarges the number of observations in Subsample 2.

4. For a justification for using the statewide congressional vote as a measure of state party strength, see Turett (1971). To the extent that the congressional vote in a state is not influenced by gubernatorial elections, it is a reasonable measure of state party strength. I should also note here that those few cases in which minor parties garnered more than 10% of the state's congressional vote were excluded from the analysis to follow.

5. The properties of the odds ratio and its natural logarithm are discussed in Novick and Jackson (1974) and Fleiss (1973).

6. A similar argument is made by Buchanan and Flowers (1969).

7. Puviani's argument is summarized in Buchanan (1967).

REFERENCES

AMACHER, R. C. (1975) "Budget size in democracy: A review of the arguments." Public Finance Quarterly 3: 99-122.

BRETON, A. (1974) The Economic Theory of Representative Government. Chicago: Aldine.

BRYAN, F. M. (1974) Yankee Politics in Rural Vermont. Hanover, N.H.: The University Press of New England.

BUCHANAN, J. M. (1967) Public Finance in Democratic Process. Chapel Hill: University of North Carolina Press.

——— and M. FLOWERS (1969) "An analytic setting for a 'taxpayers' revolution." Western Economic Journal 7: 349-359.

DOWNS, A. (1960) "Why the budget is too small in a democracy." World Politics 12: 541-563.

FLEISS, J. L. (1973) Statistical Methods for Rates and Proportions. New York: Wiley.

GALBRAITH, J. K. (1958) The Affluent Society. Boston: Houghton Mifflin.

HAIDER, D. H. (1974) When Governments Come to Washington. New York: Free Press.

HAYEK, F. A. (1961) "The non sequitur of the dependence effect." Southern Economic Journal 27: 346-348.

JOHNSTON, J. (1963) Econometric Methods. New York: McGraw-Hill.

LI, R.P.Y. (1976) "Public policy and short term fluctuations in U.S. voting behavior: A reformulation and expansion." Political Methodology 3: 49-70.

MELTZER, A. H. and M. VELLRATH (1975) "The effects of economic policies on votes for the Presidency: Some evidence from recent elections." Journal of Law and Economics 18: 781-798.

NISKANEN, W. A. (1975) "Bureaucrats and politicians." Journal of Law and Economics 18: 617-643.

NOVICK, M. R. and P. H. JACKSON (1974) Statistical Methods for Educational and Psychological Research. New York: McGraw-Hill.

PENNIMAN, C. (1971) "The politics of taxation." In H. Jacob and K. N. Vines (eds.) Politics in American States. Boston: Little Brown.

POMPER, G. M. (1968) Elections in America. New York: Dodd Mead.

REUSS, H. S. (1970) Revenue-Sharing. New York: Praeger Publishers.

SABINE, B.E.V. (1966) A History of Income Tax. London: George Allen and Unwin, Ltd.

SHERWOOD, R. E. (1950) Roosevelt and Hopkins. New York: Harper and Row.

TURETT, J. S. "The vulnerability of American governors, 1900-1969." Midwest Journal of Political Science 15: 108-132.

U.S. Advisory Commission on Intergovernmental Relations (1974) Federal-State-Local Finances: Significant Features of Fiscal Federalism. Washington, D.C.: U.S. Government Printing Office.

WALLICH, H. C. (1961) The Cost of Freedom. New York: Harper and Row.

APPENDIX I

Elections Excluded from the Analysis

1. All elections in Alaska and Hawaii were excluded.

2. All elections in the following states were excluded because these states did not have at least nominal two-party competition for the entire period 1948-1974: Alabama, Arkansas, Florida, Georgia, Louisiana, Mississippi, North Carolina, South Carolina, Tennessee, Texas, Virginia.

3. All elections in Kentucky and New Jersey were excluded because they were held in odd years. This made it impossible to control for national swings.

4. All elections in all other states were included with the following exceptions:

    A. California, 1950 (because in the previous election both parties nominated the same candidate).

    B. Idaho, 1966; Idaho, 1970; Maine, 1974; Nevada, 1974; New Hampshire, 1972; New Hampshire, 1974; New York, 1966; New York, 1970; Utah, 1956; Utah, 1960 (because in the election in question or in the previous election minor party candidates received more than 10% of the popular vote).

APPENDIX II

Data Sources

1. Voting data and incumbency data were obtained from the following sources:

   A. Paul T. David, *Party Strength in the United States* (Charlottesville: University of Virginia Press, 1972).

   B. Richard M. Scammon, ed., *America Votes 11* (Washington, D.C.: Congressional Quarterly, 1975).

2. Data about tax proposals and decisions were obtained from the following sources:

   A. *Tax Administrators News*; Volumes 11-38, 1947-1974.

   B. The Book of the States; 1947-1974; (Lexington, KY: The Council of State Governments).

   C. *The World Almanac*; 1948-1975; (New York: Newspaper Enterprise Association).

3. Data about national family median income which were used to estimate changes in the rate of state personal income taxes were obtained from *Statistical Abstract of the United States* (Washington, D.C.: U.S. Department of Commerce, 1975).

5

ELECTION EXPECTATIONS AND OUTCOMES: A THEORY OF NOMINATING CONVENTION CONFLICT 1896-1976

W. ROSS BREWER AND GARRISON NELSON

University of Vermont

As both a party activist and a historian, Arthur Schlesinger, Jr. had an opportunity to see conventions in two temporal contexts. His assessment at both points was that

> a convention is far too fluid and hysterical a phenomenon for exact history. Everything happens at once, and everything changes too quickly ... At the time it is all a confusion; in retrospect it is all a blur [1965: 33].

If professional politicians agreed with this assessment, they would have abandoned conventions long ago. However, conventions continue to function today in much the same way they did over a hundred years ago with baffled delegates, hungry campaign managers, and press alternately delighted and repulsed by the convention's activities. They survive because there is no other way in which sizable numbers of diverse party politicians can select from their own ranks the one person who has the best chance of obtaining the consti- tutionally required majority of votes in the Electoral College.

A MODEL OF CONVENTION BEHAVIOR

In order to give the political phenomena which swirl about nominating conventions some clear identification, we have constructed a simple model which relates preconvention cues and convention conflict to election results. Each of the model's six components and their operational definitions will be described here in relation to the key event itself–the Presidential election. This is the first element in the model, for it is the goal sought by the various participants in the nomination process (see Figure 1).

Election outcome is defined with both total popular and electoral votes. These data are the most common currency of Presidential election campaigns, past and present (Peterson, 1963; Congressional Quarterly, 1975).

Because of their centrality to politicians, party unity and its converse–disunity–have been used as the focal points for this study. As our operational definition of *convention con- flict*, we have used Rae's (1968, 1971) "Index of Fractional- ization" which permits a more refined distinction to be made on candidate proportions than simple ballot percentages. For example, a nominee who received 60% of the delegate vote on the first ballot in the face of opposition from four candidates who each received 10% will have a different recon- ciliation strategy than another nominee with the identical winning percentage who faced only one opponent. In the first case the fractionalization score would be .600, while in the second case the fractionalization score would be .480.

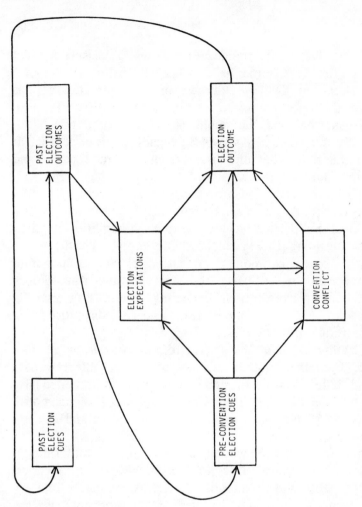

Figure 1: An Interactive Model of Convention Behavior

[153]

We have used fractionalization scores to measure conflict on the first Presidential ballot. This is the ballot which looms the largest in the consciousness of all candidates for it is often the only contested one at a convention.[1] Political commentators and the public also focus upon this ballot because it consistently shows the highest levels of conflict. It is at this point that one discovers clues to the location and depth of intraparty dissension.

Moving backward in time the next component is *election expectation*. This concept represents the beliefs held by professional politicians on the varying probabilities of their party's gaining the Presidency. Our initial hypotheses are related to this component in that we expect to encounter high conflict in out-party conventions anticipating victory and in-party conventions expecting defeat. Low conflict seems to occur within optimistic in-party conventions and pessimistic out-party ones.

Election expectations derive from *preconvention election cues*. Contained within this component are the raw data which politicians use to reduce uncertainty. In order to have genuine meaning for a large number of professional politicians, these data have to be readily accessible and directly relevant to elections.

Among these cues would be the results of midterm congressional elections, the control of statehouses by members of the party, the Presidential preference primaries, and the various public opinion polls. These are the most obvious cues.

The election predictors which we are using are accessible to all Presidential politicians, political commentators, and to the public at large. Among these are the number and percentage of seats gained and lost in the House of Representatives during the midterm election, the number and percentage of seats held by each party at the time of the conventions, and how these figures correspond to those recorded in the previous Presidential contest.[2] In addition, we have calculated the number and percentage of governors and of electoral votes which were held by each party's governors at the time of the convention.[3]

Taken in combination, the House seats and gubernatorial electoral votes are very valuable sources of data. The House seats permit Presidential politicians to detect waves of national sentiment which may impact directly upon the outcome of the Presidential contest. The governorships held by one's party and the electoral votes within those states are important to any rational campaign strategy. If the party holds the states with a majority of the votes within the Electoral College, then the rational strategy would be to build off the successful state party organizations. If the party holds no such majority in the state houses, then the strategy would be to construct a Presidential organization in the state which is separate from the unsuccessful local party.

The House cues and the gubernatorial ones have an important role in this analysis because they both exhibit cross-time comparability. Given the fact that both sets of offices have been accessible to the electorate throughout the period covered in this paper (1896-1976), they are useful guides to popular sentiment and have been so regarded by professional politicians for more than a century.

Two twentieth century cues which are available for uncertainty-reduction are the Presidential preference primaries and the public opinion polls. Unlike the gubernatorial and House cues, they are directly centered upon the Presidential contests. In addition, they are measured more frequently and at points in time closer to the convention. Although primaries have been held since 1912 and Gallup Polls have been recorded since 1936, it has only been in recent times that Presidential politicians have given them any degree of credence. President Truman dismissed primaries as "eyewash" and virtually every candidate in the land has discounted them at some point in his campaign (New York Times, 1952). How often have we all been told that the "only meaningful poll is the one conducted on election day?"

Presidential primary results have been operationally assessed in terms of the total party votes gathered by the various candidates; the overall degree of fractionalization which emerged; the number of primaries contested in; and the number of contested primaries won. Each of these measures provides partial evidence for the identity of the candidate who "won the primaries."

The polls present a different problem because they vary greatly in the type of information which they provide. For example, the most widely cited poll result is the "Presidential Job Rating" assessed by Gallup. For Presidential politicians in the opposition party, these ratings are enormously important if the next election finds the incumbent President eligible for reelection. If the rating is low, then contending ambitions will flower. If it is high, then the serious out-party contenders may choose to wait for another and more propitious opportunity.

In the President's own party, low ratings may send his fellow partisans in quest of an alternative candidate and if his ratings are high they may well repose in anticipation of a comfortable victory. However, if the President is not eligible to run again or if he withdraws at the opening of the preconvention maneuvering as did Presidents Truman and Johnson, then the Presidential approval rating loses much of its utility.

Other information provided by the polls included *intraparty* popularity ratings. Recent analysts of nominating conventions see the intraparty ratings as the most important piece of information available to the delegates and the candidate managers.[4] However, being popular within one's party may gain one the nomination but it is important to remember that half of all major-party nominations end in defeat.

The measurable characteristics of the polls which will be used in this analysis include the number of polls led by the various candidates and the overall degree of fractionalization.

With the addition of the polls and the primaries, there has been a quantitative and qualitative improvement in the data bases for successful predictions. Uncertainty is still present but the information available for its reduction is now more abundant.

The preconvention cues which are paid the most heed are those with the best track record in previous elections. This moves us further back in time to *past election outcomes* and *past election cues.* The cues which most accurately forecast the outcomes of elections will attract the most attention at Convention Hall.

Election expectations are the sum of the preconvention cues. Although these expectations are not as easily measurable as the other components in the model, we have ample anecdotal evidence that politicians' inferences about the forthcoming election affect their convention behavior. For the present, however, we will use the individual preconvention cues as a surrogate for these expectations. In addition to the six components there are important connective links. The election outcome in any given Presidential year is input for the next Presidential election. It becomes part of the collective memory of professional politicians in that its cues are studied for what results were predicted. In addition it is the outcome of that contest which determines the most important variable in this study, namely, the "in" or "out" status of the party seeking the election victory.

Other important connections include the interactive link between convention conflict and election expectations. Any reading of the proceedings of a convention indicates that party professionals sincerely believe that disunity will be fatal to a party's election prospects. Consequently, they seek to minimize the outward manifestation of conflict as soon as they can.

The components of this model interact to create what we feel is a conscious framework for professional politicians. We have tried to avoid probing into psychological recesses whenever possible but rather have treated politicians as uncertainty-reducing, power-maximizing individuals bent on attaching themselves to likely successful nominees and avoiding contact with likely unsuccessful ones.

A major virtue of this model is that it permits cross-time comparisons of nominating conventions with party and candidate situations controlled. Thus, it is possible to liberate the study of conventions from time constraints and to permit diachronic analysis. We are not the first ones to attempt this but we believe that this model integrates the nominating convention more solidly into the overall framework of American electoral politics. In this analysis the nominating convention is treated as an integral feature of the political system not as a manipulative sideshow nor as a disreputable subspecies of political events.

CONVENTION CONFLICT AND ITS CONSEQUENCES

Nothing at a convention is more menacing to party professionals than the prospect of internal conflict. It is a firmly held belief among politicians that conventions with high levels of conflict foreshadow defeat in the November elections.

They believe that convention acrimony will result in losing active party workers—supporters of candidates not nominated—who will remove their energies and cash from further involvement in the party's electoral quest. Also, the professionals fear that a public which witnesses a raucous conflict may make the reasonable assumption that a party which cannot govern itself may be unable to govern the country.

For these reasons, the proceedings of most conventions are filled with declarations of unity and harmony following the nastiest of struggles. Fingers which groped for one anothers' throats on the opening day of the convention should be interlocked and lifted skyward in victory signs on the closing day.

Our examination of this process begins with the election of 1896—the first election to foreshadow the modern Presidential campaign (Rosenbloom, 1970; Key, 1955). Using Rae's Index of Fractionalization on the first Presidential ballot in these 21 election years, it is possible to test the belief of politicians that conflict at the convention has an impact upon the party's prospects in the Presidential contest. The 42 major-party nominating conventions for our analysis reveal that the politicians are correct, convention conflict is inversely related with election outcome. The simple product-moment correlation between first-ballot fractionalization and the party's proportion of the total popular vote is -.40 and the party's proportion of the total electoral vote is -.28. The intuitive assumptions of the practical politicians have been borne out by these correlations, the figures themselves do not seem unduly high. However, if party status is controlled, a paradox emerges.

Party Status	Fractionalization w/Total Vote %	Fractionalization w/Electoral Vote %
In-Party	-.62	-.60
Out-Party	.12	.34

It seems that conflict's impact upon election outcomes is situationally determined. Conflict is apparently dysfunctional[5] for the in-party but correlates positively with the out-party's electoral success. This departure from the generally held assumption about party unity and success requires further exploration.

Table 1 presents first-ballot fractionalization means for varying party circumstances. It is apparent that the differences between the parties are not great. However, when party and candidate status are examined, significant differences emerge. In-parties are significantly less conflicted than out-parties, .282 and .532, respectively, and conventions at which an incumbent is seeking renomination are characterized by much greater consensus than conventions at which a party is seeking to nominate a successor to an incumbent, .145 and .556. This is to be expected. Not only is the incumbent the leader of his party but the leader of the country as well. To repudiate or openly challenge him is to call into question the party's record in office.

For in-party conventions without an available incumbent to nominate, first-ballot conflict levels are similar to those of the out-party conventions. This is true regardless of the successor's relationship to the incumbent President. This pattern holds whether the successor is the beneficiary of the President's goodwill or the vehicle of the President's repudiation.

Conflict is highest at conventions when the nomination is open. By definition, the out-party functions wholly under this condition. Even titular leaders—the most recently defeated Presidential nominees—are leaders in name, not necessarily in reality (Pomper, 1966; David, Goldman, and Bain, 1960). Their claims to party leadership are not automatically renewable. With this openness, out-party conflict levels are consistently high irrespective of party or era.

Table 1: Mean First Presidential Ballot Fractionalization Scores

Nominations	1896–1928	1932–1976	1896–1976
All Conventions	.457 (18)	.370 (24)	.407 (42)
Democratic	.498 (9)	.411 (12)	.448 (21)
Republican	.416 (9)	.329 (12)	.366 (21)
In-Party	.363 (9)	.221 (12)	.282 (21)
Incumbents	.139 (5)	.148 (9)	.145 (14)
Successors	.643 (4)	.439 (3)	.556 (7)
Out-Party	.551 (9)	.519 (2)	.532 (21)

N of cases in parentheses

Although Table 1 indicates that convention conflict has abated over the years, the essential differences remain. In-parties show greater consensus than out-parties, and incumbents, if they choose to run again, are assured of renomination with little or no resistance regardless of era. Similarly, in-party successors are more likely to encounter significant opposition than incumbents, and conventions at which successors are nominated more closely resemble out-party conventions. Thus, time appears to be less relevant than party situation or circumstance. This is not surprising when one considers that the presumed motivating force in all conventions is to select the one candidate who has the best chance of winning a majority of Electoral College votes. There has been no change in this most elemental structural constraint since the passage of the Twelfth Amendment in 1804, so it is unlikely that there would be any major change in the behavior of politicians regarding it.

Expectation of success is critical in understanding convention conflict for both in- and out-parties, for as the likelihood of victory increases so do the stakes involved. As the vulnerability of the in-party becomes more apparent, politicians in the out-party will see that the time is propitious for them to seek the nomination. The number of hats in the out-party ring will grow and whatever leadership vacuum may have remained from the party's previous defeat is filled by contending candidates eager to snatch the upcoming victory of the party. On the other hand, the dismal prospect of anticipated party defeat leads to the uncontested emergence of sacrificial lambs.

The case of Thomas E. Dewey, twice nominated by the Republican party, illustrates the relationship between expectation of success and convention conflict. In 1944, Dewey gained the nomination on the first ballot with 99.7% of the delegate votes and a fractionalization score of .006. Four years later, Dewey was renominated on the third ballot after polling 39.7% and 47.1% on the two previous ones. The first-ballot fractionalization score for that convention was .770. The fractionalization score of the 1944 Republican convention was .381 below the Republican mean (1896-1940: .387), while the 1948 convention was .383 above that mean.

The difference in the fractionalization scores is enormous. Ostensibly, Dewey's situation in both years was identical. He was the Republican governor of the nation's largest state facing an incumbent Democratic President.

One explanation for the higher level of conflict in the 1948 convention was that Dewey had lost previously. This may account for the 60% drop in his first-ballot delegate percentage. However, we believe that the high fractionalization score in the 1948 Republican convention would have accompanied any nomination for the simple reason that the Republicans expected to win in 1948 and to lose in 1944.

Support for this assumption was not difficult to locate in 1948. The Republicans had gained control of both houses of Congress for the first time since 1928, the incumbent President's performance in office was approved by only 36% of the public, and the Democratic Party opened the year with one sectarian departure from the supporters of Henry Wallace and were about to face another one from the Dixiecrats.[6] Every indicator predicted a Republican victory, hence, conflict at the Republican convention was high.

In February of that year, Senator Robert Taft, "Mr. Republican," chortled, "our friends, the Democrats, certainly appear to be completely demoralized here at the moment. I doubt very much if they can regain any real unity in the campaign, and so I have become an optimist" (Patterson, 1972: 388).

On the other hand, the in-party which faces dismal prospects tends to be riven with factionalism. Eager to blame the incumbent administration for the party's gloomy future, delegate conflict abounds. "Ins" on their way to becoming "outs" are a ferocious lot.

Using the 1948 example again, the Democrats, faced with impending defeat demonstrated greater disunity at their convention than any party nominating an incumbent since the 1912 Republicans. Indeed with the exception of Taft, no incumbent had been nominated in this century with a smaller proportion of first-ballot votes than Harry Truman; Gerald Ford now holds this distinction.

With these illustrations we can raise this assumption to the level of a testable proposition. We posit that a key determinant of convention conflict is expectancy of success once party status is controlled. Stated simply: in-party conventions which expect to win have lesser levels of conflict than in-party conventions which expect to lose. Conversely, out-party conventions which expect to win have greater levels of conflict than those which expect to lose.

In assessing the relationship between convention conflict and election outcome, we ranked the 42 major-party conventions since 1896 on fractionalization scores. The range was great: from .000—the score for the conventions which nominated incumbents in 1900, 1904, 1936, 1956, and 1964—to .880, the score for the 1916 Republican convention which nominated Charles Evans Hughes.

The 42 conventions were placed into three categories and the relationship noted earlier emerged once again. In looking at all of the conventions in Table 2, it seems as if high levels in convention fractionalization are associated with election defeats. However, the relationship between conflict and outcome is more complex than the statement above would indicate.

The impact of conflict on in-party prospects is devastating. Gerald Ford is merely the latest casualty of this particular fact of American political life. The .500 fractionalization score at the 1976 Republican convention placed it within the medium category. However, Ford scored seventeenth on the ranking for 21 in-party nominees and thirteenth among the 14 incumbent nominees.

Table 2:   Fractionalization Scores and Election Outcomes

Convention Fractionalization	In-Party			Out-Party			All Parties		
	Won	Lost	Win Pct.	Won	Lost	Win Pct.	Won	Lost	Pct.
High .618–.880	0	4	0%	5	5	50%	5	9	36%
Medium .208–.580	4	2	67	3	5	38	7	7	50
Low .000–.141	9	2	82	0	3	0	9	5	64
Totals	13	8	62	8	13	38	21	21	50
Gamma		–.795			+.531			–.371	

Low conflict at the in-party convention is not perfectly associated with success. However only 2 of the 11 nominees in that category—Hoover in 1932 and Nixon in 1960—failed to achieve election. And Nixon's 1960 bid came close enough to rate as a stand-off.

For the out-party, the relationship between convention conflict and elections is reversed and less strong. It is less strong because conflict is generally more evident at out-party conventions and out-party nominees have a lesser success rate. One fact which does stand out is that out-party conventions with low levels of conflict seem to nominate losers—Bryan in 1900, Landon in 1936, and Dewey in 1944.

While highly conflicted conventions have been fatal to in-party nominees, 5 of the 10 nominees of these most conflicted out-party conventions achieved the Presidency—Wilson in 1912, Harding in 1920, Franklin Roosevelt in 1932, Kennedy in 1960, and Nixon in 1968.

In order to test the relationship more fully, we have computed correlation coefficients for the fractionalization score on the first Presidential ballot with popular and electoral voting percentages. Again we find that the relationships are in the expected direction. Conflict at the in-party conven-

Table 3: Correlations between Convention Fractionalization and Presidential Results by Candidate Situation and Period

| Candidate Situation | Periods | | | | | |
| | 1896–1928 | | 1932–1976 | | 1896–1976 | |
	Elec. Vote	Pop Vote	Elec. Vote	Pop. Vote	Elec. Vote	Pop. Vote
All Candidates	−.24	−.39	−.32	−.38	−.28	−.40
In-Party	−.62	−.60	−.58	−.59	−.60	−.62
Incumbents	−.94	−.97	−.41	−.47	−.58	−.69
Successors	−.96	−.85	−.91	−.80	−.46	−.56
Out-Party	+.37	+.02	+.32	+.25	+.34	+.12

tion is associated with a declining popular and electoral vote percentage, while for the out-party the relationships are more moderate, but positive.

TRADITIONAL CUE CONSCIOUSNESS AND ELECTION OUTCOMES

Expectancy of success is not a mystical construct. While it is not as readily discernible as other elements within the political process, its impact upon convention behavior can be clearly and directly assessed.

With stakes as high as they are in Presidential politics, party professionals gather as much data as they possibly can forecasting the result of the upcoming election. Some of the data are meaningful; much are not. The criterion for meaningfulness of data is starkly simple: do they predict election outcomes?

An example of a key predictor is the number of state governorships won or lost in the midterm elections. Presumably, the President's party fortunes might be affected by the fate of his fellow partisans in the state houses. Governors with strong state party organizations can make these structures available to Presidential candidates and enhance their probability of election. Given the unique role of the Electoral College and its use of state units in allocating votes, the party with the most governors—particularly if they are in the largest states—would seem to hold a decided advantage.

In 1970 when the Republican Party lost 11 governorships, the mass media and Democratic professionals were quick to conclude that the Nixon administration was enroute to defeat in the 1972 election. To Stewart Alsop (1970) writing in *Newsweek,* Richard Nixon had become a defeatable President (see also Stewart, 1974).

Using the 1970 returns as cues for the 1972 Presidential contest, the major newsmagazines showed remarkable unanimity in appraising the worth of the upcoming Democratic nomination. *Time* stated: "Suddenly the Democratic presidential aspirants were looking at the 1972 nomination as an opportunity rather than a sacrifice" (1970: 15). *Newsweek* stated: "And suddenly, in the afterglow, the Democratic presidential nomination in 1972 seemed once again a prize worth having. All the principal contenders for it profited by the 1970 campaign" (1970: 30).

Despite the response of the media, the administration's public face showed few signs of distress. In a letter widely circulated from the White House, Robert Finch, the President's chief political adviser posed a series of rhetorical questions concerning the results. One of these questions directly addressed the governorship issue.

Does the loss of Governorships by Republicans spell disaster in 1972? Again, hardly. In 1954, the Republican Party under Dwight Eisenhower lost not only both Houses of Congress, but nine Governorships as well—and Ike came back in 1956 to win a massive landslide. In 1960, the GOP held only fourteen Governorships—yet Vice President Nixon carried twenty-six states [Finch, 1970: 2].

Rather than challenging the use of Presidential predictors, Finch attacked the validity of the media's interpretation. If this predictor was valid, then the 1972 Presidential reelection campaign might have become a futile exercise. Obviously, Finch was not inclined to trumpet its worth. His reading of the election results was more selective and unsurprisingly, more optimistic.

> The comparison with 1960 is apt. In that national deadheat Richard Nixon was running as Vice President with a political base of 14 Governorships, 36 Senators, and 154 House seats. In 1972—the GOP will have an incumbent President, with all the power and prestige of that office; and as a national base of the party not 14 but 22 Governorships; not 154 but 177 House seats; not 36 but 45 Senate seats [Finch, 1970: 3].

With this more palatable face on the 1970 results, Finch displayed the use to which predictor statistics could be put. He turned out to be correct, the Nixon victory of 1972 did in fact match in magnitude the party's differential starting base of 1970 compared to 1960's starting base and outcome.

The two cues whose predictive qualities can be assessed over the entire historical range of this study are those relating to House and gubernatorial elections. Presidential primaries made their first appearance in 1912 and the Gallup Polls made theirs in 1936. As a result, the number of predictor sets varies in the more modern elections.

HOUSE ELECTIONS

Throughout the course of American history, congressional elections have been held every two years irrespective of foreign wars or domestic catastrophes. The regularity of these contests and their sizable number make them an enormously helpful measuring tool for politicians eager to assess public sentiments. Within the professional political science literature a debate flourishes about the appropriate interpretation of congressional results vis-à-vis Presidential ones. However, politicians continue to make the same inferences about congressional elections that they have made for more than a century. Midterm elections are still seen as popular referenda on the incumbent Presidential administration, and "coat tail" anxiety about congressional candidates running in Presidential years seems as great as ever (Otten, 1976).[7]

Of all the measurable indicators emanating from congressional elections, none is easier to see than the mere fact of control of the House. In the 21 Presidential elections covered by this study, the party controlling the House at convention time has captured the Presidency 16 times (76.2%). As a predictor, this is a good but not wholly reliable measure. In recent times its utility has disappeared. Only 3 of the last 8 presidential contests have been won by the party holding the House.

This is quite a change from the years between 1860 and 1944 when the party controlling the House at convention time won 21 of 22 popular vote pluralities (95.4%) and 19 of 22 electoral vote majorities (86.4%).

The major reason for the recent decline in the predictive value of the House control cue is the emergence of a seemingly permanent Democratic majority in that body. The Democrats have organized the House in 22 of the 24 Congresses since 1930 and all of the last 12. Buoyed by incumbency and insulated from Presidential landslides by ticket-splitting, congressional candidates now seem to exist in a world apart from Presidential ones.[8]

However, this does not mean that Presidential and congressional politicians now ignore each other's political circumstances. Tufte (1975) and others (such as Pierson, 1975) have found that Presidential popularity ratings impact directly upon midterm congressional voting results. And Kernell (1974) contends that voters in midterm elections are often disproportionately "negative" and that many are indeed passing judgment on the President's performance in office when they vote for congressmen.

In lieu of the control cue, the proportion of House seats gained or lost can be used as a meaningful predictor. The percentages of seats held by the President's party both before and after the midterm elections are carefully scrutinized by politicians and commentators for signs of slippage within the Presidential majority. It has often been noted that the 1934 midterm election was the only one in this century in which the incumbent's House party did not lose ground. Because it is expected that the President's party will lose House seats, it is generally the magnitude of the loss compared to the average midterm drop which determines how much "approval" the administration has recorded. "According to the rules of the political game as played for half a century," Walter Lippman observed in 1962, "when the party in power loses little if anything in the mid-term election, it really wins a victory" (quoted in Finch, 1970:2).

In Table 4 the size of in-party seat swings in the midterm election is assessed for its impact upon the subsequent Presidential contest. Because of the varying size of the House, we have used as a measure of change the differences in the percentage of seats held by the in-party between the Presidential contest and the midterm election rather than the number of seats themselves.

As Table 4 indicates, there is a strong relationship between relatively small in-party seat losses—gain in seats or a loss below 5%—at the midterm election and victory in the following Presidential contest. Of the candidates in this category, all six won.

Large losses—15% or more—seem not to have hurt in-party prospects as much as folk wisodm would lead one to expect. Two of three in-party candidacies were successful in this category. The relationship between the size of the seat swing away from the in-party and its fortunes in the subsequent election appears to be ambiguous as losses mount.

Another House cue which can be used involves the percentage of seats held by all parties following the midterm

Table 4:   House Cues: Mid-Term Seat Swing of In-Party and Election
Results in Subsequent Presidential Contest

Size of In-Party House Seat Changes	Subsequent Presidential Contest					
	In Cases	Won	Lost	Pct.	In-Party Candidate EV%	Means PV%
Gain or Loss Held under 5%	6	6	0	100.0	87.6	59.1
Loss between 5.0 and 9.9%	4	2	2	50.0	43.1	45.5
Loss between 10.0 and 14.9%	8	3	5	37.5	40.5	44.4
Loss greater than 15.0	3	2	1	66.7	65.3	51.8
	21	13	8	61.9	58.0	49.9

gamma = +.518

contest. In keeping with our model, we expect that regardless of party, status, candidate situation, or era, the better off a party is following the midterm elections the better it will do in the upcoming Presidential contest. This can be seen in Table 5.

Of the 21 correlations relating this particular House cue to electoral votes, 20 were positive as well as 19 of the 21 between this cue and popular vote percentages. Thus, there is support for the contention that higher proportions of House seats after the midterm election will be reflected in higher proportions of both popular and electoral votes in the subsequent Presidential contest.

In the case of the exceptions involving successors in the most recent period, two points should be stressed. The first is that the number of cases in this cell is the smallest in the table—three. The other point is that each of these successions were conducted under unusual circumstances. The Nixon succession of 1960 was necessitated by the fact that Eisenhower was constitutionally ineligible to run for another term. No incumbent before or since had left the Presidential office under that constraint. The Stevenson succession of 1952 and the Humphrey succession of 1968 were also unique in that both men succeeded eligible incumbents who were their party's leading contenders at the opening of the convention year.[9] Defeats in the early primaries led to the withdrawals of both Presidents Truman and Johnson sparing both men the ignominious prospect of serious challenges in the conventions and possible repudiation in the general elections. Stevenson and Humphrey collected the wrath intended for their party chieftains. Presidents Taft, Hoover, and Ford were renominated by conventions despite the fatal House cues and went down to defeat.

The exceptions aside, Table 5 conformed to the general expectation about House seats and Presidential outcomes. Party differences in the correlations over the entire period are generally smaller than the in-out differences. The highest correlation in the popular vote column is that between mid-term House seats and the vote for incumbent Presidents. Thus, a President can gain very valuable information about

Table 5: House Cues: Correlations between Percentage of Post-Mid-Term House Seats Held and Presidential Results by Candidate Situation and Period

| Candidate Situation | Periods | | | | | |
| | 1896–1928 | | 1932–1976 | | 1896–1976 | |
	Elec. Vote	Pop Vote	Elec. Vote	Pop. Vote	Elec. Vote	Pop. Vote
All Candidates	+.67	+.48	+.32	+.32	+.42	+.37
Democratic	+.55	−.08	+.23	+.27	+.44	+.44
Republican	+.59	+.59	+.24	+.22	+.45	+.42
In-Party	+.68	+.55	+.33	+.28	+.45	+.39
Incumbents	+.94	+.98	+.45	+.44	+.49	+.46
Successors	+.69	+.46	−.57	−.99	+.28	+.17
Out-Party	+.73	+.46	+.34	+.39	+.45	+.39

his reelection prospects if he studies the midterm results carefully. This was especially true during the 1896-1928 era, when the correlation was .94 between this House cue and electoral votes and .98 with popular votes.

One final observation on this table which should be made is that the 1932-1976 popular and electoral vote correlations for Democrats, Republicans, and "ins" are all lower than the overall figures. It appears as if this particular relationship between midterm House seats and Presidential voting is in decline across each of the major nominee categories. The relationship still exists but its strength has diminished.

Of the three House cues available to party professionals at the opening of the prenomination period, the one which appears to be the most consistently reliable, irrespective of party identity and status, is the percentage of House seats following the midterm election. The recent failure of House party control as a predictor and the mixed record of seat swings obliges those who would seek out relevant cues to use the House seat percentage.

GUBERNATORIAL ELECTIONS

Expectations drawn from gubernatorial elections differ from those inferred from House results because professional politicians are less likely to see gubernatorial contests as referenda on the sitting President. Too many issues indigenous to state politics intervene in gubernatorial contests. As a result, gubernatorial election statistics are treated in a different way than the House figures.

Governorship results are interpreted as identifying sources of electoral votes in the upcoming Presidential contest. The party holding the most governorships at the time of the convention is assumed to be in a better position for gaining the Presidency than the party which holds few state houses. This is particularly true regarding the party which holds a majority among the largest states—those rich with electoral votes. Part of the postconvention Democratic party euphoria in 1976 stemmed from the fact that the Carter-Mondale ticket had fellow partisans holding the governorships of California, New York, Pennsylvania, Illinois, Texas, New Jersey, Florida, and Massachusetts. In Table 6, the relationship between gubernatorial elections and Presidential results is assessed.

In-party Presidential candidates holding strong majorities (more than 55%) among either the governorships themselves or among the electoral votes contained within those states at the time of the conventions will generally win.[10] All seven in-party nominees whose party held 55% or more of the governorships won.

The relationship between the gubernatorial cues and Presidential outcomes in Table 6 is simple and direct. Presidential victories seem to build upon gubernatorial successes, while Presidential defeats seem to be anticipated by problems in the state houses. And in the cases in which the gubernatorial

Table 6: Gubernatorial Cues and Election Results in Subsequent Presidential Contest

| Percentage Of In-Party Governors | Subsequent Presidential Contest | | | | In-Party Candidate Means | |
	In Cases	Won	Lost	Win. Pct.	EV%	PV%
Over 55.0% held	7	7	0	100.0	78.0	56.0
Between 45.0 and 54.9%	5	3	2	60.0	51.2	48.3
Under 45.0% held	9	3	6	33.3	46.2	45.9
	21	13	8	61.9	58.0	49.9
gamma = +.85						

cues appear to be evenly matched, the Presidential outcomes are competitive.

One important *caveat* which should be noted is that the recent Presidential elections are not as supportive of these cues as the earlier ones had been. In the nine presidential contests since 1944, the in-party nominee faced a deficit for his party among the governors seven times. In fact, only in 1964 did an in-party nominee, Lyndon Johnson, leave Convention Hall with his party already in control of both a majority of the nation's governorships and a majority of the electoral votes in the states. Yet in these last nine elections, the in-party nominee won five times. Franklin Roosevelt in 1944, Harry Truman in 1948, Dwight Eisenhower in 1956, and Richard Nixon in 1972 all began their successful Presidential campaigns with gubernatorial percentages below 45.0. Unsurprisingly, all four men were incumbents and the power of Presidential incumbency to surmount even the least hopeful circumstances should not be underestimated. Perhaps the most remarkable case of the decreasing utility of these cues occurred in 1960. In that contest, Nixon's Republicans held only 32.0% of the governorships and 26.3% of the electoral votes in their states (the lowest percentage since 1852) at the time of the convention, yet the election itself was one of the closest in American history.

Part of the decline in the predictive powers of the gubernatorial cue is due to the conscious effort on the part of state officials to separate the elections for governor from those for president. The increase in the length of gubernatorial terms from two years to four years in many states and the scheduling of these elections at the midpoint of Presidential administrations has made state politics more autonomous than ever.[11] Despite the recent decline in the predictive powers of this gubernatorial cue, it has been very helpful overall in forecasting the fate of the in-party.

One way to get a fuller picture of the relationship between the gubernatorial cue and election outcomes in different contexts would be to use the same format which measured the relationship fo the major House predictive cue and Presidential contests (Table 5).

In Table 7, the percentage of governors held at the time of the convention is related to percentages of popular and electoral votes with party, party status, candiate situation, and electoral era controlled. As in the case of the House cues, the model suggests that regardless of the political context, the stronger a party is in the states at convention time the better it will do in the subsequent Presidential election.

All but 3 of the 42 correlations in Table 7 are in the predicted direction. The 3 negative correlations are for the Democrats (popular vote) in the 1896-1928 period and successors in the more recent era. The Democratic anomaly may be explained by the fact that prior to Franklin Roosevelt's ascendancy, the Democratic party was more competitive in Presidential contests than in gubernatorial elections. However, after the 1932 election the Democrats were able to extend their influence into the state houses and the consequence was to link more closely their relative standing in the governorships to Presidential results (Key, 1956; Burnham, 1967). In the case of successor nominees the correlations are

Table 7: Gubernatorial Cues: Correlations between Percentage of Governorships Held and Presidential Results by Candidate Situation and Period

Candidate Situation	1896–1928		1932–1976		1896–1976	
	Elec. Vote	Pop Vote	Elec. Vote	Pop. Vote	Elec. Vote	Pop. Vote
All Candidates	+.63	+.45	+.44	+.43	+.48	+.39
Democratic	+.57	−.02	+.38	+.46	+.52	+.53
Republican	+.56	+.58	+.40	+.45	+.52	+.43
In-Party	+.63	+.61	+.53	+.51	+.52	+.45
Incumbents	+.46	+.56	+.57	+.57	+.47	+.42
Successors	+.91	+.78	−.67	−.97	+.58	+.42
Out-Party	+.62	+.23	+.50	+.53	+.50	+.40

negative and strong. These correlations are similar to the ones noted earlier between House cues and successor results for this more recent period. In two of the cases, the successor nominees, Stevenson in 1952 and Humphrey in 1968, entered the campaign with the governors of their party holding relatively competitive positions within the states. But the public hostility toward their predecessors which led to the successions contributed to their own poor showings in the elections. The successor who came the closest to victory, Richard Nixon in 1960, began his campaign with the worst state electoral base of any in-party nominee in this century. Unlike the other two recent successors, he gained his inheritance from a popular President and this fact combined with the public's uncertainty about electing a Catholic to the Presidency enabled the Nixon candidacy to make a very respectable showing even though the cues foretold disaster. (White, 1960; Converse, Campbell, Miller, and Stokes, 1961; Key, 1961).

A combination of the growing power of incumbents to overcome negative signs and the attempt by state political leaders to isolate themselves from the tide of national politics have made gubernatorial cues less useful than in the past. Nevertheless, the relationship between strength in the state houses and success in Presidential elections continues to exist.

COMBINING THE CUES: ELECTION EXPECTATIONS

Long before conventions assemble to conduct their business of selecting Presidential and vice presidential nominees, the cues regarding each party's competitive situation are in evidence. As a result, the politically knowledgeable people who serve as convention delegates have some strong indications of the likely outcome of the Presidential contest. If the cues are positive, then optimism will fill the hall. If they are negative, the delegates will assemble with a mixture of pessimism and frustration. And if the cues are mixed, as is often the case, whatever feelings they may have will derive from which set of the contradictory cues they believe to be valid.

In order to get a sense of the competitive situation within which the delegates to thse 21 in-party conventions have found themselves, we have combined three of the preconvention cues (see Table 8). If the in-party controls the House of Representatives at the time of the convention, victory has often followed in the Presidential contest. If the in-party has kept its losses in the midterm congressional election to under 10%, the probability of retaining the White House has been very high. And if the in-party holds over 55% of the nation's governorships at convention time, then success has also followed. When all three cues are positive, the in-party Presidential candidates have won five of five elections since 1896. This has occurred whether the in-party candidate was an elected incumbent (Franklin Roosevelt in 1936), an incumbent who succeeded a deceased President (Theodore Roosevelt in 1904 and Lyndon Johnson in 1964), or a nonincumbent (Taft in 1908, and Hoover in 1928). Irrespective of how the nomination was achieved, in-party nominees whose parties controlled the House, lost few midterm seats, and held a clear majority of governorships won in the November election.

When all three cues are negative, the in-party nominee loses regardless of candidate situation. Three incumbents (Taft in 1912, Hoover in 1932, and Ford in 1976) and two successors (Bryan in 1896 and Nixon in 1960) all met defeat, thus carrying out the fatal logic of these negative cues.

However, only 10 of the 21 in-party nominees faced competitive situations in which the predictors were unanimous, 11 faced mixed conditions. Some were more favorable to in-party success; others, less so.

A closer examination of the 11 cases involving mixed cues reveals that a key factor separating winners from losers was

Table 8: Combined House and Gubernatorial Cues: Competitive Situations for In-Party Nominees

House Cues	Number of Governors Held By the In-Party		
	Over 55.0%	45.0% to 54.9%	Under 45.0%
In-Party holds House	T. ROOSEVELT, 1904 TAFT, 1908 HOOVER, 1928 F. ROOSEVELT, 1936 JOHNSON, 1964	McKINLEY, 1900 Stevenson, 1952	
Seat-swing Under 10%			
In-Party holds House	WILSON, 1916 F. ROOSEVELT, 1940	F. ROOSEVELT, 1944 Humphrey, 1968	COOLIDGE, 1924
Seat-swing Over 10%			
Out-Party holds House			Cox, 1920 EISENHOWER, 1956 NIXON, 1972
Seat-swing Under 10%			
Out-Party holds House		TRUMAN, 1948	
Seat-swing Over 10%			Bryan, 1896 Taft, 1912 Hoover, 1932 Nixon, 1960 Ford, 1976

Electoral vote winners are capitalized.

Presidential incumbency. Of the eight nominated incumbents whose parties faced ambiguous electoral prospects, all won.

For nonincumbent candidates of the in-party, the situation was the opposite, none of the three nominees who faced ambiguous conditions won in November.

A simple pattern has emerged. When conditions are unequivocally favorable for the in-party, their nominees win and when conditions are unequivocally unfavorable, defeat occurs. In both sets of circumstances, the incumbency or nonincumbency of the nominee appears to be irrelevant. However, when conditions for the in-party are cloudy, incumbency plays a major role. The ability of the incumbent President to control the nomination and his power to shape national events in ways favorable to his candidacy have often been noted.[12] As a result, it is not surprising to see the last eight incumbent Presidents who have faced ambiguous electoral situations emerge victorious.

From the foregoing discussion it is possible to say that there are cues within the political environment which have high predictive capabilities and that these cues are, for the most part, known to professional politicians. There are legitimate reasons for the optimism or pessimism which they may carry into Convention Hall.

Election expectations can be identified and, with some degree of accuracy, they can be measured. However, if the model which we posited earlier represents a realistic reconstruction of convention behavior, it is essential that we relate these preconvention election expectations to levels of conflict at the nominating conventions. In the last major section of this paper, we will attempt to make this most crucial link.

CUE CONSCIOUSNESS AND CONVENTION CONFLICT

In the model, we asserted that election expectations affect the behavior of delegates to the nominating conventions.

When expectations favor the in-party retaining the White House, we assumed that conflict levels at both conventions would be low. Jubilation will reign among in-party delegates as they gather around their soon-to-be enshrined leader and the newspapers will carry accounts of "coronations" instead of nominations. For the out-party which expects to lose, the proceedings take on a funeral tone. Delegates to out-party conventions which expect to remain "out" are not angry, just depressed.

Mencken's (1960) pungent observation that nominating conventions were akin to "a revival or a hanging" scores most directly when in-party prospects are dim.[13] In-party conventions enroute to defeat have high levels of conflict. It is these which resemble hangings. Eager to punish the man who has brought party fortunes to a low estate, pessimistic in-party delegates turn their wrath on the President or on his associates. The angry delegates may fail to deny nomination to a sitting President, but they will leave discernible marks upon his candidacy.

Optimistic out-parties historically have had high levels of conflict at their conventions. Contenders for the nomination of the newly resuscitated out-party remain in the running longer and campaign more vigorously when it looks as if the nomination will have more value. And when the stakes increase, conflicts increases.

In the next two subsections of this paper we will explore the impact of preconvention cues upon conflict levels at the convention. The first section assesses how the traditional House and gubernatorial cues have been realted to conflict over the 1896-1976 range of convention history. The second section looks only at the conventions since 1936. With the emergence of the Presidential primaries and the preference polls in recent years, more preconvention cues are now available to delegates. In that section we address the seeming paradox of the 1976 Democratic convention when an out-party appeared to be both optimistic and united.

TRADITIONAL CUES AND CONVENTION FRACTIONALIZATION

Looking first at the relationship between the fractionalization scores and the traditional cues, two separate forms of analysis were conducted. The first form relies upon correlation coefficients between the House and gubernatorial cues which have interval-level properties and fractionalization.

In Table 9, correlation coefficients are presented for fractionalization scores on the first convention ballot and the two traditional cues which can be percentaged: House seats following the congressional midterm election and the number of governorships held at the time of the convention.

In keeping with the model, there is a decided difference between in-party and out-party conventions in response to preconvention cues indicating party strength in the House and in the states. The six correlations involving in-party conventions are negative. Therefore, as in-party strength increases, convention conflict decreases.

Out-party correlations are also congruent with the model. All six correlations in the out-party case are positive. As out-party strength increases in the House and the states, election expectations become optimistic and convention conflict increases.

One fascinating element in Table 9 involves the impact of time upon the fractionalization scores. For the in-party conventions, there is a decline in the correlations between each of the cues and fractionalization. In fact, there appears to be no correlation between these cues and fractionalization at in-party conventions in the 1932-1976 era. The major reason for the absence of a relationship in contemporary times would appear to be the large number of eligible incumbents who have emerged as nominees from these conventions. Nine of the 12 conventions between 1932 and 1976 nominated incumbents.

Incumbents who wish to be nominated have not been denied in this century, no matter how gloomy the prospects

Table 9: Correlations between House and Gubernatorial Cues and First Ballot Presidential Fractionalization

Candidate Situation	1896–1928		1932–1976		1896–1976	
	% of House Seats Held	% of Governors	% of House Seats Held	% of Governors	% of House Seats Held	% of Governors
All Candidates	-.25	-.24	+.08	+.07	-.04	-.02
Democratic	-.26	-.16	-.30	-.39	-.31	-.32
Republican	-.17	-.27	+.19	+.22	+.12	+.13
In-Party	-.70	-.68	-.08	-.20	-.34	-.30
Incumbents	-.99	-.67	-.51	-.42	-.54	-.44
Successors	-.86	-.99	+.86	+.92	-.02	+.15
Out-Party	+.21	+.34	+.34	+.28	+.28	+.27

have been. Delegates to in-party conventions are aware of this fact. As a result, pessimistic delegates have had to find other ways to signal their displeasure. In 1932, pessimistic in-party delegates renominated Hoover with 97.6% of the votes, but the incumbent vice president, Charles Curtis received only 55% of their votes.[14] Curtis's fractionalization score was the third highest in this century for an in-party vice presidential ballot (.648). It was only exceeded by the initial vice presidential ballots at the 1924 Republican convention (.883) and the 1944 Democratic convention (.777). All three cases involved incumbent Presidents whose election prospects were clouded by mixed-negative preconvention cues.

Another way of expressing displeasure for pessimistic in-party delegates is to challenge the proposals contained within the platform. The best-known of these challenges took place in 1948 when pessimistic Democrats nominated Harry Truman for a full term, but spent most of their energies debating the platform.[15] A similar circumstance occurred in 1960 when the Republicans were about to nominate Richard Nixon. Cues emanating from the 1958 congressional elections foretold disaster for Republican Presidential prospects and since there was to be little disagreement about the identity of the nominee, a number of delegates focused upon the platform. In order to avoid a floor fight, Nixon accepted with few reservations the platform prepared by Governor Rockefeller of New York—one perceived by contemporary observers to contain repudiations of many aspects of the Eisenhower administration (White, 1960).[16]

In the pessimistic Republican convention of 1976, it was the rules contest which elicited the greatest degree of dissension. Delegates with anxiety about President Ford's electability came within 62 votes of accepting the Reagan position that likely vice presidential candidates should be identified before the presidential balloting.

One result of the foregoing discussion is to suggest that fractionalization scores may now have less validity as a measure of convention conflict for in-party conventions with little doubt about the eventual nominees. In future analysis, we hope to expand and refine this concept to include other measurable dimensions of convention conflict.

The second form of analysis treats the traditional cues in the way in which we believe professional politicians treat them, namely, in nominal-level terms. For example, does the in-party hold or not hold the House of Representatives? Did the in-party lose a small or a large proportion of its seats in the midterm congressional elections? Does the in-party hold a decided advantage (more than 55%) among the governorships or is it at a decided disadvantage (below 45%)?

By defining these cues in the simple terms of whether they indicate in-party or out-party success, we are able to compare the fractionalization means for conventions meeting under the varying conditions (see Table 10).

All but 2 of the 24 mean differences are in the expected direction: higher fractionalization for both conventions when cues favor out-party victories. The two exceptions occur in the most recent period and both involve in-party conventions. As we have noted earlier, the power of incumbents to depress conflict levels and to obtain nominations in the face of deteriorating party circumstances has increased in recent years.

Regarding the out-party conventions, fractionalization levels seem less strongly related to the traditional cues in the more recent era than in the previous one. Their impact is still in the expected direction however. While these cues continue to have some meaning for out-party conventions, it is their declining impact upon in-party conventions which merits our attention for it is the in-parties which set the electoral context for American politics.

Circumstances change and the virtue of the model is that it can accommodate these changes. It is clear that newer cues have emerged which shape the competitive situation within

Table 10: Election Expectations and Mean Fractionalization Scores for Traditional Predictor Cues, 1896–1976

Period and Cues	Mean Fractionalization Scores					
	In-Party Conventions Cue Favors:			Out-Party Conventions Cue Favors:		
	In-Party	Out-Party	Out-In Difference	In-Party	Out-Party	Out-In Difference
1896–1928						
House Control	.158	.773	+.615	.490	.672	+.182
Seat Swing	.345	.386	+.041	.421	.713	+.292
Governors Held	.218	.599	+.381	.539	.701	+.162
Combined Cues	.174	.599	+.425	.431	.701	+.270
1932–1976						
House Control	.283	.159	−.124	.435	.602	+.167
Seat Swing	.162	.262	+.100	.458	.562	+.104
Governors Held	.084	.113	+.029	.454	.568	+.114
Combined Cues	.266	.159	−.107	.485	.602	+.117
1896–1976						
House Control	.220	.364	+.144	.463	.626	+.163
Seat Swing	.253	.308	+.055	.440	.617	+.177
Governors Held	.160	.329	+.169	.502	.627	+.125
Combined Cues	.215	.335	+.120	.455	.642	+.187

which political parties find themselves. These new cues are the Presidential primaries and the preference polls. In the following section, their impact upon convention conflict and election outcomes is directly addressed.

NEW CUES AND FRACTIONALIZATION

With the advent of polls and primaries, professional politicians have gained access to new sources of information for reducing their uncertainty about the likely outcome of the Presidential contests. Their major advantage over the traditional cues is that they focus directly upon the Presidential contenders. They are unclouded by local conditions. Also, they are measured more frequently. Thus, it is possible to sense the swings in public opinion which follow responses to changing political circumstances.

One of the new cues which has captured politicians' attention is the Presidential job rating done by George Gallup's American Institute for Public Opinion. This question, which has been asked of respondents in all but one year (1944) since 1938 asks simply, "Do you approve or disapprove of the way _____ is handling his job as president?" Not only does this question provide a ready measure of the President's popularity at the time of the poll, it also is the only relatively solid Presidential cue which is available to politicians in the year prior to the opening of the primaries.[17] Trial heats one year or two in advance of Presidential contests seldom reflect more than the Presidential job rating.

The Presidential popularity cue figures prominently in the decisional processes of candidates who may wish to enter the Presidental sweepstakes. If the President is eligible to run again and his popularity seems high, likely challengers within his own party's ranks will stay out of the running. However, if the rating is low, in-party professionals may cast about for another nominee whose candidacy may prove less disastrous to the party's overall fortunes.

The impact of high Presidential popularity ratings upon out-party contenders is less direct. No matter how popular an incumbent President may be, the out-party is obligated to produce a nominee. However, it is assumed that the more popular a President, the greater the likelihood that the out-party contenders will be fewer in number, less intense in their campaigns, and less highly placed within the party's hierarchy. Conversely, low Presidential popularity ratings are assumed to generate a large field of highly competitive and well-placed out-party contenders.

The value of the Presidential job rating as a cue seems quite high. The correlation between Presidential popularity at the opening of the election year and in-party results in November is .68 for total popular votes in the 10 elections between 1940 and 1976.

Using this new cue, in-party leaders and delegates know when a President is in trouble and they have responded accordingly. The correlation between Presidential popularity in January and fractionalization for in-party conventions is -.85. High popularity is strongly associated with low fractionalization. When Presidential popularity has dipped, challengers have marched into the in-party primaries. Prior to 1976, the in-party challengers who have been the most successful in this period—Estes Kefauver in 1952 and Eugene McCarthy in 1968—both made their moves when Presidential popularity was low, but the traditional preconvention cues indicated that party prospects were competitive. It was thus possible to convince some professionals that the party would be more likely to retain the White House if the incumbent was replaced. This was certainly the logic underlying the later entry of Robert Kennedy in 1968.[18] In both of these years, the incumbents withdrew from contention following early difficulties in the primaries.

The challenge of Ronald Reagan to President Ford was undoubtedly encouraged by the fact that the president scored above 50% only twice in the 19 job ratings conducted in 1975.[19] Unlike, the in-party challenges in 1952 and 1968, the traditional cues were clear and unambiguous. They foretold disaster for the in-party Republicans. The Democrats held the House and their numbers were swelled by a seat-swing in their direction of 12% in 1974's midterm contest. Also, the Democrats held 72% of the governorships at the opening of their convention in July. Since the appearance of these ratings, President Ford was the first incumbent to have been burdened simultaneously by low Presidential popularity in the polls and the traditional cues unambiguously forecasting defeat.

Out-party professionals have access to the same polls and cues as the in-party professionals and the relationship between Presidential popularity and fractionalization in their conventions was also negative for the 1940-1976 period (-.21). Presumably, when the Presidential job rating indicates approval for the incumbent, out-party expectations lessen and conflict diminishes. Barry Goldwater was nominated at a convention with a lower out-party fractionalization score than any since the 1944 Republican convention which sent Dewey into battle with Franklin Roosevelt.

This is what makes the 1976 Democratic convention so unique. The fractionalization score for this last convention was .423 (Congressional Quarterly Weekly Report, 1976). Only four other out-party candidates were nominated with a lower fractionalization recorded on their first ballots. All lost and their losses were expected. In three of the cases (1900, 1908, 1936) the traditional cues were all or predominantly positive for the in-party and the fourth involved Franklin Roosevelt's final run for the Presidency in a year which he entered with a 66% job approval rating.

The traditional cues in 1976 pointed clearly to the election of the out-party nominee, but the fractionalization for Carter's nomination was well below the .613 mean recorded for the other four out-party candidates who faced similarly encouraging prospects.

The reason for this occurrence is simple. Democratic professionals were so determined to avoid what they perceived to be the lessons of the two previous conventions that unity became their overriding theme. The belief of the professionals, expressed most emphatically in October 1975 by Chairman Robert Strauss, was:

> I would remind you that we were the majority party as we entered the 1968 Democratic National Convention, and we emerged as an embittered and fractured group of minority elements. I would remind you that in 1972, we entered our Miami Convention as the majority party of the United States, and emerged again as a disunited group of factions [1975:1].[20]

As a result, the out-party delegates in New York City seemed more interested in nominating Governor Carter in unity than they were interested in nominating Governor Carter. As one observer noted:

> At times, the emphasis on unity all but eclipsed the attention paid to Carter himself—as it did after the nominee's acceptance speech, when Strauss called dozens of party leaders to the podium to celebrate—and Carter and his family found themselves lost in the crowd [Ehrenhalt, 1976: 1867].

Out-party delegates in 1976 acted as if the party was renominating an incumbent. The word "coronation" appeared in print and was uttered over the airwaves. Because of the Democrats' commanding position in the traditional cues, the incumbent's own lack of popularity, and the raging battle within the Republican Party for the nomination, Democrats acted like "ins." The message which they sent out was unmistakable: all we have to do is band together behind our nominee and we will win. Thus, the 1976 Democrats

extracted from their party's "memory" the belief that only
disunity cost them the elections of 1968 and 1972. Some-
how, the Vietnam War, the riot-torn cities, and the nation's
racial tensions were less important to the outcome than the
party's own lack of unity. Unlike past optimistic out-party
contentions in which conflict was acceptable and indeed
positively associated with election performance, the organizers
of that year's Democratic convention were deeply committed
to the avoidance of even the appearance of conflict. It
seemed as if they had come to regard the convention as an
outcome cue in and of itself. Through this process, the role
of the convention was altered. It became for the out-party
Democrats what conventions had once been for optimistic
in-parties, a ceremonial stand rather than an arena where
conflict is resolved (Sullivan, Pressman, Arterton, Nakamura,
and Weinberg, 1976).

That year's alteration was made possible because of the
increased reliance upon the new cues. The two which seemed
most useful here were the primaries and the intraparty polls.
Unlike the Presidential popularity cue and the traditional
House and gubernatorial ones, these cues are not presumed to
predict the outcome of the election, but instead to identify
"the party's choice."

Intraparty popularity is regularly measured by the Gallup
Poll in two ways: Presidential preference lists with a number
of possible candidates and "showdowns" in which two contenders are matched against one another. For the purposes of
this analysis, only the Presidential preference lists will be
used.

Contemporary analysts of the nominating system such as
Hadley (1976) and Keech and Matthews (1976) stress the
importance of these polls. They have contended that these
polls generally predict the identity of the eventual nominee
and, as a corollary, when these polls are ignored and someone
other than "the party's choice" is nominated, defeat occurs.

One very useful piece of analysis by Beniger (1976) identifies the most popular intraparty candidates at four separate stages of the preconvention period: the first poll, the first poll after the midterm election, the first poll after the first major primary, and the final poll of the campaign. Summary data for these stages are presented in Table 11.

As the Beniger data indicate, selective use of the polls can either confirm or reject the proposition that the likely nominee is "the party's choice" as manifested through "the invisible primary." This appears most dramatically in the case of nonincumbent candidates. They seem to have a little better than a coin's toss probability of nomination if they lead the polls at any point prior to the final one. The advantages that presumably accrue to front runners may not be as great as generally assumed.

One last factor which should be considered relates to the eventual outcome. While it may be true that conventions nominating candidates other than their most popular possibilities may produce losers, there is no guarantee that the "party's choice" will also be "the people's choice" in Novem-

Table 11: Preferential Poll Leadership at Four Campaign Stages and Convention Success, 1936–1976

Campaign Stage	Predicted Nominee All Races		Predicted Non-Incumbent Nominee	
First Poll of Campaign	13/21	61.9%	7/14	50.0%
First Poll After Midterm Elections	13/21	61.9%	6/14	42.9%
First Poll After First Major Primary	12/19	63.2%	7/14	50.0%
Final Poll of Campaign	19/21	90.5%	12/14	85.7%

Source: Adapted from James R. Beniger, "Winning the Presidential Nomination: National Polls and State Primary Elections, 1936–1972," *Public Opinion Quarterly*, XL (Spring, 1976), p. 27.

ber. Dewey in 1944, Stevenson in 1956, and Nixon in 1960 led at every point in their intraparty polls, but all lost.

There is one fascinating relationship between intraparty poll leadership and election outcome which seems to have escaped notice. In the 11 elections since 1936, the nominee more strongly favored by his fellow partisans in the final preconvention poll has been elected 9 times over the nominee less strongly favored. Only the narrow Kennedy victory in 1960 and Carter in 1976 went against this trend.

In keeping with our foregoing discussion, we are using the mean fractionalization score of all the preconvention polls to determine the degree of clarity with which the polls could be read.[21] A low mean fractionalization score would seem to indicate that the partisan respondents were clear in their choice of a candidate to represent them in the general election. Conversely, a high fractionalization score would seem to indicate a great deal of confusion among the rank and file concerning their preferred nominee.

As expected, poll fractionalization correlates with convention fractionalization for both in-parties (.76) and out-parties (.55). If the rank and file of the party is divided in its preferences, so too will be the delegates. The relationship between poll fractionalization and election outcomes is also in accord with the model. The in-party's popular vote percentage correlates negatively with poll fractionalization, both among its own partisans (-.76) and among those of the opposition party (-.53). Although the relationship is similar, the reasons underlying it are not. Poll uncertainty about the in-party nominee is usually due to the absence of an incumbent President or serious reservations about his performance in office.

Out-party fractionalization correlates negatively with in-party election results because of lessened election expectations. The better the prospects for in-party victory, the fewer will be the out-party contenders who will announce their candidacy or make known their availability. Landon in 1936 and Stevenson in 1956 recorded the lowest mean fractionalization scores in their party's preconvention polls. Their claims to the nomination were not seriously challenged.

When out-party prospects improve, poll fractionalization increases. Out-party popular vote percentages correlate positively with both out-party and in-party poll fractionalization—.48 and .60, respectively. In-party divisiveness and those factors which lead to that divisiveness increase the prospects for out-party victories which in turn creates greater interest in the out-party nomination and more divisiveness in the out-party polls. Not surprisingly, in-party and out-party poll fractionalization are highly correlated with one another (.70). Thus, this new cue seems to operate in a fashion similar to the traditional cues.

The other source of information used to determine the party's favored nominee is the Presidential primary system. Much maligned by candidates and dismissed on a semiregular basis by political pundits, the Presidential primaries have been a feature of American political life since 1912. They were virtually ignored by Presidential politicians for almost 40 years. In both 1912 and 1932, incumbent Presidents were soundly defeated in the primaries. Taft captured only 34% of the 1912 Republican vote while Hoover captured only 33% of 1932's. Both were renominated, giving rise to Mencken's remark that "a sitting Republican President can no more fail of renomination, if he wants it, than a dry Senator can resist a drink" (1960: 243).

Primaries made their resurgence in 1952. In that year, Estes Kefauver exposed President Truman's vulnerability as a candidate in the Democratic primaries while Eisenhower and Taft competed vigorously in the Republican primaries. There was an increase of almost eight million voters in 1952's primaries over those in 1948—a percentage increase of 165%. Neither Kefauver nor Taft, the overall winners of that year's primaries, were nominated but that would not always be the case. With John Kennedy's showing in the 1960 primaries and his subsequent nomination and election, the primaries became "the road to the White House" (Davis, 1967). Richard Nixon in 1968, George McGovern in 1972, and both Jimmy Carter and Ronald Reagan in 1976 benefitted enormously from the increased role of primaries in the candidate selection process.

There is one very serious problem confronting delegates who seek to gain information from the primaries about their party's most popular candidate and that is the state laws governing the primaries are very idiosyncratic. Some states have primaries; others do not. Some primaries are closed to all but registered partisans; others permit any voter to participate. Some primaries clearly identify the names of Presidential contenders on the ballot; others only list delegates. Some primaries bind delegates for at least one convention ballot; others are merely advisory. In addition to the lack of uniformity concerning the role of the electorate and the delegates, candidates can also contribute confusion by running only in the primaries which they anticipate winning. The clearest case in recent times of a candidate rendering the primaries irrelevant occurred in 1964 when Lyndon Johnson chose not to run in any seriously contested primaries and had stand-ins do battle with George Wallace in the states of Wisconsin, Indiana, and Maryland. As it turned out, Johnson, whose Presidential approval rating soared over the 70% mark for most of the year and was favored by better than 2 to 1 in all of the trial heats between himself and any Republican candidate, received only 17% of the total Democratic primary vote. For these reasons, it is difficult to identify the "overall winner" of each party's primaries, but not impossible.

One system devised by Weinberg and Crowley (1970) used four separate standards for determining the winners of the primaries. The four standards were: (1) aggregate popular vote totals for all primaries; (2) aggregate popular vote totals in contested primaries; (3) total number of individual primary wins; and (4) total number of individual wins in contested primaries. In Table 12, each of these standards is related to the convention's decision for all candidates, for all nonincumbent candidates, and for two time periods.

The relationship between the post-1936 primary victors in all races and their probability of nomination is very similar to the Beniger findings on the polls. However, the primaries appear to be less helpful for predicting nonincumbent candidates. One major reason for the difficulties faced by nonincumbent victors of the primaries is the "late grabber" phenomenon.

The late grabber is a candidate who waits out all of the preliminaries and then makes a major lunge for the nomination early in the balloting. The late grabber should be differentiated from the all but extinct "dark horse," who emerges as the nominee after a weary convention turns toward a new face following the decimation of all the leading contenders. The late grabber is a major contender prior to the opening of the convention but deliberately makes a minor effort in the primaries.

In defining late grabs, two conditions must be met: a low percentage of votes in the party's Presidential primaries (for example, less than 15% of the total party votes) and a marked improvement in the candidate's percentage of first-ballot delegates over his primary performance (for example, a gain of 10 points or more). Using these two guidelines, we have identified 21 late grabs since the inception of the primaries in 1912; 14 have occurred since 1940.[22]

Prior to 1936, only one late grabber was nominated—Charles Evans Hughes. Since then, five were nominated: Wilkie in 1940, Dewey in 1944 and 1948, Stevenson in 1952,

Table 12:   Primary Strength on Four Measures and Convention Success,
            1912–1976

1912–1976	Predicted Nominee All Races		Predicted Non-Incumbent Nominee	
Leader in Aggregate Vote, All Primaries	20/34	58.8%	11/22	50.0%
Leader in Aggregate Vote, Contested Primaries	18/34	52.9	9/22	40.9
Leader in Total Primary Wins	21/34	61.8	11/22	50.0
Leader in Total Contested Primary Wins	22/34	64.7	12/22	54.5
1936–1976 Only				
Leader in Aggregate Vote, All Primaries	13/22	59.1	6/14	42.8
Leader in Aggregate Vote, Contested Primaries	13/22	59.1	6/14	42.8
Leader in Total Primary Wins	15/22	68.2	7/14	50.0
Leader in Total Contested Primary Wins	16/22	72.7	8/14	57.1

Source: Adapted from Leonard Weinberg and Joseph Crowley, "Primary Success
as a Measure of Presidential Election Victory: A Research Note," *Midwest Journal
of Political Science*, XIV (August, 1970), p. 507.

and Humphrey in 1968. All six candidates lost in the subsequent election.

Four of the five post-1936 late grabbing nominees led their
parties in the final preconvention poll. Stevenson was the
only exception, but he had a friend in the White House. It
appears as if the convention delegates faced with conflicting
information from the polls and the primaries seem more
inclined to support the poll leader than the primary victor.

Of the last 13 conventions without an eligible incumbent,
10 have had late grabbing candidates. The only three conventions to escape this phenomenon were the Republican conventions of 1952 and 1960 and the Democratic convention

of 1976. Only one late grab was directed at an incumbent and that was Richard Russell's challenge to Truman in 1948. Clearly, if an incumbent is to be challenged successfully, it must be done at the earliest possible point—in the primaries.

For the most part, the late grabbers appear to be better connected to the party's existing hierarchy than many of the nominees. Not only can this be said of the successful grabbers such as Dewey, Stevenson, and Humphrey but also of some of the failures such as Averill Harriman (1952 and 1956), Lyndon Johnson (1960), William Scranton (1964), and Henry Jackson (1972). It would seem as if the late grab is a tactic for "insiders" whose major constituency is the existing party apparatus.

As the primaries increase in importance and more bound delegates appear at conventions, the likelihood of successful late grabs should diminish and, given the track record of grabbers in the general election, conventions would be wise to ignore candidates who choose this particular strategy. Adding the primary-based success of President Carter to those of previous out-party nominees who chose the primary route indicates that out-party conventions may have already moved in their direction.

In order to place the primaries within the model, we computed fractionalization scores for each party's total primary vote. In Table 13, the mean fractionalization scores for polls, primaries, and conventions are presented for each of the relevant candidate situations.

Although the means vary, the relative rankings do not. Out-party nominations are accompanied by higher fractionalization in the polls, the primaries, and the conventions than in any other case. In-out differences are greater than Democratic-Republican ones. And the least fractionalization occurs consistently in the case of incumbents.

In relating the primaries to the other variables, it seems as if the out-parties exist within their own world. The ease with

Table 13:   Mean Fractionalization Scores of Intraparty Polls, State
            Primary Totals, and First Ballots for Candidate Situation,
            1936–1976

	Mean Gallup Poll. Fract.	Mean State Primary Fract.	Mean 1st Ballot. Fract.
All Conventions	.560	.587	.373
Democrats	.565	.592	.391
Republicans	.556	.582	.354
In-Party	.413	.431	.237
Incumbents	.331	.407	.160
Successors	.602	.496	.440
Out-Party	.695	.743	.509

which out-party candidates in the past could ignore the
primaries directly affects the correlations. Out-party primary
fractionalization appears totally independent of out-party
convention fractionalization (.00). Nor does it correlate with
in-party popular vote percentages (-.09). It does relate however to out-party poll fractionalization (.64). Even though
different leading candidates may emerge from these two
sources of information, uncertainty in one arena is likely to
be matched by uncertainty in the other.

For the in-party, primary fractionalization does correlate
with both convention conflict (.55) and with election outcomes (-.43). Both of these figures would have been higher
had Lyndon Johnson not opted for his antiprimary strategy
in 1964. Leaving the 1964 case out raises the correlation
between in-party primary fractionalization and that within
in-party conventions to .84 and it makes the relationship
between primary fractionalization and in-party outcomes
clearer and more negative (-.81). In-party primary fractionalization, like that in the polls or at the convention, represents
dissatisfaction with the incumbent administration and uncertainty about the party's future.

Figure 2 gives a more complete picture of the relationship
between the cues discussed and election outcomes for the

1936-1976 period. Examining Figure 2 reveals findings in keeping with the model and its response to changing circumstances. The traditional cues relate positively to in-party results, but their relative ranking has fallen below the newer cues. The almost total domination of the House by the Democrats in these elections has decreased the utility of the congressional cue. The gubernatorial cue fared better and its value as an outcome predictor persists.

The two poll-based-cues—presidential approval and intraparty preferences scored second and third as outcome indicators.

The most support for the model appears in the six fractionalization measures. As may be seen in Table 14, all six correlate negatively with in-party popular vote percentages and all six correlate positively with out-party percentages.

As has been asserted throughout this study, conflict is positively associated with out-party fortunes and negatively associated with in-party ones. When uncertainty about the identity or the popularity of the in-party's nominee arises, their party prospects decrease. And when this occurs, conflict levels rise within the optimistic out party as contenders eagerly vie with one another for the nomination.

Table 14:   Correlations between Fractionalization Scores and Election Results by Party Status 1936–1976

Fractionalization	In-party Popular Vote %	Out-Party Popular Vote %
In Party		
Primaries	−.43	+.20
Polls	−.76	+.60
Conventions	−.83	+.73
Out-Party		
Primaries	−.09	+.17
Polls	−.53	+.48
Conventions	−.32	+.21

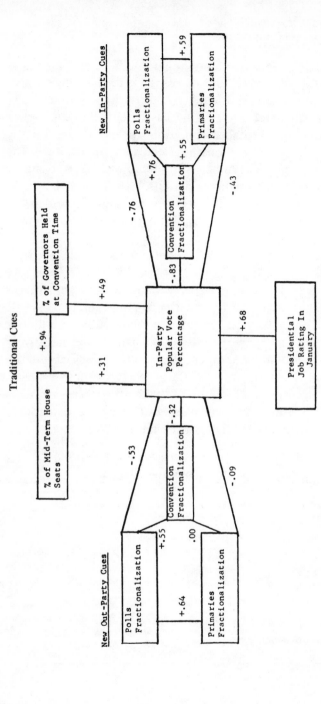

Figure 2: Correlations Between Pre-convention Cues and In-party Presidential Vote, 1936-1976

Within the fractionalization measures there is some variation. Primary fractionalization has the weakest relationship to Presidential outcomes, regardless of which party is involved or with which party's results they are being matched.

In the case of these in-party vote percentages, the fractionalization measures indicate stronger relationships between in-party conflict and defeat than out-party conflict and success. From this comparison one could conclude that out-parties do not win elections as much as in-parties lose them.

The single strongest outcome predictor is in-party convention fractionalization. The in-party convention is a focal point for all of the factors which affect Presidential elections. Whether they are there to reaffirm their allegiance or to seriously question the incumbent's management of the nation or the party, in-party convention delegates both mirror and affect the popular feelings which surround the President and his associates.

CONCLUSION

This study has treated the Presidential nominating convention as an integral part of the American political process, one which is responsive to the political climate and is related to election results. Politicians are people who understand and desire power. Most derive their power from elections; and their pursuit of power leads them into the careful scrutiny of cues which forecast outcomes. When cues indicate that in-party prospects seem dim, conflict levels increase at both in- and out-party conventions. Sensing victory, out-party politicians compete in greater numbers and with more vigor for a nomination which seems likely to lead to the White House, while the in-party, facing defeat, turns on the incumbent or his successor. When the in-party seems assured of victory, conflict levels at both conventions are lower—for the in-party there is nothing to repudiate and for the out-party the nomination is of little value.

Convention conflict in turn is related to election out-comes. For the in-party the relationship is an inverse one, that is, higher levels of conflict at the nominating convention are associated with a lower popular vote. The pattern for the out-party is the reverse. Out-parties cannot only withstand conflict but perhaps benefit from it. As convention conflict increases, so does their popular vote.

As the study has noted, the traditional election forecasting cues of congressional and gubernatorial elections have dimin-ished in importance. They no longer seem as strongly asso-ciated with Presidential outcomes and levels of convention conflict as they had been earlier in this century. They have been overshadowed by cues which focus directly upon the Presidential contest itself: Presidential approval ratings, intra-party preference polls, and state primaries. There are new cues, but the response of contemporary political leaders seems very much in accord with the behavior of past poli-ticians. Optimism decreases in-party conflict and increases out-party conflict, while pessimism fragments the in-party and depresses the contentiousness of the out-party.

The most striking recent development has been the power of incumbent Presidents to gain nominations in spite of negative party circumstances and their ability to win elec-tions in the face of these dim prospects. This development has left its impact upon conflict levels within later conven-tions. However, it is important to remember that three of the nation's most recent Presidents surrendered their ambitions long before the conventions could punish them for under-mining party fortunes.

Although the role of conventions seems to have diminished in recent years, they continue to exert an impact upon the political process. And as the nation readies itself for another election year, the key questions recur: Will the in-party Democrats of 1980 pay heed to preconvention warning sig-nals and deny renomination to President Carter? Or will they rally around their incumbent candidate and hope that Mr.

Carter's incumbency will carry them on to another term in the White House? The model is ready for yet another test.

Although the role of conventions seems to have diminished in recent years, the 1976 Republican convention gave renewed emphasis to the centrality of this most unique institution within the Presidential selection system.

NOTES

1. Of the 42 Presidential first ballots examined between 1896 and 1976, more than one candidate received votes in 36 of them. However, 32 of those contests never went beyond the first ballot.

2. Congressional seat statistics have been computed from Congressional Quarterly (1975).

3. The names and parties of the governors can be found in Congressional Quarterly (1975). The effective date used in all cases was June 1 of the convention year. Electoral votes for the states at the time of the convention came from Petersen (1963) and Congressional Quarterly (1975) for the 1840-1972 elections.

4. Intraparty ratings have been extensively used by Keech and Matthews (1976) and by Hadley (1976).

5. Since causation may run in the opposite direction, from electoral strength to convention conflict, emphasis must be placed on the word *apparent*—Editors.

6. Assessments of the Democratic Party's problems in 1948 can be found in Abels (1959) and Ross (1968).

7. Typical of the comments were those of Indiana congressional candidate David Cornwell: "We're a kind of Copperhead district, and Carter'll bring out the vote for the whole ticket. People feel he'll really make some of the changes they've been wanting, and that feeling spills over to me."

8. Rates of incumbents' success can be found in Kirby (1970). The role of ticket-splitting in accomplishing this end is discussed in Cummings (1966), DeVries and Tarrance (1971), and Erikson (1971).

9. See Matthews (1974). Truman led in the preference polls among Democrats over Senator Kefauver 36% to 21% (Gallup, 1972). The poll was taken January 20-25, 1952. Johnson trailed Robert Kennedy in Gallup's September 1967 Presidential preference list for Democratic

voters but Johnson led Kennedy in the showdown polls for January and February of 1968 (Gallup, 1975).

10. In our analysis we will deal only with the percent of governorships held by the party. This correlates highly (.90) with the percent of electoral votes held by governors of the respective parties at convention time.

11. For analyses of this practice and its impact, compare Key (1956) and Ranney (1971). According to the Council of State Governments (1974), 29 states of 48 (60.4%) elected their governors in Presidential years to either two-year (19 states) or four-year terms (10 states). The council also said that only 14 of 50 states (28%) continue to elect governors in Presidential years.

12. President Truman contended in his memoirs that "presidential control of the convention is a principle which has not been violated in political history" (Truman, 1955: 492). For a full assessment of past Presidential control over conventions, see David, Goldman, and Bain (1960) and Pomper (1966).

13. The remark referred to the 1924 Democratic convention in New York City.

14. Curtis was almost replaced by former Vice President Charles Dawes until Dawes removed himself from consideration, and even then the renomination was in trouble (Spears, 1932a, 1932b, 1932c).

15. The 1948 platform debate took 45 pages in the convention proceedings. It was the civil rights plank in that platform which received the most attention. Neither the segregationists nor the civil rights activists were happy with the statement emerging from the Resolutions Committee. The weaker civil rights position was defeated, 309-925, while the vote to strengthen the position passed, 651.5-582.5.

16. According to White (1960), Eisenhower saw the proposals as "the personal treachery of Nelson A. Rockefeller" (p. 239). White's appendix contains the July 23 statement (pp. 464-467).

17. These approval ratings are summarized in Gallup (1976). Ford's January 1976 rating comes from Gallup (1976).

18. Robert Kennedy's assessment of Democratic prospects in 1968 figured heavily in his initial decision not to run and then later to challenge Lyndon Johnson (see Chester, Hodgson, and Page, 1969, and Witcover, 1969).

19. Ford's ratings in 1975 scored above 50% only in late May and June. His approval average for the year was 43% (Gallup, 1976).

20. This was a speech to a meeting of the Democratic National Committee on October 14, 1975. Speech provided by the Democratic National Committee.

21. We would like to thank James Beniger of the University of California, Berkeley, for kindly providing us with these data which he computed from the Gallup polls (see Beniger, 1976).

22. The 14 late grabbers since 1940 were: Wendell Wilkie (1940), Thomas E. Dewey (1944 and 1948), Richard Russell (1948 and 1952), Robert Taft (1948), Adlai Stevenson (1952), Averill Harriman (1952 and 1956), Lyndon Johnson (1960), William Scranton (1964), Hubert Humphrey (1968), Nelson Rockefeller (1968), and Henry Jackson (1972).

REFERENCES

ABELS, J. (1959) Out of the Jaws of Victory. New York: Holt, Rinehart and Winston.

ALSOP, S. (1970) "A defeatable President." Newsweek (November 16) 76:124.

BENIGER, J.R. (1976) "Winning the Presidential nomination: National polls and state primary elections, 1936-1972." Public Opinion Quarterly 40:22-38.

BREWER, W.R. and G. NELSON (1976) "Convention conflict and election outcomes, 1840-1976." Paper presented at the annual meeting of the American Political Science Association, September 2-5.

BURNHAM, W.D. (1967) "Party systems and the political process." In W.N. Chambers and W.D. Burnham (eds.) The American Party Systems: Stages of Political Development. New York: Oxford Univ. Press.

CHESTER, L., G. HODGSON and B. PAGE (1969) An American Melodrama: The Presidential Campaign of 1968. New York: Dell.

Congressional Quarterly (1975) Guide to U.S. Elections. Washington, DC: Author.

CONVERSE, P.E., A. CAMPBELL, W.E. MILLER, and D.E. STOKES (1961) "Stability and change in 1960: A reinstating election." American Political Science Review 55:269-280.

CUMMINGS, M.C., Jr. (1966) Congressmen and the Electorate: Elections for the U.S. House and the President, 1920-1964. New York: Free Press.

DAVID, P.T., R.M. GOLDMAN and R.C. BAIN (1960) The Politics of National Party Conventions. Washington, DC: Brookings.

DAVIS, J.W. (1967) Presidential Primaries: Road to the White House. New York: Crowell.

DeVRIES, W. and V.L. TARRANCE (1971) The Ticket-Splitter: A New Force in American Politics. Grand Rapids, MI: Eerdmans.

EHRENHALT, A. (1976) "Harmonious Democrats rally behind Carter." Congressional Quarterly Weekly Report 34 (July 17):1,867.

ERIKSON, R.S. (1971) "The advantage of incumbency in congressional elections." Polity 3:395-405.

FINCH, R.H. (1970) Letter from the White House. (November 9)

GALLUP, G.H. (1972) The Gallup Poll: Public Opinion 1935-1971. New York: Random House.

HADLEY, A.T. (1976) The Invisible Primary. Englewood Cliffs, NJ: Prentice-Hall.

KEECH, W.R. and D.R. Matthews (1976) The Party's Choice. Washington, DC: Brookings.

KEY, V.O. (1961) "Interpreting the election results." In P.T. David (ed.) The Presidential Election and Transition 1960-1961. Washington, DC: Brookings.

——— (1956) American State Politics: An Introduction. New York: Alfred A. Knopf.

——— (1955) "A theory of critical elections." Journal of Politics 17:3-18.

KERNELL, S. (1974) "Presidential popularity and negative voting: An alternative explanation of the mid-term electoral decline of the President's party." Paper presented at the meeting of the American Political Science Association, Chicago.

KIRBY, J.C. (1970) Congress and the Public Trust. New York: Atheneum.

MATTHEWS, D.R. (1974) "Presidential nominations: Process and outcomes." In J.D. Barber (ed.) Choosing the President. Englewood Cliffs, NJ: Prentice-Hall.

MOOS, M. [ed.] (1960) H.L. Mencken on Politics: A Carnival of Buncombe. New York: Vintage Books.

New York Times (1952). February 1, p. 10.

Newsweek (1970) "Elections '70: The Democrats shape up." (November 16) 76:30.

OTTEN, A.L. (1976) "Carter's coattails: Democratic candidates for Congress consider nominee a major asset." Wall Street Journal July 15, p. 1.

PATTERSON, J.T. (1972) Mr. Republican: A Biography of Robert A. Taft. Boston: Houghton Mifflin.

PETERSON, S. (1963) A Statistical History of American Presidential Elections. New York: Ungar.

PIERSON, J.E. (1975) "Presidential popularity and midterm voting at different electoral levels." American Journal of Political Science 19:683-694.

POMPER, G. (1966) Nominating the President: The Politics of Convention Choice. New York: Norton.

RAE, D.W. (1971) The Political Consequences of Electoral Laws. New Haven: Yale Univ. Press.

——— (1968) "A note of the fractionalization of some European party systems." Comparative Political Studies (October):413-418.

RANNEY, A. (1971) "Parties in state politics." In H. Jacob and K.N. Vines (eds.) Politics in the American States: A Comparative Analysis. Boston: Little, Brown.

ROSEBOOM, E.H. (1970) A History of Presidential Elections. New York: Macmillan.

ROSS, I. (1968) The Loneliest Campaign: The Truman Victory of 1948. New York: New American Library.

SCHLESINGER, A.M., Jr. (1965) A Thousand Days: John F. Kennedy in the White House. Boston: Houghton Mifflin.

SPEERS, L.C. (1932a) "Hoover is pictured as Curtis's last hope." New York Times, June 15, pp. 1, 14.

——— (1932b) "Dawes's 'No' crushes anti-Curtis drive." New York Times, June 16, pp. 1, 12.

——— (1932c) "Curtis victory won against field of 12." New York Times, June 17, pp. 1, 13.

STEWART, J.G. (1974) One Last Chance: The Democratic Party, 1974-76. New York: Praeger.

SULLIVAN, D.G., J.L. PRESSMAN, F.C. ARTERTON, R.T. NAKAMURA and M.W. WEINBERG (1976) "Candidates, caucuses, and issues: The Democratic Convention 1976." Paper presented at the annual meeting of the American Political Science Association, September 2-5.

Time (1970) "And now, looking toward 1972." (November 16) 96:15.

TRUMAN, H. (1955) Years of Trial and Hope (Vol. 2). Garden City, NY: Doubleday.

TUFTE, E.R. (1975) "Determinants of the outcomes of midterm congressional elections." American Political Science Review 69:812-826.

WEINBERG, L. and J. CROWLEY (1970) "Primary success as a measure of Presidential election victory." Midwest Journal of Political Science 14:506-513.

WHITE, T.H. (1961) The Making of the President 1960. New York: Pocket Books.

WITCOVER, J. (1969) 85 Days: The Last Campaign of Robert Kennedy. New York: Putnam.

6

RATIONAL ALLOCATION OF CONGRESSIONAL RESOURCES: MEMBER TIME AND STAFF USE IN THE HOUSE

THOMAS E. CAVANAGH

Yale University

The behavioral revolution has greatly added to our understanding of the empirical world. But it has also had the curious effect of taking much of the politics out of political science. Such classic theorists as Machiavelli, Hobbes, and Madison premised their analyses on the attempts of political actors to attain personally desired goals. The behavioralists, however, have seemingly attempted to reduce political behavior to a deterministic vector sum of social and psychological forces.

The literature on Congress has been symptomatic of this approach. Until recently, most congressional scholarship consisted of placing congressional phenomena in a sociological framework. Congress was frequently conceptualized as an ongoing social system, composed of interacting subsystems arrayed in structures, which performed, or failed to perform, certain functions. This approach made its first vivid appearance in the work of Young (1958) and reached its apotheosis in Fenno's (1966) exhaustive study of the appropriations process.

A second, related school was concerned less with structural patterns per se than with the relationship of individuals to these structures. The behavior of individual actors was thought to be prescribed by systemic norms which defined "roles" for the actors. Early treatments of this variety included Huitt's (1954, 1957) articles on committee procedures and Matthews's (1960) research on senatorial "folkways." A more rigorous typology of legislative roles was subsequently developed by Wahlke, Eulau, Buchanan, and Ferguson (1962) in a pioneering study of state legislators and was later applied to Congress in the Davidson's (1969) work.

THE DRIFT TOWARD THE PURPOSIVE

In recent years, there have been efforts to articulate an alternative theoretical framework. Scher (1960, 1963) initiated this approach in the early 1960's with his seminal articles on the oversight process. He saw congressmen making "rational decisions about the allocation of their scarce personal resources (energy, time, etc.) so as to maximize gains to themselves in things which they value and minimize their losses in those things" (1963: 528). In a similar vein, Fenno modified his structural-functional approach in a 1973 study of committees, which posited that congressmen make use of the committee process to maximize their personal goals: "reelection, influence within the House, and good public policy" (p. 1). And the structural-functional approach has been abandoned altogether in his current research on congressional "home style," one of whose ingredients is "the congressman's allocation of his personal resources and those of his office (Fenno, 1977: 890; also see Fenno, 1978).

Taking account of these trends, Mayhew has identified "a disciplinary drift toward the purposive, a drift, so to speak, from the sociological toward the economic" (1974:3). The defining character of this emerging approach is an emphasis upon personal motivation. The goals to be maximized differ from those of the economists, but the assumption of rational calculation to attain these goals is retained. Mayhew's political universe is peopled by individuals who "struggle . . . to gain and maintain power" (1974: 6), a not implausible foundation for political analysis. His critical axiom is an adaptation of that of Downs (1957) that politicians undertake certain activities in order to win elections, rather than winning elections in order to undertake certain activities (Mayhew, 1974.)[1]

This "drift toward the purposive" has resulted in a change in the focus of congressional research. The level of analysis has shifted increasingly from the congressional system to the individual member's relationship to the system, and ultimately to the individual member; this is best exemplified by the trends in Fenno's research over the past decade.[2] And just as important, the drift is reflected in a change in the locus of attention, from the legislative maneuverings on Capitol Hill to the activities of a member as they are perceived by the constituents back home (Fenno, 1977, 1978).

The body of theory on Congress has been enriched by this shift in emphasis, but it has also been rendered more complex. In a recent pair of papers, Davidson (1977a, 1977b) has presented a model of "the two Congresses," in which he views recent congressional reform efforts as an attempt to "maintain an equilibrium between outside and inside forces" (Davidson, 1977b: 5). The "outside forces" are the demand for constituency services, counterpoised against the individual member's desire for reelection; while the "inside forces" are the demand for policy coordination, as opposed to the individual member's desire for personal power and influence (Davidson, 1977b).

Davidson's structural-functional approach is one means of integrating the study of the "two Congresses"; in this paper, I shall offer another, namely, the purposive orientation of Mayhew, as modified by a crucial insight developed by Fenno and Scher. Mayhew focuses on activities pursued in order to win reelection. I shall introduce another assumption to cover nonelectoral goals as well. That is, I shall propose that *congressmen undertake certain activities in order to win elections, which then gives them the opportunity to pursue certain other activities which may or may not be related to reelection.* Fenno makes this point nicely: "For most members most of the time, this electoral goal is primary. It is the prerequisite for a congressional career and, hence, for the pursuit of other goals" (1977: 889). Mayhew's powerful model is simply not designed to fully explain such congressional activities as oversight, legislative mobilization, and agenda setting, in which the electoral incentives are often nil.[3]

Because Scher concentrates on explaining activities in the policy area, his grappling with the problem is instructive. He notes that for each of Davidson's "two Congresses," there exists a distinct set of demands: "In a setting in which there are innumerable claims upon his time," the congressman "realizes that how he accommodates these demands is likely to be crucial to the success of his efforts to maintain and if possible improve his legislative and electoral position" (Sher, 1963: 529). It is essential to realize that these two goals may in fact be contradictory: what improves a member's position with the electorate may hurt his standing among his colleagues, and vice versa. Thus, the congressman must ask himself, "What profit and what loss can be anticipated from satisfying committee and party leadership expectations if this means rejecting, even though momentarily, constituent or interest group demands which he considers important?" (Sher, 1963: 529).

Specifically, then, what I shall propose is that congressional activities are undertaken in two competing arenas of performance: the electoral and the institutional. As Lowi did, I shall define an "arena" as a distinctive sphere of political activity exhibiting "its own characteristics political structure, political process, elites, and group relations" (1964: 689-690; cf. Price, 1965). The major actors in each arena are individual congressmen; what distinguishes one arena from the other is the environment in which these actors are placed. Each arena offers a different set of incentives for the pursuit of various activities. Other purposive individuals attempt to fulfill their personal objectives through their interaction with the congressman; and the congressman in turn has personal goals to be satisfied through this interaction.

What gives this model its bite is the potential for conflict between the incentives for performance in the two arenas. Clearly, the need to compete in the electoral arena constrains the member's ability to participate in the ultimately more attractive arena of the institution of the House. The congressman is thus faced with an excruciating problem of resource allocation, for a member's supplies of time, staff, and influence are decidedly finite. The problem is further complicated by the fact that competing successfully in the electoral arena is obviously a necessary, but of course not sufficient, condition for success in the institutional arena.

Fiorina (1974) was the first to formalize such a conceptualization of Congress, although his model is more game theoretic in its roots. He hypothesizes that members pursue a vote-maximizing strategy up until the point at which their perceived subjective probability of being reelected (p) exceeds their personally acceptable subjective probability of being reelected (p*). In other words, a congressman who is satisfied to receive 60% of the vote, and under a given expenditure of resources can expect to receive 70% of the vote, has a kind of "surplus" of electoral utiles which can then be traded off at the margin for other types of utiles which bring more personal satisfaction. Or less formally still, a safe-seat incumbent can afford to put less effort into activities geared solely to insuring reelection and, more effort into the pursuit of personal goals without fear of retribution at the polls.

Having insightfully laid the foundation for a purposive model of Congress, Fiorina (1974, ch. 1) then proceeds to restrict his focus to the question of the differing policy preferences of the electorate and the members. While the analysis is penetrating at times, it misses a central point because of its assumption that the function of a congressman is to vote on legislation. The real question is this: what if the critical difference between representative and constituents concerns not the direction of legislative policy, but rather to what extent a member should undertake the legislative function at all? What if some voters would prefer effort expended on casework, or obtaining federal funds for the district? If the congressman defines the job differently than the electorate, then who wins out?

This question is more fundamental than the one Fiorina addresses. It is certainly far more interesting. Indeed, the explanatory power inherent in his model is only partially revealed in its application to roll call voting analysis. A broader application can tell us much about the entire range of congressional behavior. What follows is a partially deductive, partially inductive exploration of the path charted by a set of signposts. While admittedly preliminary as a theoretical statement, my hope is that the reader will find the treatment to be an enlightening way of viewing the congressional world.

In the electoral arena, citizens satisfy their desires for a personally appealing mix of congressional services and activities by casting votes for the most preferred of two or more competing candidates. The marketing strategies inherent in this situation are at once subtle and critical to understanding the process, for political concerns are tangential to the daily lives of most voters. The aspiring political entrepreneur must stimulate a demand for a product—the candidate himself— which must be differentiated from a host of competitors similarly striving to attain election. His task is to seek out and tap a "clientele" of potential supporters.

All who take an active interest in an election outcome, whatever their motives, find it in their interest to aid in promoting their most preferred candidate. If the stakes are sufficiently high to the political elite, the effect of a campaign is to saturate the electorate with partisan appeals from candidates, the media, and reference group leaders. Informal conversations further increase the supply of cognitive bits in circulation. Whatever its objective accuracy or depth, there is sufficient political information provided "free of charge" to the typical prospective voter to discourage investing personal resources in acquiring additional costly information. This is particularly true when candidate and party cues remain stable over several elections, as in the person of a renominated congressional incumbent. In sum, the rational voter responds in a cost-efficient manner to the environment created by the rational calculations of the political elite.[4]

Beginning with very simple postulates analogous to those above, Mayhew derives a persuasive model of the "electoral connection." In his analysis, the entrepreneurial cast to congressional activities is striking; indeed, what he terms "advertising" involves building "what amounts to a brand name" (1974: 49). The hypothesized effects on congressional behavior have been aptly summarized by Rogowski:

> Congressmen, particularly if they come from marginal districts, will show strong tendencies toward self-advertisement in their

constituencies and toward claiming credit for particularistic benefits (dams, post offices, the satisfactory resolution of citizens'
complaints) that accrue to their constituencies. . . . Because most
citizens' knowledge of the internal processes of Congress is slight,
position taking (the introduction of bills, delivery of speeches,
casting of roll call votes) will receive far more attention than will
actual efforts to obtain results, except in areas where well-
informed and persistent pressure groups are active. In the taking
of positions, moreover, the congressman will be utterly servile to
what he perceives to be the preferences of his constituency
[1978: 314].[5]

This is far from the "fiduciary morality" posited by Riker
(1962) in his model of legislative behavior. As Mayhew notes,
"the electoral process guarantees not that there will be a
fiduciary relationship, but only that politicians will make it
appear as if there were one" (1974: 114; emphasis in original). The merchandising of an *image* of responsiveness to
constituent concerns is sufficient to satisfy the voters' limited
cognitive requirements for electoral choice.

In the institutional arena, congressmen are linked to interest groups, the bureaucracy, the press, and one another in the
intricate complex of policy networks described in Lowi's
(1964) analysis. A full analysis of the internal operations of
the House is of course well beyond the scope of this paper.
My purpose here is simply to sketch a framework of collegial
interaction within the House sufficient to bear comparison
with the electoral arena presented above.

The most basic unit of analysis within the House as an
institution is the decision. In a key early work, Fenno (1965)
begins with this premise, which implies that the central
problem of House organization is decision making. A corollary problem is that of maintenance, the means of "holding
the decision-making structure together" by enabling the
members to "work together so as to minimize disruptive
internal conflicts." The key to understanding the institution
of the House, therefore, is understanding

the problem of decision-making. That is, who shall be given influence over what, and how should he (or they) exercise that influence? Influence can be defined simply as a share in the making of House decisions. The House's first problem, then, involves the distribution of these shares among its members [Fenno, 1965: 52].

The distribution of influence is governed through an intricate maze of formal and informal rules and is constantly being readjusted through a kind of sifting and sorting process as influence is acquired and wielded in the ongoing transaction of congressional business.[6] This transaction is largely accomplished through the pervasive process of bargaining with shares of influence, in which members attempt to exercise some measure of personal control over specific legislative and political decisions. As a result of the committee system, each member's influence tends to be highly specific by policy area, giving the process as a whole an appearance of radical decentralization. The maintenance function is undertaken by the more senior members, who act as "honest brokers," steering subcommittees and committees to consensual decisions by inducing individual members to each give a little so each can get a little. The successful bargainer and, even more, the successful broker are rewarded with relatively greater shares of influence than their colleagues (Fenno, 1965).

Influence can also accrue through the "cue-giving" (or more accurately, perhaps, "cue-taking") process. The high volume of congressional decision making puts a premium on the possession of reliable information. Thus expertise is a special form of influence which is highly valued in the House, for members find it essential to locate colleagues whose policy evaluations they can consistently trust, thereby reducing their information costs. But the greatest benefits are enjoyed by the "expert," who not only gains prestige but can also influence decisions by serving as a cue giver for other members—in effect acquiring additional shares of influence at little marginal cost.

To summarize the model, congressmen compete in two arenas, electoral and institutional. In the electoral arena, they must provide services to their constituents in order to win votes; in the institutional, they use shares of influence to effect decisions in concert with their colleagues. As candidates, members are entrepreneurs; as representatives, they are policy makers. In the electoral arena, they primarily satisfy others' desires for congressional services; in the institutional arena, they hope to satisfy their own desires for power and prestige. To the extent that congressmen must divert resources from the institutional to the electoral arena, it follows that their aspirations for collegial influence will be frustrated, even though they may be more successful as electoral entrepreneurs.

To test this model, I shall be making use of data gathered in 1977 by the Commission on Administrative Review of the House of Representatives, including two surveys of House offices and a national public opinion survey conducted by Louis Harris and Associates.[8] I shall first discuss the nature of electoral demands and how they conflict with what members of the House would rather be doing while serving in the House. Next, I shall explain how these conflicts are resolved in the allocation of a member's personal time and staff. In conclusion I will detail the implications of the two arenas of Congress for the American party system.

THE ELECTORAL IMPERATIVE

In conjuring up his image of congressmen as single-minded seekers of reelection, Mayhew paints a vivid picture of a legislature whose institutional functions are imperiled by the demands of the electoral arena. In expanding the analysis beyond the "electoral connection," it must be emphasized that the two arenas have an unequal importance for the congressman. Institutional incentives may determine what a

member would *like* to do, but the electoral imperative determines what a member *has* to do. Members must live by this
distinction in allocating the precious resources of time, staff,
and influence. Those who fail to do so are rarely given a
chance to repeat their mistakes.

To ascertain the differences between voter and member
preferences on activities, a useful way to begin is to examine
the preferences of members if left to themselves. In January
1977, the Commission on Administrative Review asked a
sample of 153 congressmen, "What roles *should* the House
play in the federal government—what do you believe *ought* to
be its one or two most important functions?" The question is
intended to determine which functions of the House are
valued most highly by its members. Thus, the responses can
be interpreted as an inventory of the activities for which a
congressman is accorded influence by his colleagues. Such
activities would presumably be pursued extensively save for
the competing incentives emanating from the electoral arena.
The results are presented in Table 1.

The most striking aspect of Table 1 is the primacy of
policy determination and implementation as a desired congressional activity. The legislative role is cited by 82% of the
members, and virtually all of those mentioning it volunteer
this role as their first mention. Oversight, the review of the
administration of legislative enactments, is mentioned by
41%. The lesser importance accorded to the ombudsman and
representative roles, mentioned by 27% and 18%, respectively, indicates that intercession on behalf of constituents
and direct advocacy of district interests are much less prized
among the members as institutional activities than the
making of decisions on national policy in committee and on
the floor.[9]

The preferences of the public, which structure the incentives in the electoral arena, are at once less pronounced and
more district oriented. Table 2 presents the findings of the

Table 1: Volunteered Member Views on Roles House Should Play

	%
The legislative role	*82*
To legislate (no further information)	22
To produce legislation concerning taxation, the budget, and appropriations, an historic constitutional role	17
To produce legislation which responds to the needs of the people, defends the interests of constituents	12
To produce legislation in fulfilling of a constitutional responsibility	11
To produce legislation which responds to the needs of the nation	10
To set broad, basic policy	10
To innovate, plan for the future	7
To initiate policy and programs, independent of the President	5
To initiate policy and programs, in coordination with the President and the Senate	4
To initiate legislation and reconsider old legislation; to recognize the limit of the effectiveness of legislative solutions to problems	4
All other specific legislative roles	3
The oversight role	*41*
Monitoring the administration of programs to ensure that legislation is properly implemented	17
Oversight of government operations (no further information)	13
The House is not very effective in the oversight role, although it is very important	8
Oversight to provide a check and balance on the executive branch	7
The ombudsman role	*27*
Helping constituents with problems vis-a-vis the federal bureaucracy	16
Middleman, interface between the citizen and the government; giving citizens the feeling that someone in government cares about them and their problems	5
Ombudsman (no further information)	4
Servicing constituents and local governments on bread-and-butter issues	3
The representative role	*18*
To respond to the needs and interests of the people	11
Two-year terms keep the House close to, responsive to the people	5
To create a national consensus out of diverse needs and interests	3
Representative role (no further information)	3
The constitutional role: checks and balances; to be a coequal branch; to play a balancing role	*12*
The educational role: to make people aware of issues, government activities	*3*
The political role: to get reelected; serve as political leader	*3*
All other roles	*1*
No answer, don't know, not sure	*1*

Total weighted N = (146). Multiple responses possible.

1977 Harris survey. Legislation is valued somewhat more highly than constituency service, representation, and communication by the general public. However, the priority assigned to legislation is far less impressive than among the members, while the district-oriented functions are more in demand. Oversight is so obscure in the eyes of the electorate that it is barely mentioned frequently enough to merit a coding category. Thus, the incentives for performance in the electoral arena are clearly distinct from the prescriptions for performance in the institutional arena.

Having established the conflicting incentives for performance, we can next try to determine which set of expectations is more salient to the members—those of the public or their colleagues. This was ascertained by asking congressmen to note "the major *kinds* of jobs, duties, or functions that you feel you are expected to perform as an individual member of Congress." Due to the salience of the electoral imperative, the public's demands (presented in Table 2) are weighted far more heavily in these overall expectations than the members' own prescriptions for institutional activity (presented in Table 1). The net member expectations, encompassing the demands of both arenas, are presented in Table 3. One finds that legislation and constituency service are demands perceived by virtually all congressmen, with demands for communication (43%) and representation (26%) perceived by significant numbers and oversight (9%) far behind. Overall, one finds that congressmen perceive much stronger expectations for meeting the demands of the electoral arena than those of the institutional arena, as we assess the net expectations for congressional performance.[10]

This conclusion is confirmed when one asks the members about their most precious resource of all: "What are the *differences* between how you *actually* have to spend your time and what you would *ideally* like to do as a member of Congress?" By far the most frequent complaint, offered by

Table 2: Volunteered Public Views on Functions Expected of Congressman

	%
The legislative role	58
Attend all, as many sessions as possible; be there to vote on bills, legislation	10
Work on improving the economy; lower prices; stop inflation; create more jobs; reduce unemployment	10
Be knowledgable, well informed about the issues; study legislation, pending bills before he votes	9
Pass fair, good bills; have a good voting record; make sure the right laws are passed	8
Positions on the issues, e.g. welfare, crime, etc.	8
Be concerned with, try to pass legislation that is best for the entire country	5
Be active; stand up for what he believes; initiate programs; introduce new legislation	3
Be active on, head committees, subcommittees; be knowledgable about committee work	3
Balance the interests of his constituents with those of the country; back bills he believes in even if it's unpopular back home	2
The education and communication role	41
Keep in touch, contact with the people; visit his district; have meetings; know his constituents	17
Find out what the people need, want, think; send out polls, questionnaires	12
Use media, newsletters to keep people informed of what he's doing; explain issues, pending bills, what's going on in Washington	7
Be available; constituents should be able to visit or write and get a response; answer letters; encourage communication	5
The constituency service role: work to solve problems in his district; help the people; respond to issues, needs of our area	37
The representative role: represent the people, district; vote according to the wish of constituents, the majority	35
The personal character role	13
Be honest, fair, as truthful as possible; keep his promises; be a man of good character	10
Put the interest of government ahead of his own political career; stop playing politics; should not bow to pressure of lobbyists, sell and buy votes, etc.	3
The general competence role: know his job; do a good job; do the best he can	3
The oversight role: be aware of what is going on in government; know what the President is doing; oversee the Administration's policies	1
All other roles	6
Don't know	10

Total weighted N = (1518). Multiple responses possible.

Table 3: Volunteered Member Views on Functions Expected of Members

	%
The legislative role	87
To draft and introduce legislation	30
Committee work; to draft and introduce legislation in committee and subcommittee	19
To develop expertise, thorough knowledge in an area of specialization, in committee	19
To vote on legislation on the floor and in committee	16
To keep abreast of legislation; study and consider legislation; do legislative homework	15
To formulate solutions to national problems; formulate policy in the public interest	13
To carefully study problems; make judgments on the issues	12
All other specific legislative roles	4
The constituency service role	79
Ombudsman; constituency service; casework; helping constituents solve their problems	52
To act as an intermediary between the people and the federal bureaucracy	21
Insuring that the district secures public works, pork barrel projects	9
Aiding local officials and governments in dealing with the federal bureaucracy	6
Constituency service role too demanding; takes away time from more important concerns	3
The education and communication role	43
To educate and inform constituents about issues and legislation	25
To meet and interact with constituents; to listen to their concerns	12
To articulate positions and take the lead on issues	10
Ceremonial public, social role as a member of Congress	7
The representative role	26
To represent the district; represent constituents' interests	22
To be an advocate, spokesman for the people of the district	4
The political role: campaigning, politicking; party work and party leadership; getting reelected	*11*
The oversight role: to ensure that laws are administered properly, as the Congress intended	9
The institutional role: to deal with the executive branch, interest groups, other levels of government	7
The office management role: to supervise staff	*6*
To be everything: jack-of-all-trades	*6*
All other roles	*4*

Total weighted N = (146). Multiple responses possible.

50% of the members, is that constituent demands interfere with legislative and other congressional activity. In short, when asked to spontaneously define their priorities for congressional activities, voters and their representatives present markedly different preferences. And when asked how they reconcile these differences in their expenditure of time, members overwhelmingly voice the sentiment that their own personal prescriptions for House activity give way to the demands of the voters.

As a result, functions in the institutional arena of the House are performed less effectively than those in the electoral arena. In Table 4, one sees the members' evaluations of the House's performance of the functions volunteered as important earlier in the interview. Constituency service receives the highest rating: 42% of the House members consider their activity in this area "very effective," and another 35% regard it as "fairly effective." The rating drops to 13% "very effective" and 48% "fairly effective" for representation, while legislation is evaluated as "very effective" by 12% and "fairly effective" by only 39%. Oversight, however, is rated "very effective" by a mere 4% and "fairly effective" by only 18%, while 44% label it "not very effective." In sum: unless reinforced by electoral demand, congressional performance suffers.

Table 4: Member Ratings of Effectiveness of House Performance of Volunteered Roles House Should Play

Roles House Should Play	Very Effective %	Fairly Effective %	Only Somewhat Effective %	Not Very Effective %	Weighted Cases (N)
Ombudsman role	42	35	10	12	(35)
Representative role	13	48	35	4	(24)
Legislative role	12	39	35	14	(130)
Oversight role	4	18	33	44	(60)

Note: The number of cases varies because the question on effectiveness was only asked of respondents volunteering a given role as one that the House should play.

At this juncture, let us pause to consider the theoretical underpinnings of this performance pattern. The rational congressman seeks to maximize his position as an *individual* member of the House. As Olson (1965) has demonstrated, there are inadequate incentives for individuals to engage in organizational activity if both the responsibilities and the benefits are widely diffused throughout the membership. It is straightfoward to show that resource allocation in the House is a special instance of this problem.

When asked in the Harris survey to evaluate the job performance of Congress, the public responded with a resounding 65% negative rating, as opposed to only 22% positive. The reasons for these evaluations, presented in Table 5, indicate that Congress *as a whole* is judged for its performance on policy. The job rating for the respondent's own congressman, however, was 40% positive and 23% negative. Table 6 indicates that the members *as individuals* are evaluated in terms of their linkage with constituents.

The relevance of Olson is clear. Responsibility for policy performance is diffused and therefore deflected away from * individuals in the electoral arena. The expectation for meeting constituent demands, on the other hand, is highly focused on the individual congressman. The member thus feels constrained to allocate resources in the direction of constituency service, representation, and communication, the activities yielding the most salient public evaluations. The members as individuals are rather popular as a result, but policy performance suffers, and with it suffers the reputation of the House.

This effect can be studied in more detail by measuring the effect of response to demands for casework on member job ratings. Fiorina (1977a, 1977b) has speculated that the growing tangle of the federal bureaucracy has provided a fertile ground for congressmen to improve their standing with the electorate. A true test of the hypothesis would of course

Table 5: Volunteered Public Reasons for Performance Rating of Congress

	%
Positive evaluations	21
They've tried to help, do what they can; they can only do so much; it's a hard job	6
They are doing their work; passed a lot of bills	4
Passed many good bills that were later vetoed; weren't afraid to oppose the President, do what was best for the country	4
Their handling of Watergate, Nixon	3
They kept prices down, helped the conomy	2
They passed increases in Social Security, helped the elderly	1
They kept us out of war	1
They have done a lot about (a specific issue)	1
All other positive evaluations	5
Negative evaluations	73
Democratic Congress and Republican President couldn't get together, couldn't agree; party politics	10
Can't see that anything's changed; no signs of improvement; they haven't done anything	10
Congress opposed the President, wouldn't cooperate, stood in the way	9
They bicker, haggle, waste time; are to slow, too big, inefficient	9
Too much scandals, graft, kickbacks	7
They care only about themselves; don't work hard; don't do their job	6
Unemployment is rising; no action about jobs	6
They spend, waste money on the wrong things; never get results	6
Congress hasn't understood, acted on our problems correctly; poor program	6
Haven't done all they could; lots of problems they didn't deal with, e.g., energy, crime, etc.	6
Don't represent the people; represent themselves, special interests	4
President vetoed so many bills that were passed	2
Cleaning up scandals has diverted their attention from their work	2
They raised their own salaries	2
Lots of promises, talk, rhetoric, but they don't do anything	2
From what I read, hear	2
They give too much welfare	1
They're just trying to get reelected	1
They haven't helped the poor, old, underprivileged people	1
All other negative evaluations	8
All other evaluations	1
Hasn't affected my life one way or another; haven't paid attention	1
Don't know	5

Total weighted N = (1267). Multiple responses possible.

Table 6: Volunteered Public Reasons for Performance Rating of Member

	%
Positive evaluations	66
Represents his district well; works hard for the district	18
His contact; listens to you; is available; cares about his constituents and what they think	17
Has done a good job; is working hard; is well informed	12
Keeps you well informed; sends newsletters, bulletins	9
From what I've heard, read about him, his record	8
He keeps getting reelected	6
He stands for the good; he's fair, just, honest, conscientious, one of the better men in Congress	6
He has brought industry, jobs, government money, improvements to our area	5
He tries hard, but he's only one man	3
He works for the working man, labor	2
He has helped the elderly	1
He tries to help poor, lower income people	1
He has helped the farmer	1
All other positive evaluations	6
Negative evaluations	26
He hasn't done much; could do more; has done nothing outstanding	8
Nothing has improved; the situation hasn't improved	3
Haven't heard about him	3
All he did was vote the party line; played party politics	2
Hasn't done anything about unemployment	2
Doesn't keep in touch; doesn't keep us informed	2
Congress doesn't get much done	2
Bad relationship between the Congress and the President; too many vetoes	1
All other negative evaluations	8
All other evaluations	*1*
Don't know	9

Total weighted N = (913). Multiple responses possible.

require panel data on individuals both before and after the disposition of their cases. However, a surrogate analysis can be made by comparing the job ratings given incumbents by constituents who have requested casework with the evaluations of those who have never requested congressional assistance.

Casework has in fact touched the lives of a significant proportion of the public. Harris found in 1977 that 15% of American households had at one time "requested help or assistance from a member of Congress or his staff." More to the point, the assistance has generally been extremely successful. Of those requesting help, 63% were "very satisfied" with the help received. Even more remarkably, 66% of those requesting help *volunteered* that the congressman and his staff "did their best" or "could not have done more" to help.

With such a high success rate, it is not surprising to find an apparent improvement in member job ratings among casework alumni. Of those who have personally requested help, 76% evaluate their congressman favorably, compared to 62% (including 24% "excellent") among those whose families who have requested help, and an identical 62% (but only 19% "excellent") in households never involved in casework. The extremely weak relationship for those whose relatives received assistance may indicate that only the person *directly* affected by a case is likely to alter his evaluation of his congressman, although sampling error (N=66) may also be a factor. While not enormous in their magnitude, the results are significant at the .005 level and are presented in Table 7.

Even a mediocre performance does not seem to dispel the good feeling. Households "very satisfied" with the congressional assistance give their members a 76% positive rating, and similar effects can be seen in those "mostly" or "only somewhat satisfied" with the disposition of their cases. Only the small minority who are "not satisfied at all" give unfavorable ratings to their representative, by a 59% to 42% margin (see Table 8). Thus, two effects serve to expedite casework in congressional offices: the reward of increased approval for even a modicum of responsiveness and the fear of an unhappy constituent if a response is not forthcoming.[11]

Table 7: Performance Rating of Respondent's Congressman by
          Casework Requests

Performance Rating	Respondent Requested Assistance %	Other in Household Requested Assistance %	No One in Household Requested Assistance %
Excellent	32	24	19
Pretty good	44	38	43
Only fair	18	28	28
Poor	6	10	9
Weighted (N)	(112)	(66)	(766)

Somer's D = .125 (asymmetric with job rating dependent), $p < .005$.

To summarize, the allocation of resources to constituency
service is not only a good but a necessary investment for
members. The odds are strong that taking on a case will result
in a more favorable impression of the member, because of the
high probability of constituent satisfaction; while the fear of
possible constituent dissatisfaction provides an added incentive for performance. It seems likely that other forms of

Table 8: Performance Rating of Respondent's Congressman by
          Satisfaction with Casework Involving Respondent's
          Household

Performance Rating	Very Satisfied %	Mostly or Only Somewhat Satisfied %	Not At All Satisfied %
Excellent	35	38	7
Pretty good	43	46	35
Only fair	19	12	35
Poor	4	4	24
Weighted (N)	(108)	(26)	(38)

Somer's D = .279 (asymmetric with job rating dependent), $p < .001$.

constituent contact—such as answering mail on legislative issues, sending newsletters, and greeting visitors to Washington—are similarly likely to meet with voter favor. Saloma (1969) found that 80% of the members circulated newsletters and that an average of 17% of newsletter questionnaires were returned by constituents. Fully 66% of the public reported receiving mail, newsletters, or other communications from their congressman in the January 1977 Harris survey. The salience of casework to the individual probably makes it the most important member investment of resources in the electoral arena, but it is unlikely that these other forms of contact would be so widespread if they did not have some positive effect.

With the demand for constituent service so high, and relatively easy to satisfy, one might expect congressmen to not only increase their supply over time but to stimulate more demand as well. The scattered quantitative evidence seems to indicate an explosion of constituent service in recent years that is probably best explained by the hypothesis of demand stimulation. Johannes (cited in Commission on Administrative Review, 1977a, Vol. 2:41) estimates that the volume of casework has doubled in the last 10 years. The volume of mail entering and leaving the House tripled between 1969 and 1975, escalating from 14 million to 42 million pieces annually. In 1965, a George Gallup Survey found that 19% of the public had written to their congressman; by 1973, a Harris survey uncovered 33% who had contacted their representative.

As early as 1963, the congressmen Clapp (1964) interviewed were developing methods to stimulate correspondence. And Dexter (1969) notes that not only are the political benefits of casework important but the political costs are virtually nil. Serving as an ombudsman can never "lead to trouble, either with the congressman's colleagues in the Congress or elsewhere in politics, or from the voters in his constituency," for casework simply involves "doing something for somebody that does not demonstrably deprive somebody else of something" (p. 110). In other words, Pareto optimality lives. Casework is utterly costless in the electoral arena, hence its appeal. Its only cost is an opportunity cost—that of diverting resources out of the institutional arena. Next I will discuss the allocation of those resources.

THE ALLOCATION OF RESOURCES: MEMBER TIME

Thus far, we have seen how the demands faced by the congressman-as-entrepreneur in the electoral arena predominate over the desires of the congressman-as-decision-maker in the institutional arena. We have also presented evidence suggesting that meeting the demands of the public does indeed expand the congressman's "clientele" among the electorate. It is now time to examine the extent to which the electoral imperative determines the allocation of the member's resources of time and staff.

A member's use of his own time is a good place to start. As Fenno notes, "Time is at once what the member has least of and what he has most control over. When a congressman divides up his time, he decides by that act what kind of congressman he wants to be" (1977: 890-891). It would behoove us, therefore, to ascertain how much of a member's time is spent where, with whom, doing what. Unfortunately, such research is well nigh impossible in the district, where the congressman is constantly on the move. However, the two leading studies of congressional time use, those of Saloma (1969) and the Obey Commission in 1977 are useful as indicators of the priorities assigned to various member activities performed in Washington.

Both studies estimate that an average congressman's Washington work week is just shy of 60 hours long. It is startling to discover that not much more than half of a congressman's

Washington work week is spent on legislative activity. The Obey Commission found that only 38.6% (and Saloma 39.1%) of a member's Washington time is allotted to work on the floor and in committee. Saloma (1969) estimates that 64.6% of a member's Washington work week is devoted to legislative activity, broadly construed; while 27.6% is spent on constituency service and 7.8%, on education and publicity.

Other data permit a more complete assessment. In January 1977, the Commission on Administrative Review asked members to estimate how much time they spend on a variety of activities, as well as how important each of these activities should be. These data not only fine tune our knowledge of the conflicting incentives for performance as they are perceived by the members, enabling us to check the validity of the codes of the responses to the open-ended questions, but also permit an estimate of how members believe they do allocate their time resources.

Despite the importance of policy functions to the members, they feel that such activities are given insufficient time. Table 9 indicates that studying and doing basic research is rated very important by 73% of the members, but it is given a great deal of time by only 25%. The gap is almost as great for oversight (56% vs. 16%), floor work (64% vs. 30%), and mobilization on legislation (55% vs. 22%). However, one finds close to optimal expenditures of time on constituency-oriented activities. For example, getting back to the district is considered very important by 74% of the members and accorded a great deal of time by 67%, a much closer fit. A similar pattern holds for casework (58% vs. 35%), pork barrel grantsmanship (44% vs. 24%), and explaining government activities to the public (53% vs. 32%). Once again, the electoral imperative wins out.

Are congressmen doomed to follow the dictates of the voters as to how they can spend their own time? It might be

Table 9: Member Views on Actual vs. Ideal Priorities for Time Expenditure

Member Activities	Actually Spend Great Deal of Time %	Should Be Considered Very Important %
Getting back to your district to stay in touch with your constituents	67	74
Working in subcommittees to develop legislation	60	82
Working in full committees to develop legislation	46	71
Helping people in your district who have personal problems with the government	35	58
Taking the time to explain to citizens what their government is doing to solve important problems and why	32	53
Debating and voting on legislation on the floor of the House	30	64
Giving speeches and personal appearances to talk to interested groups about legislative matters before the Congress	25	32
Studying and doing basic research on proposed legislation	25	73
Making sure your district gets its fair share of government money and projects	24	44
Working informally with other members to build support for legislation about which you are personally concerned	22	55
Taking the time to gain a first-hand knowledge of foreign affairs	16	44
Staying in touch with local government officials in your district	16	26
Working in committee or subcommittee on oversight activities	16	56
Managing and administering your office	15	29
Meeting personally with constituents when they come to Washington	13	35
Sending newsletters about the activities of Congress to people in your district	10	35
Keeping track of the way government agencies are administering laws passed by the Congress	9	53

Minimum weighted N = (144).

useful at this juncture to recall our adaptation of Fiorina's resource allocation model: if a congressman's seat is safe, he can then divert resources out of the electoral arena and into the institutional arena, in order to satisfy his own desires. Unfortunately, the available data do not contain a measure of district marginality. This may not be much of a flaw, because it is often found that a member's perception of electoral safety is unrelated to any objective measure.[12] However, it is possible to break down the sample by seniority level. Because longevity ordinarily implies a safe seat, one would expect that the more senior the member, the more time the member could afford to spend on personal goals, which for most members would involve participating in legislative activity.

Table 10 suggests that members do indeed enjoy more freedom to pursue policy activities as they attain seniority. Senior members can afford to spend more time on floor work, mobilization, and oversight than their junior colleagues. Consequently, they are more successful in actualizing their priorities for time expenditure. Curiously, however, the closing of the gap between actual and ideal priorities does not begin to appear until about the sixth term in office, although evidence of electoral safety is often quite persuasive to political scientists as early as the second or third term (Cover and Mayhew, 1977). It may be that subjective safety lags a few years behind objective safety. But it is important to remember that seniority implies more than just electoral safety. It also brings added responsibilities in its wake, and this change obviously necessitates revisions in time expenditure. Either explanation is consistent with the directional change observed, and there is probably considerable validity to both.

Indeed, it is even possible to integrate both explanations in a more inclusive, if perhaps less rigorous, purposive model. The emoluments of institutional authority—chairmanships, committee staff, power, and prestige—are granted only to those who satisfy their constituencies well enough to survive several election campaigns. The responsibilities of power certainly alter the senior congressman's schedule, but it is the desire to *possess* these responsibilities, and to *live* this schedule, which motivates the young member to cultivate a satisfied core constituency—for the biennial war of attrition insures that the electoral imperative has been honored in the early stages of an emerging congressional leader's career.

THE ALLOCATION OF RESOURCES: MEMBER STAFF

A congressman's time is a precious resource; it is also, as with all mortals, finite. Because the demand for the congressman's time has tended to be well in excess of supply, the tendency has been to increase the supply of the next best thing: surrogate congressmen or, more properly, congressional staff. It is the staff which handles most of the mail, does most of the research, and is empowered to invoke the congressman's name with regard to virtually any matter other than signing payroll vouchers and voting in committee and on the floor.

Congressional staff come in two varieties: committee and personal. Because access to committee staff is generally restricted to committee and subcommittee chairmen, we shall limit our focus to the staff assigned directly to member offices. The activities of personal office staff tend to supplement, rather than mirror, those of the member. Priorities come into play: whatever is not important enough to require the member's attention is left for the staff to handle. Thus, not only should the performance of functions by the staff be examined but the division of functions between member and staff can be instructive as well.

The best treatment of the latter question is that of Saloma. As noted earlier, he found 64.6% of a member's time in 1965 devoted to legislative activity and the remaining 35.4% spent on constituency service, education, and publicity. The con-

Table 10: Member Views on Actual vs. Ideal Priorities for Time Expenditure on Selected Member Activities, Controlling for Tenure

Member Activities	2 Terms		3 to 5 Terms		6 or More Terms	
	Should Be Very Important %	Spend Great Deal of Time %	Should Be Very Important %	Spend Great Deal of Time %	Should Be Very Important %	Spend Great Deal of Time %
Studying and doing basic research on proposed legislation	78	24	72	18	76	32
Debating and voting on legislation on the floor of the House	60	27	75	22	61	40
Working in committee or subcommittee on oversight activities	62	11	54	4	57	30
Working informally with other members to build support for legislation about which you are personally concerned	62	15	56	24	51	25
Weighted N	(38)		(50)		(58)	

trast with the staff workload is extraordinary: in the House offices surveyed by Saloma, personal staff spent only 14.3% of their time on legislative support, with fully 75.8% assigned to constituency service, education, and publicity. Saloma concludes,

> [T]he congressman's staff, functioning as an extension of the congressman, relieves much of his burden relating to his constituency. . . . The congressman uses his staff to reduce his non-legislative work burden (or conversely to increase constituency service), and to screen himself from excessive interruptions from constituents and the public [1969: 187].

Given the autocratic control structure of the typical Capitol Hill office, the inference to be drawn is that this division of function occurs because the members *prefer* it this way. That is, they prefer legislating to signing calendars, meeting with Boy Scouts, giving tours of the Capitol, and the other trivialities with which constituents expect to be indulged.

An updating of Saloma's findings was attempted by the Commission on Administrative Review in June 1977. The

Table 11: Functional Allocation of Member Office Staff as Estimated by Administrative Assistants

Function	Mean Office Staff Slots #
Casework	4.2
Clerical	3.1
Legislative research	2.2
Office supervision	2.2
Legislative mail	1.4
Communications	1.3
Personal secretary	1.2
Other	0.2
Total	15.7

Weighted N = (143)

commission asked administrative assistants in member offices to list the number of people performing a given function in their office. The results are presented in Table 11 and confirm the impression that staff time is overwhelmingly taken up by the demand for constituency service. Although the data are calculated according to staff slots rather than work hours, the estimate that 13.9% of staff resources are devoted to legislative support is virtually identical to the 14.3% figure cited by Saloma. The figures for casework (26.9% and 24.7%, respectively) are also very similar.

In some ways, the most intriguing finding concerns the division of staff resources between the Washington and district offices. Of the 15.7 people employed in the average House office, 9.5 are situated on Capitol Hill and 6.2 are working in the field. Not surprisingly, virtually all of the district-based personnel are involved in some aspect of constituency service: 3.0 perform casework, 1.2 are clerical staff, 0.9 manage the office, and 0.6 specialize in communications (that is, press and field representative work).

Recalling my adaptation of Fiorina's model, one would expect that a senior member, happily esconced in a safe seat, would be likely to shift resources from constituency service to legislation and from the district to the Washington office, as a policy-making focus becomes more feasible. We can consider this a "life cycle" model of resource allocation. On the other hand, if the acquisition of committee staff is the more important aspect of seniority, then one would expect that the added legislative workload concomitant with institutional responsibilities could be passed on to the committee staff, with little or no disruption in the existing staff operation within the member's office. It should be noted at this point that committee chairmen were excluded from the June 1977 sample, thereby excluding the most interesting but also the most atypical cases from the population of senior members.

It should also be noted that the total number of staff slots within an office varies with tenure. The mean staff allotment peaks at 16.6 (out of an authorized limit of 18) among sophomore members, declining to a trough of 15.0 among those with six or more terms of service. The percentage allocation of resources within categories of offices will therefore be employed as an indicator in the remainder of the paper. [13]

Upon recalculating the data, one's first impression is that a "life cycle" model of resource allocation is confirmed. The percentage of staff assigned to the district office declines monotonically with tenure level, from 45% among freshmen members to 36% among those serving six terms or more. The relationship is not overly strong, suggesting adjustment along the margins rather than a wholesale overhaul of staff assignments, but it is unmistakably in the predicted direction. Moreover, one finds a similar monotonic decline in caseworkers, from 30% of staff among the most junior members to 23% among the most senior.

Unfortunately, the apparent trend conceals more than it illuminates. For one thing, the drift away from casework does not seem to result in an increase in legislative research—since the peak in legislative support allocation (15%) is reached among *sophomore* members. One might argue that policy-oriented Democrats can turn to committee and subcommittee staffs for such support after their second terms. However, there is no difference attributable to party in the allocation of personal staff to legislative activity; among members with three to five terms of service, the figure is 14% for Democrats and 13% for Republicans, while among those with six or more terms of tenure the proportion is an identical 14% for members of both parties. The best explanation is probably that an optimal mix of staff activities is achieved early in the "life cycle" of a congressional office and undergoes little adjustment thereafter. Access to committee and subcommittee staff permits a dramatic expansion into policy activities and supplements the constituency service orientation predominant among the personal office staff of senior Democrats.

Let me summarize my extension of Fiorina's model to congressional resource allocation. The hypothesized trade-off between electoral and institutional activities clearly occurs in the increasing allocation of a member's time to personally satisfying decision-making responsibilities as seniority is attained. These responsibilities, and hence the trade-off, are sought after by individuals and enforced by the institution; regardless of which incentive is more important, the trade-off in time expenditure is quite real, because the resource of a member's time is fixed and finite.

However, no trade-off is observed in the allocation of a member's personal staff, because none is necessary. An increase in legislative support is made possible through obtaining access to a whole new source of such support with a rise in tenure: committee and subcommittee staff. In other words, the resource of staff support is not fixed over time. As a result, it is possible for a senior member, and especially a senior Democrat, to enjoy greater overall staff support on legislation than his junior colleagues without seriously altering the proportion of staff assigned to district-oriented activities in his personal office. Therefore the nature of the resource in question—that is, whether it is fixed or amenable to supplementation—determines whether a trade-off of resources is necessary between the electoral and institutional arenas.

To the extent that a member has a taste for legislative activity in the institutional arena is reflected in the member's personal allocation of time. The composition of the member's personal staff, which is basically an appendage used to service constituent demands, is unlikely to change much over time because the nature of the demands generated by a given constituency is unlikely to change much over time. It is the congressman who is free, up to a point, to pursue power and policy making in the House. The staff must be content to perform the more mundane services that keep him there.

CONCLUSION

A model delimiting electoral and institutional arenas of performance can tell us much about the workings of the House. As we have seen, the members' prescriptions for institutional activity are dominated by the policy adoption and implementation functions of legislation and oversight. The demands of the public for more district-oriented activities introduce a conflicting set of incentives. In allocating the resources of personal time and staff, the members generally resolve this conflict in favor of the demands of the electorate. The result is better congressional performance on constituency service and representation than on legislation and oversight.

This framework also enables one to gain a perspective on some of the changes in congressional behavior that have been so apparent during the contemporary period. Politicians and political analysts alike have generally exhibited a single-minded concern with the legislative aspects of representation, to the exclusion of other functions. This has naturally implied a concentration on the structures which express, aggregate, and resolve conflicting opinions on the great issues of the day. These structures, operating both in the electorate and in the government, have come to be known as parties.

In recent years, legislators have begun to get out of the business of legislating. In economic parlance, they have begun to diversify. The reason is simple: there are incentives for the supply of services other than legislative. Congressional entrepreneurs have become convinced of something that courthouse politicians and ward heelers have known for years—

that for most people, most of the time, politics means something other than passing laws. The electorate is most concerned with the things that hit closest to home. By heeding the widespread demand for constituency service, members can improve their positions in the electoral arena. By stimulating the demand for these services, members can strengthen their positions even more.

The result is the phenomenon of the vanishing marginals (Mayhew, 1974). As legislative activity is increasingly overshadowed by constituency service in the public eye, parties as organizations are becoming increasingly irrelevant as forces in the electoral arena. An incumbent who provides the right mix of services acquires a recognizable brand name that is simply more salient to the voters. If the congressman's activities are in line with the district's demand, the member stays in office; if not, the member's competitive position erodes until a more suitable mix is promised and delivered by the member or by an opposing candidate. Like all competitive mechanisms, this evolution by attrition is sloppy and imperfect, yet it is nonetheless animated by an innate logic of its own.

Parties may be reliable purveyors of legislation, but they are next to useless as participants in other congressional activities. Parties do not find lost Social Security checks or bring home dams. Congressmen do. It is that simple. Parties organize the houses of Congress, structure the committees, and provide cues on legislation. These functions are essential in the institutional arena—*in Washington*. They are peripheral to all but a handful of political activists in a congressional district. But when a federal contract creates jobs or a veteran's disability check fails to arrive, the impact of the government is stark and immediate. People take notice of how it affects them and who deserves the praise for helping them out—or the blame for failing to do so.

Individuals, not parties, are the relevant actors in the nonlegislative realm. Politicians and voters have known this instinctively for years; political scientists are only beginning to catch on. It will be a formidable task of future research to comprehend these dynamics and to contribute to understanding the clashing incentives for performance in the two arenas of Congress.

NOTES

1. Fenno (1973: xvii) has ruminated at some length on this change in his approach, and his comments are worth noting: "What struck me most forcefully in observing the House Appropriations Committee was the degree to which it was a self-contained social system. . . . Having observed six committees, however, I find the conceptualization of the social systems literature less appealing as a framework for description. All committees are not pre-eminently social systems. All committees do not have an easily differentiable set of roles. In both respects, Appropriations lies at one end of a spectrum—or so it now appears. . . . In comparative perspective, the member contribution seems both large and distinctive. The point comes through very strongly in my interviews; and I have made goal seeking by the members a keystone of this analysis. The resulting conceptual framework is, therefore, somewhat more individualistic than the previous one."

2. Mayhew (1974: 110-111) explains the manner and extent of these activities as "the products of an interplay between credit-claiming and position-taking impulsions," which seems less compelling than Fenno's notion of goals regarding policy and congressional influence independent of electoral considerations. This point is also one of the central criticisms levelled against Mayhew (in Rogowski, 1978: 314-316).

3. Many observers have commented upon this sorting process. Former Congressman Clem Miller (1962: 106) notes, "While congressmen are quite ordinary in general outline, their practice of the political art has made them knowledgeable in assessing one another. Their instincts, sharpened by this conflict of the personal and the impersonal, enable them to characterize each other to the finest hair. Thus, each congressman is given his own little pigeonhole, with all his strengths and weaknesses, foibles and tricks, duly noted for use on proper occasions. Power, then, is the respect which accrues and adheres to those individuals who are best able to stand this daily etching process." And as

Fenno (1965: 71) records, "House members believe there is no better judge of a man's worth than the institutional judgment of the House. The assessment and reassessment of one's colleagues—the calculation of each member's 'Dow Jones average'—goes on without end."

4. The two surveys of House offices made use of a multistage stratified quota sample because a strict random probability sample was not feasible. For this reason, the usual sampling statistics are not applicable to the data. Despite the quota basis of the sample, it appears to be highly representative of the House on such characteristics as tenure, party, region, and the propensity to support House reform efforts, as measured by roll call voting on the two packages of legislation submitted to the House by the Commission on Administrative Review. A detailed description of the Commission's sampling methodology can be found in Commission on Administrative Review (1977b, Vol. 2: 771-790).

5. This conclusion is markedly different from that of Davidson (1970: 666), who found that "an impressive degree of congruence exists in the role orientations of incumbent representatives and their clientele citizens." Because of differences in both the interview schedules and the coding methodologies employed, the studies are not directly comparable. The Davidson study produced a single set of codes on member roles, which summarized member responses to questions tapping role prescriptions for both the individual member and the institution of the House (see Davidson, 1969: 78). The Commission's analysts, on the other hand, built coding categories separately for the member responses to questions on institutional role prescriptions and member role expectations, permitting a comparison of these two dimensions. (For a description of the coding methodology employed, see Commission on Administrative Review, 1977b, Vol. 2: 798-801.) The conflict of expectations, which is so evident in the Commission's 1977 data, has probably intensified since the time of the Davidson study, due to an escalation in both the legislative workload and the volume of constituency service activities. However, this tension has probably always been present to some extent due to the inherent nature of the congressman's job.

6. This relationship remains even when controls are applied for socioeconomic status of the respondent. It is conceivable that those who contact a representative are likely to be favorably disposed toward the representative to begin with; in other words, a favorable job rating may stimulate casework, rather than casework improving a member's job rating. Unfortunately, there is no way to test this proposition without panel data.

7. In making these calculations, member offices were first divided into categories by party and tenure of the members. The number of staff slots associated with a given function was then summed for *all* of the offices in a given party-by-tenure category. This figure was then divided by the sum of all staff slots in those offices to arrive at a percentage allocation figure within each office category. While this indicator has the disadvantage of ignoring differences among offices in the total number of staff slots, it has the enormous advantage of being sensitive to small differences in allocation patterns, because the number of employees is a larger data base than the number of offices in a given office category (cf. Fenno, 1977: 894-897).

REFERENCES

CAVANAGH, T.E. (1979) "The Two Arenas of Congress," in J. Cooper and G.C. Mackenzie (ed.) Congress at Work. Austin: Univ. of Texas Press.

CLAPP, C.L. (1964) The Congressman: His Work as He Sees It. Garden City: Anchor.

Commission on Administrative Review (1977a) Administrative Reorganization and Legislative Management. Washington, DC: U.S. Government Printing Office.

――― (1977b) Final Report of the Commission on Administrative Review. Washington, DC: U.S. Government Printing Office.

――― (1977c) Scheduling the Work of the House. Washington, DC: U.S. Government Printing Office.

COVER, A.D. and D.R. MAYHEW (1977) "Congressional dynamics and the decline of competitive congressional elections," in L.C. Dodd and B.I. Oppenheimer (eds.) Congress Reconsidered. New York: Praeger.

DAVIDSON, R.H. (1969) The Role of the Congressman. New York: Pegasus.

――― (1970) "Public Prescriptions for the Job of Congressman." Midwest Journal of Political Science 14, 4 (November): 648-666.

――― (1977a) "Our changing Congress: The inside (and outside) story." Presented at the Conference on Congress and the Presidency (November).

――― (1977b) "Our two Congresses: Where have they been? Where are they going?" Presented at the convention of the Southern Political Science Association (November).

DEXTER, L.A. (1969) The Sociology and Politics of Congress. Chicago: Rand McNally.

DOWNS, A. (1957) An Economic Theory of Democracy. New York: Harper and Row.

FENNO, R.F. (1965) "The Internal Distribution of Influence: The House," in D.B. Truman (ed.) The Congress and America's Future. Englewood Cliffs, NJ: Prentice-Hall.

——— (1966) The Power of the Purse: Appropriations Politics in Congress. Boston: Little, Brown.

——— (1973) Congressmen in Committees. Boston: Little, Brown.

——— (1975) "If, as Ralph Nader Says, Congress is 'the Broken Branch,' How Come We Love Our Congressmen So Much?" in N.J. Ornstein (ed.) Congress in Change: Evolution and Reform. New York: Praeger.

——— (1977) "U.S. House Members in Their Constituencies: An Exploration." American Political Science Review 71, 3 (September): 883-917.

——— (1978) Home Style: House Members and Their Districts. Boston: Little, Brown.

FIORINA, M.P. (1974) Representatives, Roll Calls, and Constituencies. Lexington: D.C. Heath.

——— (1977) Congress: Keystone of the Washington Establishment. New Haven: Yale Univ. Press.

HUITT, R.K. (1954) "The Congressional Committee: A Case Study." American Political Science Review 48, 2 (June): 340-365.

——— (1957) "The Morse Committee Assignment Controversy: A Study in Senate Norms." Amer. Pol. Sci. Rev. 51, 2 (June): 313-329.

LOWI, T.J. (1964) "American Business, Public Policy, Case Studies, and Political Theory." World Politics 16, 3 (July): 677-715.

MATTHEWS, D.R. (1960) U.S. Senators and Their World. New York: Random House.

MAYHEW, D.R. (1974) Congress: The Electoral Connection. New Haven: Yale Univ. Press.

MILLER, C. (1962) Member of the House: Letters of a Congressman. New York: Charles Scribner's Sons.

OLSON, M. (1965) The Logic of Collective Action. Cambridge: Harvard Univ. Press.

RIKER, W.H. (1962) The Theory of Political Coalitions. New Haven: Yale Univ. Press.

ROGOWSKI, R. (1978) "Rationalist Theories of Politics: A Midterm Report." World Politics 30, 1 (January): 296-323.

SALOMA, J.S. (1969) Congress and the New Politics. Boston: Little, Brown.

SCHER, S. (1960) "Congressional Committee Members as Independent Agency Overseers: A Case Study." American Political Science Review 54, 4 (December): 911-920.

——— (1963) "Conditions for Legislative Control." Journal of Politics 25, 3 (August): 526-551.

WAHLKE, J.C., et al. (1962) The Legislative System: Explorations in Legislative Behavior. New York: John Wiley.

WEISBERG, H.F. (1977) "Congressional Elections as Random Terror." Presented at the convention of the American Political Science Association (September).

YOUNG, R. (1958) The American Congress. New York: Harper and Row.

THE ROLE OF INSTITUTIONAL STRUCTURE IN THE CREATION OF POLICY EQUILIBRIUM

KENNETH A. SHEPSLE

Washington University

The past 20 years have witnessed an impressive flowering of formal, deductive theory in political science. Although not universal, many students in political science today are exposed to Arrow's (1963) Impossibility Theorem, von Neumann and Morgenstern's (1964) theory of games, Riker's (1962) size principle, Olson's (1965) logic of collective action, Buchanan and Tullock's (1962) theory of constitutional choice, Black's (1958) single-peakedness theorem, and Downs's (1957) spatial theory of party competition, to name but a few of the high points in this research program (a survey of which is found in Riker and Ordeshook (1973)). During this same period, students of political institutions have begun moving beyond the crude behavioralism that had previously dominated their empirical research and, while they have not reverted to detailed historical studies of institutional development or to descriptions of institutional minutiae—a style of scholarship typical in an earlier era—they have begun to blend a concern with motives and personal characteristics of institutional actors, on the one hand, and a concern with institutional structure and process, on the other.[1] It is ironic, then, that much of the recent formal political theory had proceeded in virtual ignorance of this new institutional scholarship while institutional scholars have failed to integrate and exploit the theoretical leverage of formal models of political phenomena.[2] That this is both an unhappy and an unnecessary state of affairs is the message of this paper.

In the first section the general argument of the paper is spelled out and a model of institutional choice described. The second section focuses on three recent studies—Isaac and Plott (1978), Romer and Rosenthal (1977), and Mackay and Weaver (1978—that illustrate the prospects for formal political models rich in institutional detail. In the third and fourth sections a general model of institutional choice is formalized and some implications developed. In the fifth section specific attention is given to one important institutional phenomenon—that of institutional monitoring of its own activities. In particular, this takes the form of amendment procedures in legislative institutions.

MOTIVATION

The underlying structure of most formal models in political science is highly atomistic and institutionally sparse. Normally such models are variants of a game-theoretic or social choice-theoretic approach in which:

(1) Individuals are represented by "well-behaved" preferences (reflexive, complete, transitive) and are assumed to pursue the objectives represented in their preferences rationally.

(2) Decisive coalitions are identified as those sets of actors who, by some form of cooperation, collusion or jointly correlated behav-

ior, are empowered under the rules of aggregation to make choices in behalf of the institution.

(3) The equilibria of the process are among those alternatives that, in some sense, are supported by some decisive coalition or, somewhat weaker, are not dominated by any other alternative.

The principal emphasis on individual rationality, decisive coalitions of actors, and an induced dominance relation among choice alternatives is normally not supplemented by other aspects of institutional arrangements. Many institutional aspects and practices, including agenda construction,[3] division-of-labor arrangements, jurisdictions, resource distinctions, and so on remain implicit in the construction of decisive sets and dominance relations. It is, however, often the case that variations in precisely these kinds of institutional variables distinguish institutions from one another structurally, differentiate policy processes, and determine policy outcomes.

In this paper institutional properties and their policy consequences are given more prominence. In particular, I focus on three aspects of organization: a division-of-labor arrangement called a *committee system,* a specialization-of-labor system called a *jurisdictional arrangement,* and a monitoring mechanism called an *amendment control rule.* The conceptual language has a legislative flavor but, in fact, the concepts are broadly applicable to diverse organizational forms possessing a modicum of decentralization in tasks and authority.[4] With this conceptual apparatus I seek to demonstrate the ways institutional arrangements may conspire with individual preferences to produce structure-induced policy equilibria.

To provide a base line against which to appraise the more institutionally rich models reviewed in the next section and the one offered in the third section, I devote the remainder of this section to a brief description and critique of the *simple game.* The theory of simple games (see Bloomfield and Wilson, 1972, and Shapley and Shubik, 1973) which underlies many political models, is described by four axioms. Notationally, let $N = [1,2,\ldots,n]$ be the set of players and $P(N) = [A,B,C,\ldots]$ be the collection of subsets of N, called coalitions, blocs, factions, or alliances among the players in N. The axioms are:

(1) Every coalition is either winning or losing.
(2) The empty set, ϕ, is losing.
(3) The all-player set, N, is winning.
(4) No losing set contains a winning set, that is, if C is losing and $B < C$, then B is losing.

If, in addition, the following axiom is satisfied:

(5) The complement of any winning set is losing, that is, if C is winning, then N-C is losing.

then the game is said to be *proper.* Additionally, if

(6) The complement of a losing set is winning, that is, if C is losing, then N-C is winning.

then the game is said to be *strong.* Proper games, in effect, are those in which a coalition and its complement are not simultaneously winning, while strong games are those in which a coalition and its complement are not simultaneously losing (as when two nonwinning coalitions block one another). Games satisfying Axioms 1-6 are said to be *decisive simple games,* and their winning coalitions are called *decisive sets.*

This simple underlying power structure induces a *dominance relation* on the set X of alternatives:

For any alternatives $x,y \in X$, $xDy \leftrightarrow$ there exists a coalition $C \in P(N)$ with C decisive and $x \underset{i}{>} y$ for all $i \in C$ (where $\underset{i}{>}$ is the preference relation for the ith player.

That is, x dominates y if and only if a coalition deemed decisive by the rules unamimously prefers x to y. For decisive simple games with players all of whom have strict preferences, the dominance relation is complete in the sense that, for any two alternatives $x,y \in X$, either xDy or yDx. A decisive simple game, then, has two important properties:

(1) All pairs of alternatives are related by the induced dominance relation
(2) Decisiveness is a property of a coalition so that if C is decisive as between $x,y \in X$, then it is also decisive as between $u,v \in X$.

I believe that both of these properties are inaccurate as statements of social facts about most political institutions and, consequently, that the simple game is an inappropriate model of most institutional processes. The first property prohibits the outcome "not xDy and not yDx," yet institutions typically have agenda formation rules that prohibit certain comparisons, for example, rule of germaneness. The second property states that a winning coalition is a winning coalition is a winning coalition. Yet any institution with a division- and specialization-of-labor normally delimits jurisdictional domains in which some coalitions, for example, those that contain a majority of a relevant committee, but not others are decisive, and those decisive coalitions do not remain decisive in other jurisdictional domains.

These properties (and their inapplicability to many institutional settings) are conveniently illustrated by an *effectiveness form*. An effectiveness form is a correspondence associating with each coalition $C \in P(N)$ the set of alternatives in X for which it is effective if the members of C are in agreement. For the general simple game, the effectiveness form is given by

$$E(C) = \begin{array}{ll} \phi & \text{if } C \in L \\ X & \text{if } C \in W \end{array} \qquad [1]$$

where L and W are the collections of losing and winning coalitions, respectively. For the simple majority game, for example, Equation 1 specializes to:

$$E(C) = \begin{array}{l} \phi \;\; \text{if} \mid C \mid < \frac{n}{2} \\ X \;\; \text{if} \mid C \mid > \frac{n}{2} \end{array} \qquad [2]$$

where $\mid C \mid$ is the number of players in C and n is the cardinality of N. As Equations 1 and 2 suggest, all coalitions are either winning or losing, and a winning coalition is effective for any alternative, while a losing coalition is effective for none.

I argue that few institutional processes are adequately characterized by Equations 1 or 2. Rarely is a coalition within an institution either universally effective or universally ineffective; rarely is every alternative in the range of some coalition's effectiveness. These points have recently been illustrated in three studies—Isaac and Plott (1978), Romer and Rosenthal (forthcoming), and Mackay and Weaver (1978)—which I now examine.

A TALE OF THREE STUDIES

ISAAC-PLOTT

Isaac and Plott have designed a series of experiments to study majority rule decision-making institutions. The structure of these experiments include the following factors:

(1) The experimental group consists of three players, N= [1,2,3]
(2) Their task is to choose an outcome from the set X = [A,B,C,D,E,-F,G,H,I,J]
(3) Each $i \in N$ has preferences over X induced by a monetary pay off schedule displayed in Table 1.
(4) The decision rule is a variation of simple majority rule—Equation 2 above.

Table 1: Incentive Charts*

	1		2		3
B	26.00	F	33.00	E	21.20
G	22.60	E	26.40	F	18.00
J	19.40	I	20.60	H	15.20
A	16.40	D	15.60	J	12.40
H	13.60	H	11.40	D	9.75
C	11.00	C	8.00	I	7.40
D	8.60	G	5.40	B	5.15
I	6.40	A	3.60	G	3.15
E	4.40	J	2.60	A	2.40
F	2.60	B	2.40	C	1.00

*payoffs in dollars

During the play of the games, players could communicate ordinal information to one another (for example, "I like J better than C"), but could not talk about the amount they would win and could not discuss side payments (positive inducements or threats).

So far the description is that of a three person majority rule game in which Equation 2 becomes

$$E(\phi) = E(1) = E(2) = E(3) = \phi$$
$$E(12) = E(13) = E(23) = E(123) = X. \qquad [3]$$

The dominance relation induced by all-powerful majority coalitions and individual preferences given in Table 1 determines a Condarcet winner—alternative E dominates alternative F via the coalition [1,3] and dominates all other alternatives via the coalition [2,3]. In the experimental trials, the group ended up at E or "close" to it on most occasions.

What is of special relevance to this discussion is two additional experimental series run by Isaac and Plott. In these experiments two important institutional alterations of the simple majority rule game were examined. One of the individuals—Mr. 1—was arbitrarily designated the *convener* and one of the alternatives–D–was arbitrarily designated the status quo. The convener was given the monopoly power to suggest changes in the status quo. These suggestions could be voted up or down by a simple majority, *but they could not be amended.* The process continued until either:

(1) a majority approved one of the convener's proposals,
(2) the convener declared the meeting adjourned, in which case D was the outcome, or
(3) the two nonconveners declared the meeting adjourned (for lack of a quorum), in which case D was the outcome.

The effectiveness form for this game is no longer Equation 3 but rather

$$E(\phi) = E(2) = E(3) = \phi$$
$$E(1) = E(23) = D$$
$$E(12) = E(13) = E(123) = X. \qquad [4]$$

Alternative E is still the Condorcet winner, but because D ⪰ E (see Table 1), the convener will never propose E. The dominance relation among the elements of X differs under Equations 3 and 4. The unique undominated element under Equation 3 is alternative H. And, experimentally, alternative H was the outcome on every occasion.

A second alteration allowed the convener to propose *only one* change in the status quo. If a majority approved, the proposal was declared the winner; otherwise D obtained. Although it was a procedural change, it did *not* change the effectiveness form (Equation 4) or the dominance relation it induces. H is still the unique undominated outcome and, once again, each experimental trial produced H, underscoring the fact that some institutional "reforms" may only be cosmetic.

The Isaac-Plott experiments are of interest here because they demonstrated one consequence of taking the simple game (Equation 3) and altering it by introducing a division of labor. Not all coalitions are equally powerful under Equation 3. Player 1, the convener is more powerful than the others, though constrained by unanimous opposition. Thus, the game is no longer simple. Also, given the specialized task of the convener, not all alternatives are comparable. Alternative E, the Condorcet winner, will never appear on the agenda. Thus, alternative H is undominated not because it can defeat all possible alternatives (as is required in decisive simple games), but rather because it can defeat all of a restricted set of alternatives (those alternatives the convener prefers to the status quo, D).

ROMER-ROSENTHAL

In a somewhat more substantive context than Isaac and Plott, Romer and Rosenthal (forthcoming) explore a collective decision-making situation in which majority rule prevails but a specific individual or group—called the *agenda setter*—puts forth the alternatives to the status quo which are voted upon. Their paper is directed toward collective expenditure decisions in which a "high-demand" group dominates the agenda setting, as may be the case when

(1) a school board proposes a tax and expenditure package which must be approved by voters; if it fails, a status quo tax and expenditure arrangement prevails or
(2) a legislative committee, consisting of legislators who represent "high demand" districts and/or are spokesmen for an administrative agency, propose an authorization or appropriation which may not be amended by the legislature; it either passes or fails.[5]

As Romer and Rosenthal note (forthcoming):

By facing the voters with a "take it or leave it" choice, the setter exercises a threat over the voters. The worse the status quo [to the voters], the greater this threat and, consequently, the greater the gain to the setter from being able to propose the alternative.

Two features of their inquiry should be emphasized. First, their agenda setter, as the Isaac-Plott convener, is a *monopoly* provider of alterations in the status quo. Thus, as in the Isaac-Plott study, the simple game formulation is no longer appropriate. Any majority is effective for the status quo, but only majorities containing the agenda setter are effective for changes in the status quo. Thus, the dominance relation among alternatives takes account of the monopoly status of the agenda setter. Second, Romer and Rosenthal (and Isaac and Plott as well) give their agenda setter *exclusive* control of the agenda, thereby permitting monopoly rents to be earned. In a context of competing agenda setters—as is typically assumed in models of electoral competition—those rents are competed away. The monopoly model and the competitive model, as shall be seen below, are the extreme versions of a phenomenon I call *monitoring.* The former allows the "parent body" little control over its agenda setter, while the latter mitigates to a considerable extent the power of agenda formulation.

MACKAY-WEAVER

Mackay and Weaver (1978), as Romer and Rosenthal, are concerned with agenda monopoly by public bureaus. In the several models they construct,

> the source of monopoly power in bureaus is shown to derive from political failure in the agenda formation process; in particular, from an undersupply of competing proposals. This failure can result from several sources: a free-rider problem among citizen-voters in putting forth costly proposals, a failure of the legislative review process, or significant barriers to entry into political markets. In each case, this political failure establishes the potential for monopoly power by allowing bureaus a degree of control over the formation of the agenda [Mackay and Weaver, 1978: 141].

They examine several different kinds of monopoly practice including all-or-nothing offers, benefit and tax share discrimination, and commodity bundling.

Theirs is an important paper not only because they examine a range of potential practices in which an agenda setter/convener can engage but also because they exploit a key insight about the agenda formation process. They note that there are two essential aspects of agenda formation—access to the agenda and scope of the agenda. The first concerns who has access to the agenda. In the model I propose in the next section, the *rules* of the institution determine who has access. Mackay and Weaver, however, treat a wider set of institutional phenomena in which *incentives,* as well as rules, play a significant role. A citizen, for example, may have *access* to the agenda in proposing, say, a school expenditure and tax plan, but have little *incentive* to exercise his option to engage in this relatively costly form of participation. Thus, a school board, though not a de jure monopoly provider of proposals, may well be a de facto monopolist owing to the free-rider phenomenon. The second aspect of the agenda formation process to which Mackay and Weaver refer—scope of the agenda—concerns the range of alternatives that ultimately comes under consideration. They argue that when rules or incentives limit access to the agenda, they also constrict the range of proposals that are included on the agenda. Following Niskanen (1971) and others, they hypothesize a bias in favor of high-demand proposals when there are barriers to agenda participation. Below I take a slightly different course, suggesting that institutional procedures define jurisdictions and restrict agency proposals to be, in some sense, jurisdictionally homogeneous. Under a jurisdiction rule, apples can never be compared to oranges, so to speak, so that in this sense social comparisons are limited.

Each of these studies departs from the simple game orientation by establishing a structural condition that not only distinguishes winning from losing coalitions but also distinguishes the outcomes for which the various winning coalitions are effective. Ironically, each study employs the most extreme version of a monitoring device, the *closed rule.* In the next section I propose a general framework for examining various effectiveness structures. The framework focuses on three institutional features common to most legislatures and, I claim, most other organizations as well. They are a division-of-labor arrangement called a *committee system,* a specialization-of-labor system called a *juridictional arrangement,* and a monitoring system called an *amendment control rule.*

A BAREBONES MODEL OF ORGANIZATION[6]

In this section I propose a multidimensional choice model that is institutionally richer than previous models. $N = [1,...,n]$ is a finite set of voters or organizational players and X, the set of alternatives, is some subset of an m-dimensional Euclidean space. That is, an alternative $x \in X$ is an m-tuple, that is $x = (x_1, x_2, ..., x_m)$, where the components x_i of x are the levels on each of the dimensions of the space. The dimensions can be interpreted as characteristic of the outcomes, issues, public good quantities, and so on. Their meaning varies from context to context as the following examples illustrate:

(1) In multidimensional voting models of electoral phenomena, the dimensions respresent salient political issues, ideology, candidate personal characteristics, and, perhaps, partisan factors (see the literature on spatial modeling summarized in Davis, Hinich, and Ordeshook, 1970; also see Downs, 1957; Plott, 1967; Sloss, 1973; McKelvey and Wendell, 1976; Slutsky, 1977b; Matthews, forthcoming; and Kramer, 1977).

(2) In models of legislative choice, the multidimensional space represents policy decisions, where each dimension corresponds to a characteristic of policy (see Ferejohn and Fiorina, 1975; Ferejohn, Fiorina, Weisberg, 1978; Ferejohn, Fiorina, Packel, 1978).

(3) In models of political economy, the multidimensional space is a consumption space—dimensions 1 through ℓ are private goods and $\ell+1$ through m are public goods (see Denzau and Parks, 1973; Slutsky, 1977a).

(4) In models of bureaucracy, the dimensions reflect quantities of the goods and services provided by the bureau (see Niskanen, 1971; Mackay and Weaver, 1978).

The conceptual language and illustrations of this paper have a legislative flavor, but appropriate alterations in interpretation render the model applicable to other organizational contests.

Each $i \in N$ has preferences defined on X that are represented by a utility function, u_i. Thus, for $x,y \in X$, if i prefers x to y, or y to x, or is indifferent between them, then this is reflected by $u_i(x) > u_i(y)$, $u_i(x) < u_i(y)$, and $u_i(x) = u_i(y)$, respectively. Two technical properties of u_i are assumed: continuity and strict quasi-concavity.[7]

We now define two finite coverings.[8] The first is a division of labor among the institutional actors in N. Call the family of sets $C = [C_1, \ldots, C_s]$ a *committee system* if and only if it covers N. Each $C_i \in C$ is called a *committee*. Committee systems, as defined here, are really quite general representations of organizations with varying degrees of decentralization, as the following examples suggest:

C.1 A degenerate form of committee system is the *committee of the whole*—one big committee composed of all $i \in N$. In the literature on social choice and spatial modeling, it is varyingly called group, committee, electorate, society, citizenry, and so on.

C.2 Let $C = [C_1, \ldots, C_s]$ be the various departments of a university. If there are no joint appointments and every faculty member has a departmental affiliation, then C is a partiition of N inasmuch as each $i \in N$ is in one and only $C_j \in C$.

C.3 Let $C = [C_1, C_2]$ with $C_1 = [i]$ and $C_2 = [1, 2, \ldots, i-1, i+1, \ldots, n]$. If we call C_1 the "convener set" or the "agenda setter," then we have the organizational structure of the Isaac-Plott and Romer-Rosenthal studies.

C.4   As a slight generalization of C.3, let $C = [C_1, C_2]$, $C_1 = [1, \ldots, r]$ $C_2 = [1, \ldots, n]$. Notice that C_1 is a subset of C_2 so that C does not partition N. Call C_1 the Rules Committee and C_2 the House of Representatives. As in C.3, for an alternative to be victorious, it must obtain a majority from C_1 and C_2.

C.5   Let $C = [C_1, \ldots, C_s]$ and let each $C_i \in C$ be a standing committee of the House of Representatives. Since $i \in C_k \cap C_\ell$, that is, multiple committee assignments are permitted, and since, for every $i \in N$, $i \in C_j$ for some C_j, that is, every congressman is assigned to at least one committee, C covers N but does not partition it.

The second covering is a specialization-of-labor arrangement defined on the m-dimensional space of alternatives, X. Specifically, let $E = [e_1, \ldots, e_m]$ be the set of dimensions (basis vectors) that span X. Call the family of sets $J = [J_1, \ldots, J_t]$ a *jurisdictional arrangement* if and only if it covers E. Each $J_k \in J$ is a subset of dimensions called a *jurisdiction*. The committee system covering reflects personnel decentralization whereas the jurisdictional covering reflects a task or substance decentralization. To capture this distinction, imagine the two following methods of delivering postsecondary education. Create an organization (called a university) and establish a committee system $C = [C_1, \ldots, C_s]$ (called a system of colleges) with each college identical to each other college in the sense that each provides the same common set of products. Here there is a division of labor (each faculty member and student is affiliated with a particular college) but no specialization of labor (each college is a perfect substitute for any other college). A number of English and continental universities have this structure (though colleges do acquire some reputation for specialization).[9] On the other hand, instead of a system of colleges, let $C = [C_1, \ldots, C_s]$ be a set of departments, each with a (relatively!) well-defined intellectual domain. Now each of the university's subunits is a specialized entity. To sum up, the committee system creates personnel subunits, whereas the jurisdictional arrangement establishes substantive domains.

This is not to say, however, that the substantive domains are necessarily very specialized. Two extreme examples of jurisdictional arrangement are:

J.1 Let $J = [J_1, \ldots, J_n]$ with $J_k = [e_k]$, $k=1,\ldots,m$. This is the set of *simple jurisdictions* in which each jurisdiction is a single dimension.

J.2 Let $J = [e_1, \ldots, e_m]$. That is, all the dimensions of X fall in a single jurisdiction—*global jurisdiction.*

The combination of C.1 and J.2 is characteristic of most of the social choice and spatial modeling literature, and lends itself to a simple game interpretation. As the reader can see, it is a very specific organizational form and, in many respects, is rather extreme. Two other jurisdictional arrangements are worth noting in passing:

J.3 Let $J = [J_1, \ldots, J_t]$, $t < m$. Here some of the $J_k \in J$ contain more than one basis vector (dimension); J is a set of *complex jurisdictions.*

J.4 Let $J = [J_1, \ldots, J_t]$ with $J_k \cap J_\ell \neq \phi$ for some $J_k, J_\ell \in J$. J now contains *overlapping jurisdictions,* a condition now found in the House of Representatives and Senate more than 30 years after the Legislative Reorganization Act of 1946.

I assume that each $C_j \in C$ is associated with a unique $J_k \in J$,[10] which I write $f(C_j)$. It will also be useful to define the correspondence g that assigns to each $C_j \in C$ and distinct point $x^o \in X$ (called the status quo) the set

$$g(C_j, x^o) = [x \in X \mid x = x^o + \Sigma \ \lambda_i e_i, \ e_i \in f(C_j)]$$

For a given status quo, $g(C_j, x^o)$ defines the set of alternatives in X falling in C_j's jurisdiction that represent jurisdictionally channeled changes in the status quo. In particular, the set of *feasible proposals* for change in the status quo, x^o, is

$$P = \underset{j}{U}g(C_j, x^o) = [x \mid x = x^o + \underset{e_i \in I}{\Sigma} \lambda_{i} e_i, I \subseteq J_k \text{ for some } J_k \in J].$$

According to this definition and the division- and speciali-zation-of-labor systems supporting it, the institutional status quo is vulnerable to changes, but those prospective changes with which the status quo must contend need not be the full set of alternatives, X. The set of feasible proposals is (ordi-narily) a proper subset of X. Thus, in contrast to the simple game model, in this model a given status quo can be *undomi-nated* without *dominating* all other alternatives if it can defeat all $x \in P$; it does not matter that some $x' \in X-P$ could defeat x^o since x^o will never be compared to x'. Some examples will be given in the next section.

The "story," as yet incomplete, associated with my model is this: each $C_j \in C$ is a *monopoly provider* of proposed changes in x^o from its respective jurisdiction $f(C_j)$. Each C_j plays a role analogous to the Isaac-Plott convener or the Romer-Rosenthal agenda setter, except that its monopoly agenda power is limited to its jurisdiction.

The story is incomplete inasmuch as most organizations do not extend decentralization to the point that they grant their subunits the authority to decide in the organization's be-half.[11] Deans, for example, monitor the personnel, research, and curriculum decisions of a university's departments. Cor-porations, even the most decentralized, often establish "profit centers" and auditing procedures as devices by which to monitor the performance of its corporate divisions. And, of course, legislatures reserve the right of final decision for proposals from their committees. In order to incorporate this monitoring phenomenon, suppose a $C_j \in C$ proposes $x \in g(C_j, x^o)$ as a change in the status quo. For any proposal $x \in g(C_j, x^o)$, the set $M(x) \subset X$ consists of the modifications the parent organization (N) can make in x. M(x) is said to be an *amendment control rule*. Thus, C_j proposes $x \in g(C_j, x^o)$. The parent organization can then select a point $x' \in x \cup M$

(x); the parent organization then chooses between x ' (which may be an amended version of x or x, itself) and the status quo, x^o.

In Shepsle (1978a) I provide a number of different amendment control rules. Here I focus on four:

A.1   If $M(x) = [x]$, then the organization is governed by a *closed rule*.

A.2   If $M(x) = X$, then the organization is governed by an *open rule*.

A.3   If $M(x) = [x' \mid x_i' = x_i^o$ if $x_i = x_i^o]$, then the organization is said to be governed by a *germaneness rule*.

A.4   If $M(x) = [x' \mid x' < x]$ or $M(x) = [x' \mid x' > x]$, then the organization is said to be governed by a *boundary rule* (reduction and expansion rules, respectively).

The question to be examined in the next section is: What are the equilibrium properties of an organization characterized by a committee system, jurisdictional arrangement, and amendment control rule? In the fifth section special attention is given to amendment rules in a comparative framework.

ORGANIZATIONAL EQUILIBRIUM

An organizational equilibrium is an alternative $x \in X$ that cannot be "unseated" in the sense that it can defeat any proposed change (or permissible modification thereof). Two equilibrium concepts are defined shortly in terms of *replaceability* and *vulnerability*, defined as follows: the status quo, x^o is *replaceable* by a proposal $x \in X$ (called a *replacement*) if

(i) $x \in g(C_j, x^o)$ for some $C_j \in C$,

(ii) $x = C_j(x, x^o)$, where $C_j(\cdot, \cdot)$ is the binary choice function for the jth committee,

(iii) $x \in C(x, x')$ for all $x' \in M(x)$, where $C(\cdot, \cdot)$ is the choice function of the full organization, and

(iv) $x = C(x, x^o)$.

That is, x is a replacement for the status quo if it is feasible, that is, lies in the jurisdiction of some committee in the sense of (i), is preferred by that committee to the status quo (ii), is preferred by the parent organization in comparison to all possible modifications in it (iii), and finally is preferred by the parent organization to x^o (iv).

The status quo, x^o, is *vulnerable* if there exists a replacement for it or if there exists a feasible proposal preferred by a committee to x^o, that is, an $x \in g(C_j,x^o) \cap c_j(x,x^o)$, some permissible modification of which is preferred to it and to the status quo by the parent organization, that is, an $x' \in M(x) \cap C(x,x') \cap C(x',x^o)$.

The notion of vulnerability suggests the following equilibrium concept: a status quo, x^o is a *structure-induced equilibrium* (SIE) if and only if it is invulnerable. Before commenting on this notion of equilibrium, it is valuable to contrast it to the more traditional solution concept of multidimensional voting games: a status quo, x^o, is a *preference-induced equilibrium* (PIE) if and only if it is a global binary winner, namely, $x^o \in \underset{x \in X}{\cap} C(x,x^o)$. A PIE is a Condorcet point. That is, it is undominated precisely because it dominates every other alternative in X (see the earlier discussion of simple games). An SIE, too, is undominated, but *not* because it dominates every other alternative in X; rather it is undominated because it dominates all the points *against which it feasibly may be compared.* The two equilibrium concepts are related in the following theorem, a proof of which is found in Shepsle (1978a):

   (i) PIE $\rightarrow$ SIE
   (ii) $\sim$ (SIE $\rightarrow$ PIE).

That is, every global winner is invulnerable, but there are invulnerable alternatives that are not global winners.

There are at least three important reasons for distinguishing SIEs from PIEs. First, SIEs reflect a *conspiracy* between preferences of institutional actors, on the one hand, and institutional structure and procedures, on the other. An SIE can exist as much because institutional division-of-labor, specialization-of-labor, and monitoring practices prohibit certain alternatives from access to the institutional agenda as because, in some sense, it is preferred by the organization. The "mobilization of bias" that Schattschneider (1960) long ago warned about—not to speak of more recent manifestations of "cozy little triangles," "policy whirlpools," "policy reciprocity," and "policy by subgovernment" that Lowi (1964) and Freeman (1965) have discussed—are captured nicely by the SIE concept of equilibrium.

Second, and perhaps of more narrow theoretical interest, PIEs are a rather delicate affair. The seminal paper by Plott (1967) and recent extensions by Sloss (1973), McKelvey and Wendell (1976), Matthews (forthcoming), and Slutsky (1977b), provide the *stringent* necessary and sufficient conditions for the existence of a PIE and comment on the low likelihood such conditions will materialize in empirical settings. Moreover, the recent papers by McKelvey (1976, forthcoming), Cohen (1977), Cohen and Matthews (1977), Schofield (forthcoming), and Bell (1978) show that even if the conditions are met, the slightest perturbation destroys that equilibrium totally.

Third, as the theorem above states, an SIE may emerge even if a PIE fails to exist. That is, the SIE set contains the PIE set and the former set is nonempty even when the latter is.

These contrasting equilibrium concepts are illustrated in the following example (see Figure 1). Let $N = [1,2,3]$ be a three-person organization which must choose a point in a three-dimensional Euclidean space. The organization is characterized by no division of labor—$C = [N]$—but there is a specialization of labor consisting of simple jurisdictions (see J.1). In effect, then, the organization can consider changes in the status quo one dimension at a time. If the $i \in N$ have ideal points at $(1,0,0)$, $(0,1,0)$, and $(0,0,1)$, respectively, and spherical indifference contours, if $C(\cdot,\cdot)$ is the simple majority rule and if only germane amendments are allowed, it is easy to see that $x^o = (0,0,0)$ is an SIE.

Two things are of interest in this example. First, $PIE = \phi$ — there is no point that can defeat every other point in a simple majority vote. If Mr. 3's ideal point were moved to the point $(t, 1-t, 0)$ $0 \leqslant t \leqslant 1$, then that point, a convex combination of the ideal points of 1 and 2, would be a PIE; otherwise none

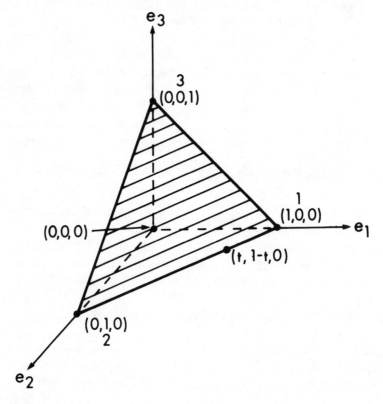

Figure 1

exists. This serves as our first firm demonstration of the existence of an SIE in the absence of any PIEs. Second, this particular SIE does not lie on the Pareto optimal surface (the shaded triangle in Figure 1). Thus, there are points in X that all three voters prefer to x^o, yet they can never be compared to x^o because of jurisdictional constraints that prohibit packaging alternatives involving simultaneous changes in more than one jurisdiction.

Elsewhere (Shepsle, 1979) I examine a number of situations producing institutional equilibrium of the SIE variety. In the remainder of this section I examine a rather special case characterized by the following axioms:

   I. The preference of each $i \in N$ on the alternative set X (a subset of m-dimensional Euclidean space) are represented by a strictly quasi-concave, continuous, real-valued utility function.

  II. The committee system $C = [C_1, \ldots, C_s]$ is an arbitrary covering of N, except that $s \leqslant m$.

 III. The jurisdictional arrangement is simple (J.1) and nonoverlapping; thus
   i. $J = [[e_1], [e_2], \ldots, [e_m]]$
   ii. $f(C_i) \cap f(C_j) = \phi$ for all $C_i, C_j \in C$.

  IV. $C(\cdot, \cdot)$ and $C_j(\cdot, \cdot)$ are the simple majority choice rule.

   V. The amendment control rule is the germaneness rule (A.3).

The condition $s \leqslant m$ is necessary for nonoverlapping jurisdictions; and $f(C_j) \subset [[e_1], \ldots, [e_m]]$. That is, if $s < m$, then some committees can be assigned several jurisdictions. This does *not* mean they can propose policies that change the status quo in more than one of their jurisdictions at the same time.

The following consequences are derived from these axioms.

THEOREM: SIEs always exist.

GERMANENESS RULE THEOREM: If individual preferences are separable by jurisdiction,[12] then x^o is an SIE if and only if

$$x_j^o = \text{median } [\bar{x}_j^i] \text{ or median } [\bar{x}_j^i]$$
$$\quad\quad i \in N \quad\quad\quad\quad i \in C_j$$

where x_j^i is the jth component of i's ideal point.

COROLLARY: If individual preferences are separable by jurisdiction and if C is the committee-of-the-whole arrangement (C.1), then a necessary and sufficient condition for x^o to be an SIE is

$$x_j^o = \text{median } [\bar{x}_j^i].$$
$$\quad\quad i \in N$$

In effect, these results tell us that SIEs always exist and, under the hypothesized conditions, will produce policies in each jurisdiction that reflect either the median committee preference or the median preference of the parent organization. The hypothesized conditions permit the parent organization to monitor via a germaneness rule and, as well, permit committees to "keep the gates closed" in their jurisdiction if they so choose.

With what effect? Consider the example constructed in Figure 2. $N = [1,2,\ldots,7]$ and each $i \in N$ is assumed to have circular indifference curves centered at this ideal point. $C = [C_1, C_2]$ with $f(C_i) = [e_i]$, $C_1 = [1,2,3]$ and $C_2 = [4,5,6,7]$. The set of equilibria is SIE = $[A,B,C,D]$. Point B has each committee keeping the gates closed in its assigned jurisdiction, that is, the first component is median $[x_1^1, x_1^2, x_1^3]$ and the second component is median $[x_2^4, x_2^5, x_2^6, x_2^7]$. Point C is an equilibrium in which the organization, N, vetoes any change proposed by either of its committees. A and D reflect mixes of these two—a committee median in one jurisdiction and the organizational median in the other jurisdiction. No other point is an SIE and the PIE set is empty. Notice that two of the four SIEs are not Pareto optimal. In the next section I explore what happens to the SIE set as I vary the monitoring rule.

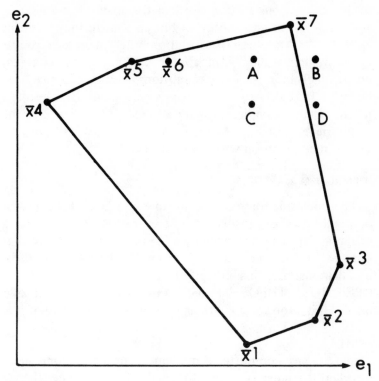

Figure 2

SOME COMPARATIVE STATICS OF AMENDMENT CONTROL

In order to illustrate the kind of organizational analysis that is possible with the family of models described in the third and fourth sections, I inquire in this section into some of the comparative statics of amendment procedures. In effect, I adopt Axioms I-IV of the previous section and, instead of Axiom V, employ one of the following variations:

V′ . The amendment control rule is the open rule (A.2).
V″ . The amendment control rule is the closed rule (A.1).
V‴. The amendment control rule is a boundary rule (A.4).

As in the previous section, I retain the assumption of separable preferences (see Note 12) but emphasize that I do this only to facilitate the presentation; the theoretical results below remain valid (with appropriate notational changes) under much more general assumptions about preferences (see Shepsle, 1978a). After presenting some theoretical results I return to the example in Figure 2 to see what happens to the equilibria as we adopt Axiom V, V ' , V '' , and V ''' , respectively, in conjunction with Axioms I-IV.

OPEN RULE (A.2)

The open rule for amendments undoes much of the impact on equilibrium of jurisdictional decentralization since, once a proposal for change is made by a $C_j \in C$, amendments to that proposal do not have to be germane.[13] The following theorem demonstrates this unhappy fact.

OPEN RULE THEOREM: With Axioms I-IV and V', if $x_j^o \neq$ median $[\bar{x}_j^i]$ for some C_j, then x^o is an SIE if and only if it is
$i \in C_j$
a PIE.

That is, if any committee is unhappy with the outcome in its jurisdiction under x^o, then it will propose some change $x = x^o + \lambda e_j$. Since $M(x) = X$, the committee's proposal can be amended in any way and, in particular, in ways that also upset the status quo. Therefore, in order to be invulnerable, x^o must be undominated in the large—it must be a PIE. Of course, if $x_j^o =$ median $[\bar{x}_j^i]$, then x^o is an SIE since each
$i \in C_j$
committee will "keep the gates closed," so that at least in this one circumstance the gatekeeping monopoly of committees is not without substance. In most instances, however, the open rule on amendments enables the parent organization to monitor and modify committee proposals at the price of maximal uncertainty over the final outcome. If x^o is not optimal for each committee, then x^o must satisfy Plott's

(1967) "severe symmetry of preferences" condition in order for it to be an equilibrium.

CLOSED RULE (A.1)

The closed rule forces an "up" or "down" vote on any proposal; no amendments are permitted. The rule describes the practice of the U.S. House in dealing with most legislation from the Ways and Means Committee, the practice of most universities in allowing a dean to veto or approve (but not modify) a departmental hiring proposal, and the practices involving the monitoring of the Isaac-Plott "convener" and the Romer-Rosenthal "agenda setter." For each jurisdiction, define

$$S_j = [x \mid x = x^o + \lambda \, e_j, \lambda \neq 0, x = C_j(x,x^o)]$$
$$T_j = [x \mid x = x^o + \lambda \, e_j, \lambda \neq 0, x = C(x,x^o)].$$

S_j and T_j are the modifications of x^o in the jth jurisdiction preferred, respectively, by C_j and the parent organization. CLOSED RULE THEOREM: With Axioms I-IV and V ", x^o is an SIE if and only if $S_j \cap T_j = \phi$ for all j. Two straightforward consequences of this theorem are:

(1) x^o is an SIE if $T_j = \phi$ for all j, in which case x^o is the jurisdiction-by-jurisdiction median of the parent organization.
(2) x^o is an SIE if $S_j = \phi$ for all j, in which case the C_j's are veto groups for any possible changes.

Of course, combinations of 1 and 2 also produce SIEs.

BOUNDARY RULES (A.4)

Without germaneness,[14] this amendment rule is equivalent to an open rule over a bounded region of X. From our earlier results it remains true that x^o is an SIE if $x_j^o = \underset{i \in C_j}{\mathrm{median}} \, [\bar{x}_j^i]$

for all C_j. A stronger claim, however, can be proved for *germane* boundary rules (V and V iii together).

BOUNDARY RULE THEOREM: With Axioms I-V and V''', x^o is an SIE whenever x_j^o is indistinct from median $[\bar{x}_j^i]$.
$$i \in C_j$$
If distinct then it is an SIE if and only if, for all j, median
$$i \in C_j$$
$[\bar{x}_j^i] < x_j^o <$ median $[\bar{x}_j^i]$ for the reduction rule or median
$$i \in N \qquad\qquad i \in N$$
$[\bar{x}_j^i] < x_j^o <$ median $[\bar{x}_j^i]$ for the expansion rule.
$$i \in C_j$$

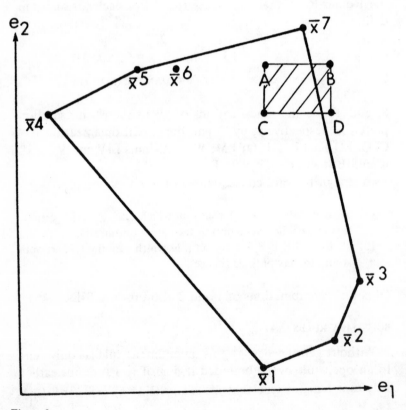

Figure 3

AMENDMENT RULES COMPARED

In order to assess the impact of the four amendment rules I have reproduced the example of Figure 2 as Figure 3. With the stated axioms, SIEs exist under each of the monitoring arrangements, but the associated equilibrium sets are not equal:

> *germaneness rule (A.3)*–as indicated earlier, the SIE set is the vertices of the shaded box in Figure 3, namely, SIE = [A,B,C,D]. This is consistent with the Germaneness Rule Theorem.
>
> *closed rule (A.1)*–the Closed Rule Theorem tells us that x^o is an equilibrium in this example if each component, x^o_j, of x^o satisfies one of
>
> (i) $x^o_j = \underset{i \in C_j}{\text{median}} \, [\bar{x}^i_j]$,
>
> (ii) $x^o_j = \underset{i \in N}{\text{median}} \, [\bar{x}^i_j]$, or
>
> (iii) wherever C_j prefers $x^o_j + \lambda e_j$ to x^o_j, N prefers x^o_j to $x^o_j + \lambda e_j$.

Every point in the closed box satisfies one of these conditions so that the SIE set is the entire shaded area.

> *open rule (A.2)*–the Open Rule Theorem requires that $x^o_j = \underset{i \in C_j}{\text{median}}$ $[\bar{x}^i_j]$ or x^o a PIE in order for x^o to be an SIE. In Figure 3, PIE = ϕ since Plott's "severe symmetry" condition does not hold. Therefore, the unique SIE under the open rule is the vertex B, namely, SIE = [B].
>
> *Boundary rule (A.4)*–according to the Boundary Rule Theorem the point B is an SIE since no committee will make a proposal. With the reduction boundary rule it is the only such equilibrium, since median $\underset{i \in C_j}{[\bar{x}^i_j]}$ is not less then median $\underset{i \in N}{[\bar{x}^i_j]}$ for either jurisdiction. With the expansion boundary rule, every point in the shaded box satisfies median $\underset{i \in N}{[\bar{x}^i_j]} \leqslant x^o_j < \text{median} \underset{i \in C_j}{[\bar{x}^i_j]}$ and thus constitutes an SIE.

DISCUSSION

In order to understand the ways in which institutions make policy, it is important to incorporate into one's thinking the peculiar details of institutional practices. I have endeavored to demonstrate the inappropriateness, in many institutional contexts, of the simple game model precisely because it fails to provide or make room for relevant institutional details. A second purpose of this paper has been to provide a framework that captures the ideas of decentralization and monitoring. There are, of course, other institutional features on which my model is silent, but I do believe the features I have incorporated are in some sense central to a proper institutional analysis of policy making. Third, I have demonstrated, under one set of assumptions, that institutional games have policy equilibria, a property that is not possessed (except under very extreme conditions) by simple majority-rule games. Finally, I devoted specific attention to monitoring practices in the form of amendment control rules and, in one example, showed how different monitoring practices produce different equilibrium states.

I have said little about one variable that, I believe, is of central importance in the operation of American political institutions—what might generically be called *committee assignments*. In the context of the House of Representatives I have written on this subject (Rohde and Shepsle, 1973; Shepsle, 1978b). In the more general context of this model, it becomes increasingly clear that structural characteristics produce equilibria, *but committee assignments determine what those equilibria are like.* As the example of the last section shows (though I did not make much of this fact in discussing Figure 3), committee systems that assign actors to committees in which they are "high demanders"—that is, members whose preferences are unrepresentative of the parent body—generate equilibrium states that may not rank high in any actor's preferences. A decline in institutional legitimacy and popularity is a not very surprising consequence. For those students of American public policy interested in the phenomena associated with clientelism and in the (concomitant?) decline in institutional reputation, the model presented here may be of some practical utility.

NOTES

1. For a detailed statement of this synthetic spirit in legislative research, see Rohde and Shepsle (1978).

2. A notable exception is Ferejohn and Fiorina (1975).

3. But see Levine and Plott (1977) and McKelvey (forthcoming).

4. For a general discourse, consult Williamson (1975).

5. Niskanen (1971) examines the consequences for a bureaucracy whose activities are controlled and monitored by a legislative committee dominated by "high-demand" legislators. Fiorina (1977) explores the same ground from the point of view of incentive incompatibilities between the executive and legislative branches. Shepsle (1978b) provides the theoretical rationale and empirical evidence for the gravitation of "high-demand" legislators to appropriate committees.

6. This and the following section are based on Shepsle (1978a, 1979).

7. Essentially, continuity is a smoothness property; the utility function rises or falls smoothly without sudden jumps or breaks. Strict quasi-concavity prohibits "thick" indifference contours and straight-line indifference contours. Indifference curves are smoothly convex to the origin. Technically, u_i is strictly quasi-concave if and only if

$$x,y \in X, \ x \neq y, \text{ and } u_i(x) \geqslant u_i(y) \rightarrow u_i(x') > u_i(y)$$

where $x' = \lambda x + (1-\lambda)y$, $0 < \lambda < 1$.

8. A *finite covering* of set B is a finite collection $\beta = [\beta_1, \beta_2, \ldots, \beta_t]$,
where $\bigcup_{i=1}^{t} \beta_i = B$. The $\beta_i \in \beta$ are said to cover B. If, in addition, $\beta_i \cap \beta_j = \phi$
for all $\beta_i, \beta_j \in \beta$, then β is a *finite partition* of B.

9. Prior to the Subcommittee Bill of Rights in the U.S. House of Representatives, a number of House committees had a subcommittee structure consisting of numbered subcommittees with no permanent jurisdiction. Perhaps these committee chairmen had Oxford or Cambridge in mind.

10. In Shepsle (1978a, 1979) I allow a committee to be associated with more than one jurisdiction and/or the same jurisdiction to be assigned to more than one committee. These complicating factors need not delay us here.

11. An exception is a constitutional provision to the contrary in some federal systems in which some policy areas are "reserved for the Several States," in effect a constitutional guarantee that the "organization" will *not* meddle in the affairs of its subunits.

12. Preferences are separable by jurisdiction if an individual's preference between alternatives that differ only in components falling in a single jurisdiction does not depend upon the *levels* of components in other jurisdictions. This is, in some situations at least, a rather restrictive condition. Fortunately a theorem that does not depend on the separability assumption is found in Shepsle (1979).

13. The reader should not confuse what I call the open rule with what is called the open rule in the U.S. House of Representatives. The House employs a rule which is really the germaneness rule. The U.S. Senate, with its permission of nongermane riders, is a genuine example of an institution using A.2.

14. Without germaneness, a committee is still restricted by its jurisdiction in the proposals it is permitted to offer, but once proposed, nongermane amendments are in order.

REFERENCES

ARROW, K. A. (1963) Social Choice and Individual Values. New York: Wiley.

BELL, C. E. (1978) "What happens when majority rule breaks down?: some probability calculations." Public Choice 33 (Summer): 121-127.

BLACK, D. (1958) The Theory of Committees and Elections. Cambridge: Cambridge University Press.

BLOOMFIELD, S. and R. WILSON (1972) "The postulates of game theory." Journal of Mathematical Sociology 2 (June): 221-234.

BUCHANAN, J. and G. TULLOCK (1962) The Calculus of Consent. Ann Arbor: University of Michigan Press.

COHEN, L. (1977) "The structure of maximum majority rule cycles." Paper presented at the annual meeting of the American Economic Association, New York.

——— and S. MATTHEWS (1977) "Constrained Plott equilibria, directional equilibria, and global cycling sets." Working Paper #178, California Institute of Technology.

DAVIS, O., M. HINICH and P. ORDESHOOK (1970) "An expository development of a mathematical model of the electoral process." American Political Science Review 64 (March): 426-449.

DENZAU, A. and R. PARKS (1973) "Equilibrium in an economy with private and spatial political dimensions." Presented at the Winter Meeting of the Econometrics Society.

DOWNS, A. (1957) An Economic Theory of Democracy. New York: Harper and Row.

FEREJOHN, J. and M. FIORINA (1975) "Purposive models of legislative behavior." American Economic Review 65 (May): 407-415.

——— and E. W. PACKEL (1978) "A non-equilibrium approach to legislative decision theory." Paper presented at the annual meeting of the Public Choice Society, New Orleans.

FEREJOHN, J., M. FIORINA, and H. W. WEISBERG (1978) "Toward a theory of legislative decision." In P. Ordeshook (ed.) Game Theory and Political Science. New York: New York University Press.

FIORINA, M. (1977) "Control of the bureaucracy: a mismatch of incentives and capabilities." Paper presented at a conference on "Congress and the Presidency: A Shifting Balance of Power?" Lyndon Johnson School, Austin, Texas.

FREEMAN, J. L. (1965) The Political Process: Executive Bureau-Legislative Committee Relations. New York: Random House.

ISAAC, M. and C. PLOTT (1978) "Cooperative game models of the influence of the closed rule in three person, majority rule committees: theory and experiment." In P. Ordeshook (ed.) Game Theory and Political Science. New York: New York University Press.

KRAMER, G. (1977) "A dynamical model of political equilibrium." Journal of Economic Theory 16 (December): 310-334.

LEVINE, M. and C. PLOTT (1977) "Agenda influence and its implications." Virginia Law Review 63 (May): 561-604.

LOWI, T. (1964) "American business and public policy, case studies and political theory." World Politics 16 (July): 677-715.

MACKAY, R. J. and C. WEAVER (1978) "Monopoly bureaus and

fiscal outcomes: deductive models and implications for reform." In G. Tullock and R. E. Wagner (eds.) Policy Analysis and Deductive Reasoning. Lexington: Lexington Books.

McKELVEY, R. D. (forthcoming) "General conditions for global intransitivities in formal voting models." Econometrica.

——— (1978) "A theory of optimal agenda design." Paper presented at Conference on Political Science and the Study of Public Policy, Hickory Corners, Michigan.

———. (1976) "Intransitivities in multidimensional voting models and some implications for agenda control." Journal of Economic Theory 12 (June): 472-482.

——— and R. E. Wendell (1976) "Voting equilibria in multidimensional choice spaces." Mathematics of Operation Research 1 (May): 144-158.

MATTHEWS, S. (forthcoming) "The possibility of voting equilibria." Public Choice.

NISKANEN, W. (1971) Bureaucracy and Representative Government. Chicago: Aldine-Atherton.

OLSON, M. (1965) The Logic of Collective Action. Cambridge: Harvard University Press.

PLOTT, C. R. (1967) "The notion of equilibrium and its possibility under majority rule." American Economic Review 57 (September): 787-806.

RIKER, W. H. (1962) The Theory of Political Coalitions. New Haven: Yale University Press.

——— and P. C. ORDESHOOK (1973) An Introduction to Positive Political Theory. Englewood Cliffs: Prentice-Hall.

ROHDE, D. W. and K. A. SHEPSLE (1978) "Taking stock of congressional research: the new institutionalism." Paper presented at the annual meeting of the Midwest Political Science Association, Chicago.

——— (1973) "Democratic committee assignments in the House of Representatives: strategic aspects of a social choice process." American Political Science Review 67 (September): 889-905.

ROMER, T. and H. ROSENTHAL (forthcoming) "Political resource allocation, controlled agendas, and the status quo." Public Choice.

SCHATTSCHNEIDER, E. E. (1960) The Semisovereign People. New York: Holt, Rinehart, and Winston.

SCHOFIELD, N. (forthcoming) "Generic instability of simple voting games on policy spaces." Review of Economic Studies.

SHAPLEY, L. S. and M. SHUBIK (1973) "Game theory in economics:

characteristic function, core, and stable set." R-904-NSF/6 Santa Monica: Rand.

SHEPSLE, K. A. (1979) "Institutional arrangements and equilibrium in multidimensional voting models." American Journal of Political Science 23 (February): 23-57.

——— (1978a) "Institutional structure and policy choice: some comparative statics of amendment control procedures." Paper presented at the annual meeting of the American Political Science Association, New York.

——— (1978b) The Giant Jigsaw Puzzle: Democratic Committee Assignments in the Modern House. Chicago: University of Chicago Press.

SLOSS, J. (1973) "Stable outcomes in majority rule voting games." Public Choice 15 (Summer): 19-48.

SLUTSKY, S. M. (1977a) "A voting model for the allocation of public goods: existence of an equilibrium." Journal of Economic Theory 14 (June): 299-325.

——— (1977b) "Equilibrium under plurality voting." Paper presented at the annual meetings of the Public Choice Society, New Orleans.

von NEUMANN, J. and O. MORGENSTERN (1964) The Theory of Games and Economic Behavior (science edition). New York: Wiley.

WILLIAMSON, O. E. (1975) Markets and Hierarchies: Analysis and Antitrust Implications. New York: Free Press.

ABOUT THE CONTRIBUTORS

CHRISTOPHER H. ACHEN is Assistant Professor at the University of California, Berkeley. He is interested in the development of statistical and mathematical theory for political science applications, and his work in that area has appeared in the *American Political Science Review,* the *American Journal of Political Science, Political Methodology,* and elsewhere. He is currently at work on econometric techniques for public policy evaluation when the experimental and control groups are not randomly assigned.

W. ROSS BREWER teaches in the Department of Political Science of the University of Vermont at Burlington. He is the coauthor with Garrison Nelson of "Convention conflict and election outcomes, 1840-1976," a paper presented at the annual meeting of the American Political Science Association in 1976.

THOMAS E. CAVANAGH is a Danforth Graduate Fellow in political science at Yale University. He received his B.A. from Yale in 1975, and his M.Phil. in 1978. In 1977, he served as assistant survey research director of the Commission on Administrative Review of the U.S. House of Representatives, popularly known as the Obey Commission. He has also worked as a research analyst for Peter D. Hart Research Associates and as a research consultant for the Committee for the Study of the American Electorate.

THEODORE J. EISMEIER is Assistant Professor of Government at Hamilton College, where he teaches courses in American politics and public policy. He is currently completing a book about the politics of taxation.

JENNIFER HOCHSCHILD is an Instructor in the Institute of Policy Sciences and Public Affairs at Duke University. Her dissertation is on "Norms of Distributive Justice among Rich and Poor Americans" and she specializes in welfare policy, normative analysis of public policies, and the relationship between political ideology and political results.

GARRISON NELSON teaches in the Department of Political Science of the University of Vermont at Burlington. He is the coauthor with W. Ross Brewer of "Convention conflict and election outcomes, 1840-1976," a paper presented at the annual meeting of the American Political Science Association in 1976.

WILLIAM A. NISKANEN is the Director—Economics of the Ford Motor Company. He previously served as Professor, Graduate School of Public Policy, Berkeley, and in various positions at the Office of Management and Budget, the Institute for Defense Analyses, the Department of Defense, and the RAND Corp. He is the author of *Bureaucracy and Representative Government* and numerous articles.

KENNETH A. SHEPSLE is a Professor of Political Science and Research Associate of the Center for the Study of American Business at Washington University. He is the author of *The Giant Jigsaw Puzzle: Democratic Committee Assignments in the Modern House* (University of Chicago Press).